The Imperial Tense

THE
Imperial Tense

PROSPECTS AND PROBLEMS OF
AMERICAN EMPIRE

Edited with an Introduction by

ANDREW J. BACEVICH

Ivan R. Dee
CHICAGO

Library of Congress Cataloging-in-Publication Data:
The imperial tense : prospects and problems of American empire / edited with an introduction by Andrew J. Bacevich.
    p. cm.
    Includes bibliographical references and index.
    ISBN 1-56663-532-2 (cloth : alk. paper) — ISBN 1-56663-533-0 (paper : alk. paper)
    1. United States—Foreign relations—2001- 2. United States—Foreign relations—Philosophy. 3. Imperialism. I. Bacevich, A. J.

E902.I57 2003
327.73—dc21   2003048484

To

Rick Lynch

Barrye Price

Dan Williamson

Steadfast and True

Contents

Introduction

THE UNITED STATES OF AMERICA was born in opposition to empire. Enumerating their grievances against the crown, the signers of the Declaration of Independence described in detail the "long train of abuses and usurpations" that by 1776 had rendered King George III "unfit to be the ruler of a free People." Among his other offenses, the British monarch had imposed on his North American subjects "a jurisdiction foreign to our constitutions, and unacknowledged by our laws." The delegates to the Continental Congress proceeded to find that foreign jurisdiction null and void.

In fixing their names to the Declaration, those delegates were acknowledging a reality that events had already established. The revolution then well under way had, in effect, already declared British imperial rule illegitimate. That revolution testified to a popular determination, widespread and heartfelt if by no means unanimous, to break free of empire, if need be through bloody and protracted armed struggle. Americans would not be subjects. They would be citizens.

The republic established as the chief product of that revolution was—and in the view of most Americans was intended to remain—the very antithesis of empire. Starry-eyed politicians might beguile themselves with talk of establishing in the New World an "empire of liberty." But when it came to the real thing—the exercise of dominion over populations beyond the nation's borders or across the seas—Americans wanted no part of it. After all, empire signified pomp and privilege, corruption and excess—the inverse of the virtues informing the political order to which Americans now swore allegiance. Empire came in a package that included power politics, war, and militarism. These Old World afflictions were to have no place in the *novus ordo seclorum* arising on this side of the ocean.

Thus did a presumed antipathy to empire and imperialism take its place among the founding myths of the American republic. Long after that myth had ceased to have any real meaning, Americans continued to fancy themselves in some vague way standing shoulder-to-shoulder with those around the world yearning to liberate themselves from the yoke of imperial oppression.

Evidence that the United States, from 1898 onward increasingly willing to flex its muscles on the world stage, was comporting itself in ways that smacked of the very best traditions of European empire did little to shake this conviction. Critics might charge the United States with imperial behavior, but the charges never stuck. Thus, following the war with Spain, genteel members of the Anti-Imperialist League took exception to President William McKinley's decision to annex the Philippines and convert Cuba into a submissive protectorate. During the period between the two world wars, left-leaning journals like *The Nation* railed against Yankee imperialism throughout the Caribbean Basin. In the months running up to December 1941, America Firsters accused Franklin D. Roosevelt of plotting to maneuver the United States into an imperial war that was none of our business. More recently and especially memorably, opponents of the Vietnam War cited that conflict as *prima facie* evidence proving that the project called "liberal internationalism" amounted to little more than a subterfuge for empire.

But true-blue patriots remained unpersuaded. Indeed, on that score, in official circles, even today opinion has not budged. Politicians committed to reciting whatever they think voters want to hear speak as one in rejecting categorically the notion of the United States ever entertaining imperial ambitions. Thus, as a candidate in the 2000 presidential campaign, Governor George W. Bush affirmed the conventional wisdom to which Republicans and Democrats alike subscribe: "America has never been an empire."[1]

---

[1]George W. Bush, "A Distinctly American Internationalism," November 19, 1999, Simi Valley, California.

And yet well before 2000, outside of official circles, a different and somewhat subversive idea had begun to insinuate itself into discussions of America's role in the world. The essence of that idea—emerging during the decade following the Soviet collapse—was that to describe the United States, perched in solitary splendor atop the international order, as merely a great power failed to do justice to reality. As the sole superpower, the "indispensable nation," the embodiment of *hyperpuissance*, America had become something much more. Enjoying a position of unprecedented economic, cultural, technological, and above all military dominance, the United States by the 1990s was shouldering responsibilities, wielding authority, and facing challenges that, in the eyes of some observers, could best be likened to those of an imperial power.

Then came the horrific events of September 11. In their aftermath, the administration of now President George Bush cited the war on terror as a basis for staking out even broader claims. His administration asserted for the United States the exclusive prerogative of waging preventive war. It declared that it would not be bound by the strictures of the international community but would act when and how it saw fit, if necessary doing so unilaterally. It decreed that democratic capitalism offered the only route by which any nation could prosper and succeed. And it announced that it would not permit the rise of a rival capable of challenging American preeminence. American values and American power would reign supreme.

Although President Bush himself continued to reject the charge that Washington entertained imperial ambitions, in many quarters the evidence that the Great Republic had now become the seat of a global imperium appeared incontrovertible.

Was the imperial label justified this time? If so, what precisely was the nature of America's empire? What were its prospects? What were the implications of empire for the American people?

By early 2003, these and related questions had become a staple on talk shows and had spurred writers to produce a flurry of op-eds, essays, and books. But this new debate over American empire—one unlikely to end anytime soon—differs in tone and substance from that which had occurred, say, in the aftermath of 1898 or during the 1960s.

To be sure, some contributors to this debate hew to the hallowed establishment line, dismissing the very idea of empire as un-American and rejecting as absurd the claim that the United States has become or could ever become an imperial power. Others, both at home and abroad, having dusted off and updated the traditional anti-imperialist line, affirm the existence of an American empire only to denounce it as evil and to call for its immediate dismantling.

But at least two new camps have made their appearance. Inhabiting the third camp are those who acknowledge the reality of empire (although often substituting for the E-word euphemisms like benign hegemony or unipolarity) and who enthusiastically endorse that reality as good for the United States and good for everyone else too. As one of the more fevered adherents of this school has proclaimed, "America's Destiny Is to Police the World."[2]

Those inhabiting the fourth camp find it difficult to share that enthusiasm. The United States may well find itself today presiding over some form of empire, they concede, but the appropriate response to that reality is not chest-thumping celebration but sober reflection. If guided by the utopian attractions to which today's heirs of Woodrow Wilson are inclined, America's empire, they believe, is likely to prove far more costly than its proponents let on and could well end in tragedy. In their view, the empire is less an opportunity than a predicament, a burden that, if ill-managed, poses great dangers, not least of all to the United States itself.

This book collects the best writing from each of these four camps. *The Imperial Tense* does not attempt to proselytize or persuade. Rather, it offers a wide range of views and invites readers to draw their own conclusions.

With a single exception, all the essays that follow accept the fact that by the beginning of the twenty-first century the United

[2]Max Boot, "America's Destiny Is to Police the World," *Financial Times*, February 18, 2003.

States, for better or worse, has become an imperial power. (That exception, the contribution by Victor Davis Hanson, categorically rejects the notion of an American empire.)

With a single exception, all of the essays were written after September 11, 2001. Many of them were inspired at least in part by the reorientation of U.S. national security strategy to which the Bush administration's global war on terror gave birth. (The exception is David Rieff's proposal for a "liberal imperialism," inspired by the humanitarian crises that before September 11 had formed a defining feature of the post–cold war international landscape.)

The Imperial Tense derives from my own conviction that the conventional debate over U.S. foreign policy has reached a dead end and that the language informing that debate has become bereft of real meaning. The architects of American statecraft no longer argue seriously about opting for realism or idealism, engagement or withdrawal, internationalism or isolation. If those putative dichotomies ever had any real meaning, that day is long gone.

But to a remarkable extent the lexicon of those old debates—traceable at least as far back as the 1930s but persisting throughout the postwar era—survives. Even today it litters the speeches and writings of elected and appointed officials who purport to describe America's role in the world.

But the persistence of this familiar language today does less to illuminate than to conceal. It serves mostly as a veil. As a consequence, discourse about foreign policy, such as it is, tends to be insipid and unhelpful. As a further consequence, ordinary citizens, who as far back as World War II have been conditioned to defer to "experts" on matters pertaining to America's relations with the larger world, find themselves left largely in the dark.

This collection of essays is offered in the belief that the idea of "America as empire" has the potential to change all that. Embracing a new vocabulary, shedding hoary old axioms, and entertaining thoughts once thought to be unthinkable may make it possible to see America's global role in a new and clearer light. Examining U.S. policy through the prism of empire may promote greater candor and seriousness and, in doing so, may bring ordinary Americans into the discussion of matters from which they have too long been excluded. In that way, we may take a large step in reasserting our claim to citizenship.

A. J. B.

Walpole, Massachusetts
April 2003

The Imperial Tense

I

Back to an Imperial Future?

GEORGE W. BUSH

America's Responsibility, America's Mission

*In the face of grave threats, American power
will ensure the ultimate triumph of freedom.*

THE GREAT STRUGGLES of the twentieth century between liberty and totalitarianism ended with a decisive victory for the forces of freedom—and a single sustainable model for national success: freedom, democracy, and free enterprise. In the twenty-first century, only nations that share a commitment to protecting basic human rights and guaranteeing political and economic freedom will be able to unleash the potential of their people and assure their future prosperity. People everywhere want to be able to speak freely; choose who will govern them; worship as they please; educate their children—male and female; own property; and enjoy the benefits of their labor. These values of freedom are right and true for every person, in every society—and the duty of protecting these values against their enemies is the common calling of freedom-loving people across the globe and across the ages.

George W. Bush is 43d president of the United States. This essay originally appeared as an introduction to The National Security Strategy of the United States, *published by the White House on September 17, 2002.*

5

Today, the United States enjoys a position of unparalleled military strength and great economic and political influence. In keeping with our heritage and principles, we do not use our strength to press for unilateral advantage. We seek instead to create a balance of power that favors human freedom: conditions in which all nations and all societies can choose for themselves the rewards and challenges of political and economic liberty. In a world that is safe, people will be able to make their own lives better. We will defend the peace by fighting terrorists and tyrants. We will preserve the peace by building good relations among the great powers. We will extend the peace by encouraging free and open societies on every continent.

Defending our Nation against its enemies is the first and fundamental commitment of the Federal Government. Today, that task has changed dramatically. Enemies in the past needed great armies and great industrial capabilities to endanger America. Now, shadowy networks of individuals can bring great chaos and suffering to our shores for less than it costs to purchase a single tank. Terrorists are organized to penetrate open societies and to turn the power of modern technologies against us.

To defeat this threat we must make use of every tool in our arsenal—military power, better homeland defenses, law enforcement, intelligence, and vigorous efforts to cut off terrorist financing. The war against terrorists of global reach is a global enterprise of uncertain duration. America will help nations that need our assistance in combating terror. And America will hold to account nations that are compromised by terror, including those who harbor terrorists—because the allies of terror are the enemies of civilization. The United States and countries cooperating with us must not allow the terrorists to develop new home bases. Together, we will seek to deny them sanctuary at every turn.

The gravest danger our Nation faces lies at the crossroads of radicalism and technology. Our enemies have openly declared that they are seeking weapons of mass destruction, and evidence indicates that they are doing so with determination. The United States will not allow these efforts to succeed. We will build defenses against ballistic missiles and other means of delivery. We will co-operate with other nations to deny, contain, and curtail our enemies' efforts to acquire dangerous technologies. And, as a matter of common sense and self-defense, America will act against such emerging threats before they are fully formed. We cannot defend America and our friends by hoping for the best. So we must be prepared to defeat our enemies' plans, using the best intelligence and proceeding with deliberation. History will judge harshly those who saw this coming danger but failed to act. In the new world we have entered, the only path to peace and security is the path of action.

As we defend the peace, we will also take advantage of an historic opportunity to preserve the peace. Today, the international community has the best chance since the rise of the nation-state in the seventeenth century to build a world where great powers compete in peace instead of continually prepare for war. Today, the world's great powers find ourselves on the same side—united by common dangers of terrorist violence and chaos. The United States will build on these common interests to promote global security. We are also increasingly united by common values. Russia is in the midst of a hopeful transition, reaching for its democratic future and a partner in the war on terror. Chinese leaders are discovering that economic freedom is the only source of national wealth. In time, they will find that social and political freedom is the only source of national greatness. America will encourage the advancement of democracy and economic openness in both nations, because these are the best foundations for domestic stability and international order. We will strongly resist aggression from other great powers—even as we welcome their peaceful pursuit of prosperity, trade, and cultural advancement.

Finally, the United States will use this moment of opportunity to extend the benefits of freedom across the globe. We will actively work to bring the hope of democracy, development, free markets, and free trade to every corner of the world. The events of September 11, 2001, taught us that weak states, like Afghanistan, can pose as great a danger to our national interests as strong states. Poverty does not make poor people into terrorists and murderers. Yet poverty, weak institutions, and corruption can make weak states vulnerable to terrorist networks and drug cartels within their borders.

The United States will stand beside any nation determined to build a better future by seeking the rewards of liberty for its people. Free trade and free markets have proven their ability to lift whole societies out of poverty—so the United States will work with individual nations, entire regions, and the entire global trading community to build a world that trades in freedom and therefore grows in prosperity. The United States will deliver greater development assistance through the New Millennium Challenge Account to nations that govern justly, invest in their people, and encourage economic freedom. We will also continue to lead the world in efforts to reduce the terrible toll of HIV/AIDS and other infectious diseases.

In building a balance of power that favors freedom, the United States is guided by the conviction that all nations have important responsibilities. Nations that enjoy freedom must actively fight terror. Nations that depend on international stability must help prevent the spread of weapons of mass destruction. Nations that seek international aid must govern themselves wisely, so that aid is well spent. For freedom to thrive, accountability must be expected and required.

We are also guided by the conviction that no nation can build a safer, better world alone. Alliances and multilateral institutions can multiply the strength of freedom-loving nations. The United States is committed to lasting institutions like the United Nations, the World Trade Organization, the Organization of American States, and NATO as well as other long-standing alliances. Coalitions of the willing can augment these permanent institutions. In all cases, international obligations are to be taken seriously. They are not to be undertaken symbolically to rally support for an ideal without furthering its attainment.

Freedom is the non-negotiable demand of human dignity; the birthright of every person—in every civilization. Throughout history, freedom has been threatened by war and terror; it has been challenged by the clashing wills of powerful states and the evil designs of tyrants; and it has been tested by widespread poverty and disease. Today, humanity holds in its hands the opportunity to further freedom's triumph over all these foes. The United States welcomes our responsibility to lead in this great mission.

DAVID RIEFF

Liberal Imperialism

*Dealing with the humanitarian crises of our
age demands a new sort of imperialism. Like it
or not, only the United States can fill the role.*

IF ANYTHING should be clear from the Kosovo crisis, and, for
that matter, from the unhappy experiences that outside intervention forces, whether serving under their own flags, the U.N.'s, or
NATO's, have had over the past decade in places like Somalia,
Rwanda, and Bosnia, it is that ad hoc responses to state failure and
humanitarian catastrophe are rarely, if ever, successful. At the same
time, the fact that there is now demonstrably a willingness on the
part at least of the NATO countries to intervene militarily in the
internal conflicts of other nations represents a radical change in
international affairs. The conflict over Kosovo in 1999, the first
war ever waged by the NATO alliance, was undertaken more in
the name of human rights and moral obligation than out of any
traditional conception of national interest. Indeed, had strictly

David Rieff is the author of several books, including Slaughterhouse: Bosnia and
the Failure of the West *(1996) and, most recently,* A Bed for the Night: Humanitarianism in Crisis *(2002). This essay appeared in slightly different form in the*
Summer 1999 *issue of* World Policy Journal *and is printed by permission of The
Wylie Agency, Inc.*

practical criteria been applied to Kosovo, NATO as a whole might well have taken the same tack its European members did in Bosnia and attempted to prevent the conflict from spreading rather than trying, however halfheartedly, to reverse Slobodan Milosevic's campaign of murder and mass deportation.

The longer-term implications of this further step in the post–Cold War moralization of international politics are not yet clear. Realists, whether they belong to the pure national-interest school of a Henry Kissinger or the "lead by moral example" of a George Kennan, are alarmed, as well they should be. For it is now clear that half a century of campaigning by human rights activists has had a profound effect on the conduct of international affairs. The old Westphalian system, in which state sovereignty was held to be well nigh absolute, is under challenge as never before. As former U.N. secretary general Javier Pérez de Cuellar put it in 1991, "We are clearly witnessing what is probably an irresistible shift in public attitudes toward the belief that the defense of the oppressed in the name of morality should prevail over frontiers and legal documents."

Whether it is really "irresistible" is of course debatable. Sometimes what appears at first glance as a prescient description of the future can turn out to be little more than an accurate diagnosis of the present. But Pérez de Cuellar, who, for all his grandee's aloofness, was a far abler diagnostician of his times than he is usually given credit for being, does seem to have discerned an essential shift and discerned it early. The Westphalian system in which he was formed as a diplomat now had challengers, many of whom spoke the language of human rights and derived from this language the belief that, in extreme cases at least, human rights abuses necessitated international intervention. The Franco-Italian legal scholar Mario Bettati and the French humanitarian activist and politician Bernard Kouchner even formulated a doctrine: the right of intervention.

And they and those who took a similar line had a profound effect on the thinking of Western governments. Human rights became an organizing principle for action in the 1990s the way anticommunism had been throughout the Cold War. The result was that most of the interventions of the 1990s, whether they were meant to protect civilians in states that had fallen apart, as in Somalia, or to shield an ethnic group from the murderous intent of its own government, as in Kosovo, were undertaken under the banner of preventing human rights abuses or righting humanitarian wrongs. Kosovo offered yet another example of this, as President Bill Clinton made clear when he said that NATO had acted to prevent "the slaughter of innocents on its doorstep."

ENDS AND MEANS

However, the fact that while the NATO powers are often willing to intervene they have also shown themselves almost never willing to take casualties suggests that this commitment is as much about having fallen into a rhetorical trap as about being guided by a new moralizing principle. The means employed simply do not match the high-flown rhetoric about ends. There have been times during the Kosovo crisis, as there were during the Bosnian war and the Rwandan emergency, when it has appeared that Western involvement came about because the leaders of the Western countries no longer found it politically possible to get up at a press conference before a television audience and say, in effect, "Sorry about the starving X's or the ethnically cleansed Y's. It's just awful what's happening to them, but frankly they don't have any oil, nor are those that oppress them a threat to us. So you, Mr. and Ms. Voter, will have to continue to watch the slaughter on the evening news until it burns itself out."

Of course, that is precisely what members of the policy elites in Washington, Brussels, Paris, London, or Berlin say in private to one another all the time. But public language, along with public pressure, is often what drives policy. By now, commonplace expressions of realism in international affairs have become, to borrow the Early Christian theological distinction between elite and mass Christianity, an esoteric language restricted by and large to policymakers when they are out of public view. It is the language of human rights and humanitarianism that now stands as the exoteric language of public discourse about such questions. What this demonstrates is the degree to which there really has been a human rights revolution in the attitudes, though not to nearly the same degree in the practices, of the Western public and its poll-addicted, pandering governments.

The fact that it is all but inconceivable that a responsible Western leader could say of the Kosovo conflict what Neville Chamberlain said of Czechoslovakia, that this was "a quarrel in a faraway country between people of whom we know nothing," should be demonstration enough—even though, strictly speaking, this would be no more than a simple statement of fact, all the rhetoric about Albania being in the "heart of Europe" to the contrary notwithstanding. To be sure, a politician or cabinet official will occasionally flout, intentionally or unintentionally, the new moral bilingualism. When, famously, then Secretary of State James Baker said of the breakup of Yugoslavia, "We don't have a dog in that fight," he was breaking the unwritten rule that held that, in public, representatives of the Western democracies were always supposed to insist that they stood ready to defend high moral principles.

But for the most part, what a human rights advocate would probably describe as the triumph of the categorical imperative of human rights—an imperative that, in extreme cases anyway, is held to trump all other political or economic interests or criteria—and what a realist might describe as the hypermoralization of international political action, has taken hold not just as a rhetorical but as an operating principle in all the major Western capitals on issues that concern political crises in poor countries and failing states. The fact that there is a human rights double standard where powerful countries like China are concerned does not mean nothing has changed.

The problem lies in separating the cosmetic from the fundamental, the makeover from the moral and political sea change. In all likelihood, elements of both figure in. It is not just that the possibility of any senior government official of any Western government speaking as bluntly as Baker did about the former Yugoslavia has receded, at least when the press microphones are on. The changes are deeper than that. The writer Michael Ignatieff is surely correct when he insists that "the military campaign in Kosovo depends for its legitimacy on what fifty years of human rights has done to our moral instincts, weakening the presumption in favor of state sovereignty, strengthening the presumption in favor of intervention when massacre and deportation become state policy."[1]

By "our," of course, Ignatieff means the Western public that is, as he says, perturbed by distant crimes in a way that it would probably not have been 50 or 75 years ago. Obviously, some sectors of public opinion in all Western states have viewed international affairs largely through a moral lens. U.S. relations with China before the Second World War, to cite only one obvious example, were highly influenced by the agenda of the missionaries. What is impressive is the degree to which these largely Christian missionary (and imperial) habits of thought and categories of analysis find their much broader echo in the secular human rights movement of the past 30 years, and how successfully that movement has been in persuading governments to act at least publicly as if they shared the same concerns and at least some of the same priorities.

MORAL AMBITIONS

Had the consequences of this ascendancy largely been beneficial, and had the actions undertaken by governments in the name of human rights and humanitarian imperatives been as successful as activists initially expected them to be, it would be possible simply to welcome the changed rhetorical and, perhaps, even moral circumstances in which international politics must be conducted. But this is not the case. From Somalia to Rwanda, Cambodia to Haiti, and Congo to Bosnia, the bad news is that the failure rate of these interventions spawned by the categorical imperatives of human rights and humanitarianism in altering the situation on the ground

[1]Michael Ignatieff, "Human Rights: The Midlife Crisis," *New York Review of Books*, May 20, 1999.

in any enduring way approaches 100 percent. Time and time again, our moral ambitions have been revealed as being far larger than our political, military, or even cognitive means. And there is no easy way out.

It is undeniable that the Western television viewer does indeed—and surveys support this contention—see some scene of horror in Central Africa or the Balkans and want something to be done. But "something" is the operative word. Even in situations where the media pays intense attention over a long period of time, there is rarely a consensus that military force should be used, while there is usually a great deal of anxiety about involvement in any operation whose end point is not fixed in advance.

No matter how profoundly the influence of the human rights movement has led to a questioning of the inviolability of state sovereignty, the wish to help and the increasing consensus, at least in elite opinion in most NATO countries, that the West has not just the right but the duty to intervene in certain egregious cases is not matched by any coherent idea of what comes next. This is assuming—and as Kosovo demonstrated, success is anything but assured—that the intervention has succeeded in bringing the particular horror to an end.

Perhaps this is why, in Western Europe at least, the prestige of humanitarianism increased so dramatically over the past 15 years. The humanitarian enterprise—giving help to people desperately in need of it—has seemed to cut through the complexities and corruptions of politics and national interest. Here at last, it seemed, was something morally uncomplicated, something altruistic, something above politics. Of course, what the humanitarian movement discovered painfully over the past decade (though many aid workers had understood this much earlier), starting in Bosnia and culminating in the refugee camps of eastern Zaire where aid helped not only people in need but those who had perpetrated the Rwandan genocide, was that there was no transcending politics. Aid undeniably did good things. A vaccinated child is a vaccinated child. But at least in some instances, it also prolonged wars, distorted resource allocations, and, as in Bosnia, where the humanitarian effort became the focus of Western intervention, offered the great powers an alibi for not stopping the genocide of the Muslims. And Somalia demonstrated that what the West saw as a humanitarian intervention might well be understood by the locals as an imperial invasion, which, whatever its intentions, to a certain extent it almost always is.

AN UNSTABLE MIXTURE

As the limitations of humanitarianism have increasingly become apparent, human rights has taken center stage in the imaginations of those in the West who continue to believe in human progress. Even many humanitarian aid workers have increasingly come to believe that they too must uphold rights, and most of the major private voluntary groups like Doctors Without Borders, Save the Children, or the International Rescue Committee are taking bolder and bolder positions on the need to redress wrongs as well as build latrines, set up clinics, or provide food.

As aid becomes more and more of a business, and private-sector companies expert in construction projects increasingly vie with aid agencies for contracts from principal funders like the U.S. Agency for International Development (USAID) and the European Commission Humanitarian Office (ECHO), some humanitarian workers are coming to believe that the more emphasis they place on human rights (something that private companies are hardly likely to have much taste or aptitude for), the more important a role they will retain. But it is more than a question of corporate self-interest; the way out of the crisis of confidence humanitarianism has undergone has seemed to lie in the quasi-religious moral absolutism and intellectual self-confidence of the human rights movement.

For Western leaders, these distinctions have very little resonance. The Clinton administration, like its European counterparts, routinely conflated human rights and humanitarian concerns. Kosovo was probably the most extreme example of this, but the pattern has been consistent. The best one can say is that most post–Cold War interventions have been undertaken out of an unstable mixture of human rights and humanitarian concerns. And yet the categorical imperative of upholding human rights and the categorical imperative of getting relief to populations who desperately need it are almost as often in conflict as they are complementary.

The human rights activist seeks, first and foremost, to halt abuses. Usually, this involves denouncing the states or movements that are violating the laws of war or the rights of their citizens. In contrast, the humanitarian aid worker usually finds that he or she must deal with the abusive government or rampaging militia if the aid is to get through safely and be distributed.

So far at least, there is more confusion than any new synthesis between human rights and humanitarianism. And the consequences of this have been immensely serious, both operationally and in terms of rallying support for interventions like the ones that took place in Rwanda, Somalia, or Bosnia. Somalia, in particular, revealed the difficulty of engaging in an operation that was supposed to end a famine but that ended up as a war between the foreign army deployed to help the humanitarian effort and one of the Somali factions. Americans were appalled to see soldiers killed in such circumstances, and their revulsion cannot be attributed solely, or even fundamentally, either to the pictures of a dead U.S. soldier being dragged naked through the streets of Mogadishu or to the trauma of Vietnam.

Soldiers are expected to die in a war, but the Somali operation was not presented as a war; it was presented as a humanitarian mission. And soldiers are not supposed to die in such circumstances. Even when the U.S. government declared Mohamad Farah Aideed its enemy, and set out to hunt him down through the back alleys of Mogadishu, it did so using the language of police work. Aideed was a criminal, U.S. officials kept saying.

The result was that the American public came to think of the hunt for Aideed, even though they knew it was being carried out by U.S. Army Rangers, not as war but as police work. Casualties in war are understood to be inevitable. Soldiers are not only supposed to be ready to kill, they are supposed to be able to die. But casualties in police work are a different matter entirely. There, it is only criminals who are supposed to get hurt or, if necessary, killed, not the cops. Again, the fundamental problem has not been some peculiar American aversion to military casualties. Rather, there has been an essential mistake in the way such operations are presented to the public, and, perhaps, even in the way they are conceived of by policymakers. Under the circumstances, it should hardly be surprising that public pressure on Congress and the president to withdraw U.S. troops predictably arises at the first moment an operation cannot be presented in simple moral terms, or when the casualties or even the costs start to mount.

CONFLATING WAR AND CRIME

The emphasis, both in Bosnia and Rwanda, on tribunals and apprehending war criminals, however understandable, only further muddied the moral and political waters. For it cemented this conflation of war and crime. One deals with an enemy in war very differently from how one deals with a war criminal. And wars against war crimes, which is how Kosovo was presented, must either be waged as the Second World War was waged—that is, until unconditional surrender—or run the risk of seeming utterly pointless when, as in most noncrusading wars, a deal is struck between the belligerents that leaves those who have previously been described as war criminals in power. The tensions of such a policy were apparent at the end of the Bosnian war when Slobodan Milosevic, who had quite correctly been described previously by U.S. officials, at least in private, as the architect of the catastrophe, was seen as the indispensable guarantor of the Dayton Accords.

If the tensions are inevitable, so too is a crime-based outlook about war. Ours is an era when most conflicts are within states, and have for their goal less the defeat of an adversary's forces on the battlefield than either the extermination or expulsion of populations. Actually, there are few wars that do not seem to involve widespread and systematic violations of international humanitarian law, so thinking about war as crime is not just an understand-able but in many ways a rational response to objective conditions.

And yet the emphasis on the Yugoslav and Rwandan ad hoc international tribunals, and, more recently, on the International Criminal Court (ICC), not only created false hopes but false perceptions of what a human rights–based international order implies. The false hopes are easier to categorize. Such tribunals may, like the death penalty, deter the individual in question, breaking, as Michael Ignatieff put it, " 'the cycle of impunity' for [certain] particular barbarians," but they cannot hope to seriously deter future criminals or crimes any more than the death penalty deters future murderers—a fact one might have expected the largely anti–death penalty, pro-ICC activists to have confronted more seriously.

But it is by insisting that there is no intellectual or moral problem with demanding that international law should be upheld as strenuously as the domestic laws of democratic states that human rights activists, and the governments that are influenced by them, however intermittently, are engaged in a project that almost certainly seems doomed to failure. Starkly put, its presuppositions do not withstand scrutiny. It is all very well to talk about these laws, or courts, or imperatives, as expressing the will of the "international community." In practice, however, the definition of this "community" is highly if not exclusively legalistic and consists of the states that sign various treaties and conventions and the activist non-governmental organizations that lobby them to do so.

In finessing this fundamental problem of legitimacy—the ICC, as one of its American defenders once conceded, was largely the concern of "hobbyists and specialists"—and in asserting that a body of law that is the product of a treaty has the same authority as a body of law that is the result of long historical processes that involve parliaments, elections, and popular debate, the activists have in effect constructed a legal system for a political and social system that neither exists nor is likely to exist any time in the foreseeable future. Presented as the product of some new global consensus, it is in fact the legal code of a world government.

NO WORLD GOVERNMENT

But there is no world government. There is only world trade and national governments. To say this is not simply to indulge in nostalgia for the Westphalian system or to deny that, in the West anyway, there has been a shift in consciousness toward believing that certain conduct by nations within their borders should not be tolerated whatever the current legal status of state sovereignty may be. Obviously, the power of nation-states to control their destiny is less today than it was half a century ago. And in trade law, there has been a real ceding of sovereignty. Where politics and, above all, the conduct of international relations that can result in war are concerned, however, the picture is much more mixed. States must wage war, and only the state's inherent legitimacy can make it plausible both for young soldiers to kill and die and for their fellow citizens to support or at least tolerate such a tragedy.

The problem with the human rights approach—and in this Western governments that have eagerly seized on the rhetoric of human rights are, if anything, far more blameworthy than the activists themselves—is less that it is wrong than that it is unsustainable in the absence of a world government, or, at the very least, of a United Nations system with far more money, autonomy, and power than it is ever likely to be granted by its member states.

A U.N. mercenary army might well have been able to break the back of the Khmer Rouge in Cambodia or the warlords in Somalia. In places where the interests of the great powers are not involved, the Security Council may at times be willing to grant a mandate for intervention to the secretary general. And open-ended U.N. protectorates in those or similar places, backed up by military force and the mandate to use it, unlike such short-lived operations along the lines of the U.N. Transitional Authority in Cambodia (UNTAC) that have actually taken place, would theoretically have a chance of restoring the broken societies over which they had taken control.

But even leaving aside the question of whether such a move toward world government would be in humanity's best interest, it is obvious that no such option is now available. Even the prospect, seemingly quite realistic in the late 1980s, that U.N. peacekeeping would become a central instrument of international peace and security receded over the course of the 1990s, with peacekeeping reduced to a narrower and more traditional role of postconflict cease-fire monitoring and truce enforcement. But if the United Nations has been marginalized, and if the demands of the emerging human rights consensus among the Western elites have proved to be not just hard to satisfy but hard even to define except in the broadest and most nebulous terms, it is equally clear that the current ad hoc-ism is also unsustainable.

"JUST DO IT"

Kosovo saw to that. The conflict there revealed more than simply the fact that NATO was willing to bomb but not—at least not before it was too late to prevent a second slaughter in the Balkans in a single decade—to take the kinds of military action that might have prevented the ethnic cleansing of almost the entire Kosovar population. In Pristina, before the NATO air war began, young Kosovars walked around wearing T-shirts with the Nike logo and their own gloss on the Nike slogan. "NATO," it read, "Just do it!"

In a sense, that is what important constituencies within the human rights community had been saying as well. Obviously, neither the activists nor the Kosovars themselves imagined the kind of limited, hesitant, politically hamstrung military campaign NATO would undertake when they called for action. And yet this was the predictable, perhaps even the inevitable consequence of not defining that "it." The new language of rights, so prevalent in Western capitals, has been revealed to be at least as misleading about what is and is not possible, what it did and did not commit Western states to, as it is a departure from the old language of state sovereignty.

It is not just that the issues over what the future of a postwar Kosovo would be were fudged from the start. Was the province to be liberated by force? If so, was it to be turned into a NATO or an Organization for Security and Cooperation in Europe (OSCE) protectorate? Or was it to be given its independence? These are only some of the questions that were never answered satisfactorily in Washington or in Brussels before the air campaign began.

More gravely still, there is no evidence that a Marshall Plan for the Balkans, clearly a sine qua non for regional stability even before the bombing started and the mass deportation began, had been worked out. The World Bank was barely consulted; the U.N. specialized agencies, on whom responsibility for the predictable refugee crisis rests, were caught flat-footed. And most Western governments had to run to their parliaments just to get supplemental appropriations to pay for the war; they had no coherent plan for the future whatsoever. Thus, on the political level, the economic level, and the military level, the West was improvising from the start.

But war, even war undertaken on human rights grounds, is not like jazz singing. Improvisation is fatal—as the Kosovars have learned. Just do it, indeed! A country that ran its central bank this way would soon collapse. And yet it continues to be the implicit assumption of the NATO powers that they can confront the crisis of failed states by making it up as they go along. In Somalia, in Rwanda, and in Congo, the Western powers chose to respond with disaster relief, which both guaranteed that the political crises in those countries would continue and represented a terrible misuse of humanitarian aid. In Bosnia, the emphasis was on containing the crisis. In Algeria and Kurdistan, it was either to ignore it or exploit it.

FINESSING THE DISASTER

And yet in Kosovo (this had almost happened in Bosnia), the West was finally hoist on the petard of its own lip service to the categorical imperative of human rights. It was ashamed not to intervene, but it lacked the will to do so with either vision or coherence. Kosovo is probably a lost cause; it is certainly ruined for a generation, whatever eventual deal is worked out, as Bosnia, whose future is to be a ward of NATO, America, and the European Union, probably for decades, has also been ruined for a generation, Dayton or no Dayton.

It is to be hoped that in the wake of Kosovo, the realization that this kind of geo-strategic frivolity and ad hoc-ism, this resolve to act out of moral paradigms that now command the sympathy but do not yet command the deep allegiance of Western public opinion—at least not to the extent that people are willing to sacrifice in order to see that they are upheld—will no longer do. To say this is not to suggest that there are any obvious alternatives. Even if one accepts more of its premises than I do, the human rights perspective clearly is insufficient.

As for the United Nations, it has been shown to be incapable of playing the dual role of both succoring populations at risk while simultaneously acting like a colonial power and imposing some kind of order and rebuilding civic institutions. The important Third World countries seem to have neither the resources nor the ideological inclination to intervene even in their own regions, as Africa's failure to act in Rwanda in 1994 demonstrated so painfully.

The conclusion is inescapable. At the present time, only the West has both the power and, however intermittently, the readiness to act. And by the West, one really means the United States. Obviously, to say that America could act effectively if it chose to do so as, yes, the world's policeman of last resort, is not the same thing as saying that it should. Those who argue, as George Kennan has done, that we overestimate ourselves when we believe we can right the wrongs of the world, must be listened to seriously. So should the views of principled isolationists. And those on what remains of the left who insist that the result of such a broad licensing of American power will be a further entrenchment of America's hegemony over the rest of the world are also unquestionably correct.

WHAT IS TO BE DONE

But the implications of not doing anything are equally clear. Those who fear American power are—this is absolutely certain—condemning other people to death. Had the U.S. armed forces not set up the air bridge to eastern Zaire in the wake of the Rwandan genocide, hundreds of thousands of people would have perished, rather than the tens of thousands who did die. This does not excuse the Clinton administration for failing to act to stop the genocide militarily; but it is a fact. And analogous situations were found in Bosnia and even, for all its failings, in the operation in Somalia.

What is to be done? The Office of the United Nations High Commissioner for Refugees cannot solve crises of such magnitude; these days, it is hard-pressed even to alleviate one without logistical help from NATO military forces. The humanitarian movement has even fewer means. In becoming dependent on NATO's logistical support, or, as in Kosovo, in effect serving as a humanitarian subcontractor to one of the belligerents, its intellectual and moral coherence, which is based on impartiality, has been undermined. And human rights activists, for the valuable work they do in exposing brutality and violations of international law, are demanding a regime of intervention whose implications they clearly have failed to think through seriously.

By this I do not mean the issue of consistency—a debate that, these days is usually framed, "If Kosovo, then why not Sierra Leone?"—although the distorting effect of concentrating exclusively on the south Balkans and channeling what monies exist for aid in its direction cannot but have a devastating effect on Africa in particular. To insist on this point is, when all is said and done, to make the great the enemy of the good. There will be no serious intervention in Sierra Leone; that is no reason for us to turn our collective backs on the Kosovars.

But Kosovo is an anomaly—a crisis at the edge of Europe that came on the heels of the Bosnian crisis about which the NATO powers had a bad conscience. Even had the NATO countries responded more effectively, Kosovo would not have provided a model for how to do post–Cold War interventions.

A deeper problem is how to replace a chaotic post–Cold War disorder with some kind of order that does what it can to prevent both the worst sorts of repression and ethnic cleansing. A realist would say the effort is not worth it. For those who believe differently, whether it is simply because they find the suffering of people in places like Kosovo or the Great Lakes region of Africa as unconscionable when their countries have the means to set it right, or because they believe that too much disorder, even at the periphery of the rich world, is a clear and present danger, the task is to think through how such an order might be imposed.

A more active, attentive, and consistent diplomacy will certainly be necessary, but so will the occasional use of force. Realistically, this means either NATO or the army of the Russian Federation, or both, since only these military establishments have the logistical capacity to move troops long distances in short periods of time. But it is hard to imagine, after the experience of Kosovo, that there will be much appetite for further improvisation. At the same time, it is evident that America's strategic partners will not be disposed to support a renewed Pax Americana in which the United States acts as the global policeman of last resort, even if America were willing to reassume that role. And it never will, since the American consensus is strongly against such an arrangement.

BACK TO THE FUTURE

Where does this leave us? One possible solution would be to revisit the mandatory system that was instituted after the Versailles Treaty. Its pitfalls are obvious. In practice, League of Nations mandates became thinly disguised extensions of the old colonial empires, with trusteeships distributed more on strategic than on humanitarian grounds, and neither improved the situation of the peoples of the territories in question nor brought about any great improvement in regional stability. Woodrow Wilson's warning during the negotiations at the Paris Peace Conference that "the world would say that the Great Powers first portioned out the helpless parts of the world and then formed the League of Nations," needs to be borne in mind.

But Wilson's original idea, which was, as he put it, to take temporary control over certain territories in order "to build up in as short a time as possible . . . a political unit that can take charge of its own affairs," may be one way out of the current impasse. The unhappy experience of the United Nations in Cambodia suggests that an ad hoc imposition of a trusteeship is doomed to failure, if for no other reason than supervisory control is simply too diffuse and too subject to political pressure. Had the United Nations stayed in Cambodia for a generation, as, to his credit, then Secretary General Boutros-Ghali argued that it should, it might indeed have improved that unhappy country's prospects; by staying two years, it provided little more than a short respite. Haiti represents a similar failure to stay the course.

To insist on this point is not to bash the United Nations. The structure of the institution, above all the cross-currents and conflicting interests that find their expression in the work of the Security Council, simply makes it the wrong organization to undertake to administer a new trusteeship system. Regional organizations and great powers are far likelier to be able to devise a system of burden sharing. For all its faults (and the "imperialistic" interests involved), the Nigerian invasion of Sierra Leone was a positive development. The problem was not that the Nigerians came; it was that once there, they had neither the will nor the money to follow up their military conquest with state reconstruction.

Obviously, behind the scenes the NATO countries, and above all the United States, would have to exercise some degree of supervisory control over the trusteeships and underwrite efforts at nation building. Funding would be politically controversial (obviously, most would have to come from the Western powers and possibly from the Bretton Woods institutions) and difficult to appropriate wisely. But, on balance, the costs would still be less than the astronomical figures that were required to rebuild Kosovo, or, for that matter, to deal with the humanitarian crisis in Central Africa in the mid-1990s. Waste and mismanagement are facts of life. They should not become the impediment to actually dealing with the current disorder and tragedy in so much of the poor world.

It is likely that, were such a system to be put in place, the role of American power might actually diminish over the long term, although in the short run it would probably increase. For the most part, however, except in emergencies, or where the rapid dispatch of troops is required, other, mid-sized nations—rather than NATO powers—could do the actual administrating and the policing. And a structure that would necessarily involve this degree of burden sharing between small, medium, and great powers might also serve useful purposes in other fields of international relations, although it would be foolish to expect too much on that score.

The central point is that a mandatory system could take the insights of the human rights revolution into account without overreaching; it could provide a framework for action that could only be an improvement over the current system—if it can even be called that—in which each crisis comes as a kind of lightning bolt from the blue; and it would not be constrained by the kinds of divisions that make any sort of serious action through the U.N. Security Council all but impossible to imagine.

Is this proposal tantamount to calling for a recolonization of part of the world? Would such a system make the United States even more powerful than it is already? Clearly it is, and clearly it would. But what are the alternatives? Kosovo demonstrated how little stomach the United States has for the kind of military action that its moral ambitions impel it to undertake. And there will be many more Kosovos in the coming decades. With the victory of capitalism nearly absolute, the choice is not between systems but about what kind of capitalist system we are going to have and what kind of world order that system requires. However controversial it may be to say this, our choice at the millennium seems to boil down to imperialism or barbarism. Half-measures of the type we have seen in various humanitarian interventions and in Kosovo represent the worst of both worlds. Better to grasp the nettle and accept that liberal imperialism may be the best we are going to do in these callous and sentimental times.

Indeed, the real task for people who reject both realism and the utopian nihilism of a left that would prefer to see genocide in Bosnia and the mass deportation of the Kosovars rather than strengthen, however marginally, the hegemony of the United States, is to try to humanize this new imperial order—assuming it can come into being—and to curb the excesses that it will doubtless produce. The alternative is not liberation, or the triumph of some global consensus of conscience, but, to paraphrase Che Guevara, one, two, three, many Kosovos.

DEEPAK LAL

In Defense of Empires

*The world needs a Pax Americana; an essential
first step is for the United States to face up to its
imperial obligations.*

THE MAJOR ARGUMENT in favor of empires is that they provide
the most basic of public goods—order—in an anarchical international society of states. This is akin to maintaining order in social
life. The three basic values of all social life, which any international order should seek to protect, were cogently summarized by
the late Hedley Bull as: first, to secure life against violence which
leads to death or bodily harm; second, that promises once made
are kept; third, that "the possession of things will remain stable to
some degree and will not be subject to challenges that are constant
and without limit."

Empires—which for our purposes can be simply defined as
"multiethnic conglomerates held together by transnational organizational and cultural ties"—have historically both maintained

*Deepak Lal is the James S. Coleman Professor of International Development Studies
at the University of California, Los Angeles. The present essay, reprinted with the
author's permission, derives from Professor Lal's Henry Wendt Lecture presented in
October 2002 under the auspices of the American Enterprise Institute.*

peace and promoted prosperity for a simple reason.[1] The centers of the ancient civilizations in Eurasia—where sedentary agriculture could be practiced and yielded a surplus to feed the towns—were bordered in the north and south by areas of nomadic pastoralism: the steppes of the north and the semi-desert of the Arabian peninsula to the south. In these regions the inhabitants had kept up many of the warlike traditions of our hunter-gatherer ancestors, and were prone to prey upon the inhabitants of the sedentary "plains" and at times attempted to convert them into their chattel, like cattle. This meant that the provision of one of the classical public goods—protection of its citizens from invaders—required the extension of territory to some natural barriers that could keep the barbarians at bay. The Roman, Chinese, and various Indian empires were partly created to provide this pax, which was essential to keep their labor intensive and sedentary forms of making a living intact. The pax of various imperiums has thus been essential in providing one of the basic public goods required for prosperity.

These empires can further be distinguished as being either multi-cultural or homogenizing. The former included the Abbasids, the various Indian empires, the Ottoman, Austro-Hungarian, and the British, where little attempt was made to change "the habits of the heart" of the constituent groups—or if it was, as in the early British Raj, an ensuing backlash led to a reversal of this policy.

The homogenizing empires, by contrast, sought to create a "national" identity out of the multifarious groups in their territory. The best example of these is China, where the ethnic mix was unified as Hans through the bureaucratic device of writing their names in Chinese characters in a Chinese form, and suppressing any subsequent discontent through the subtle repression of a bureaucratic authoritarian state. In our own time the American "melting pot," creating Americans out of a multitude of ethnicities

---

[1] P. J. Cain and A. G. Hopkins, *British Imperialism, 1699–2000* (Harlow, 2002), p. 664.

by adherence to a shared civic culture and a common language, has created a similar homogenized imperial state. Similarly, the supposedly ancient "nations" of Britain and France were created through a state-led homogenizing process. India, by contrast, is another imperial state whose political unity is a legacy of the British Raj but whose multiethnic character is underwritten by an ancient hierarchical structure which accommodates these different groups as different castes.

The imperial pax or order has also historically been associated with globalization—which is not a new phenomenon—and the prosperity it breeds. This is for two important reasons. First, in the language of institutional economics, transaction costs were reduced by these transnational organizations through their extension of metropolitan property rights to other countries. Second, by integrating previously loosely linked or even autarkic countries and regions—through free flows of goods, capital, and people—into a common economic space, they promote those gains from trade and specialization emphasized by Adam Smith. Thus the Graeco-Roman empires linked the areas around the Mediterranean, the Abbasid empire of the Arabs linked the worlds of the Mediterranean and the Indian Ocean, the Mongol empire linked China with the Near East. Similarly, the various Indian empires created a common economic space in the sub-continent, while the expanding Chinese empire linked the economic spaces of the Yellow River with those of the Yangtze. It was the British who for the first time knit the whole world through their empire.

But most of these empires have ultimately declined. Given the existing technology and the inevitable predatoriness of the state, most of them overextended themselves.

In our own times, the death of nineteenth-century liberal economic order (LIEO) built by Pax Britannica fell on the fields of Flanders and led to a near century of economic disintegration and disorder. Only in the last decade, with the undisputed emergence of the United States as the world hegemon, has this been repaired. But is the U.S. willing and able to maintain its pax, which will underwrite the resurrection of another LIEO like the British in the nineteenth century? And if it is not willing, what are likely to be the consequences?

I

Although Adam Smith did not have much to say about empire per se, his followers Cobden and Bright maintained correctly—following in the master's footsteps—that the arguments used by the imperial lobby that empire was in the economic interests of the general British populace were flawed. Even today economic historians are unable to agree on whether or not the benefits of retaining and expanding the formal British empire after 1850 exceeded its costs. These nineteenth-century classical liberals rightly maintained that, as foreign trade and investment were mutually advantageous (a non-zero-sum game), no empire was needed to obtain these gains from trade. All that was required was free trade and laissez-faire.

Also (and unlike their American cousins) they believed that despite other countries' protectionism, unilateral free trade was in the national interest. They did not want an empire to force other countries to free their foreign trade and investment. They rightly urged and succeeded in Britain's unilateral adoption of free trade with the repeal of the Corn Laws in 1846. By contrast, the current hegemon—the U.S.—has never accepted the case for unilateral free trade and has insisted on reciprocity, based on the erroneous doctrine that foreign trade is a zero-sum game. This, as we shall see, has poisoned the wells of the nascent new imperium.

But these classical liberals went further, believing that the interdependence resulting from a world knit by mutually advantageous trade and investment would also lead to universal peace. They were projecting the spontaneous order of a market economy, in which seemingly conflicting interests are unintentionally harmonized, onto the international arena. This was of course the view of the Enlightenment as codified in Kant's Perpetual Peace. The apotheosis of this English Liberalism was the pacifist book written by Sir Norman Angell in 1910 called *The Great Illusion*. Angell argues that war is economically irrational. It imposes excessive fiscal burdens, defeated powers seldom pay indemnities, colonies do not provide a profit, and "trade cannot be destroyed or captured by a military power." What, then, "is the real guarantee of the good behavior of one state to another? It is the elaborate interdependence which, not only in the economic sense, but in every sense, makes an unwarrantable aggression of one state upon another react upon the interests of the aggressor."[2]

But the liberals did not altogether eschew empire. For as Angell states: "Where the condition of a territory is such that the social and economic cooperation of other countries with it is impossible, we may expect the intervention of military force, not as the result of the 'annexationist illusion,' but as the outcome of real social forces pushing to the maintenance of order."[3] That is the story of England in Egypt, or, for that matter, in India. This is the argument for a "white man's burden," indicating that even liberals were in favor of an empire to maintain a pax.

It was Woodrow Wilson who questioned this "policing" justification for empire. He was a utopian whose worldview combined classical liberalism, Burkean conservatism, Presbyterianism, and socialism. We know that Wilson referred to himself as an imperialist on two occasions, but this was to be a form of economic imperialism. But "for every sentence he uttered on commerce, he spoke two on the moral responsibility of the United States to sustain its historic idealism and render the service of its democracy." During his campaign for the Democratic presidential nomination in 1912, he said: "I believe that God planted in us visions of liberty . . . that we are chosen and prominently chosen to show the way to the nations of the world how they shall walk in the paths of liberty." The instrument for achieving this utopia was to be the League of Nations, maintaining collective security with transgressors being brought into line through sanctions. The traditional notion of "national interest" that had governed the European balance-of-

[2]Norman Angell, *The Great Illusion* (New York, 1911), p. 302.
[3]Angell, *The Great Illusion*, p. 139.

power system was eschewed, to be replaced by a community of nation-states in which the weak and the strong would have equal rights. In his new world order, said Wilson, the only questions would be: "Is it right? Is it just? Is it in the interest of mankind?"

This Wilsonian universal moralism was resurrected after the Second World War with the United Nations. Once again the anthropomorphic identification of states as persons, and the presumption of an essential harmony of interests between these equal world "citizens," was proclaimed, with those breaking international norms being brought into line through collective economic sanctions. These have been ineffective and inefficient in serving their foreign policy goals. By contrast, the nineteenth-century British pax was not maintained through economic sanctions to change states' behavior. Direct or indirect imperialism was used instead. The contrasting lessons from the last two centuries are clear and are of obvious relevance in the current confrontation with the countries in the "Axis of Evil" and the global "war on terror."

II

It was this global network of law protecting foreign capital that allowed the worldwide expansion of the "gentlemanly capitalism" of the City of London which was the hallmark and the real motive force behind the British empire. This legal framework was an integral element of Pax Britannica. Together with the economic integration through free trade and an international payments system based in the City of London, it allowed the empire to fulfill a "wider mission which can be summarized as the world's first comprehensive development program." After 1815, Britain aimed to put in place a set of like-minded allies who would cooperate in keeping the world safe from what Canning called the "youthful and stirring nations," such as the United States, which proclaimed the virtues of republican democracy, and from a "league of worn-out governments" in Europe whose future lay too obviously in the past. Britain offered an alternative vision of a liberal international order bound together by mutual interest in commercial progress and underpinned by a respect for property, credit, and responsible government, preferably of the kind found at home. And compared with the previous millennia, the results were stupendous. It was at the height of this nineteenth-century LIEO from 1850–1914 that many parts of the third world for the first time experienced intensive growth for a sustained period.

The First World War marked the beginning of the end of this nineteenth-century LIEO. Worse, the turmoil of the interwar period also unraveled that complex web of international law and practice the British had woven to protect foreign capital. From the start of the First World War till 1929 (when international capital markets effectively closed down) the United States was the largest lender, with U.S. foreign investments increasing sixfold in the period. But the weakening of British hegemony meant that the enforcement of the international rules created in the nineteenth century became problematic.

After the Second World War, the United States, chastened by the global disorder its interwar isolationism had caused, sought a partial restoration of these nineteenth-century international rules. But that effort did not extend to the newly decolonized third world, which experienced an explosion of economic nationalism. The "embedded liberalism"—which is just another label for democratic socialism—promoted by both Wilson and then Roosevelt within the U.S., also meant that the sanctity of property rights that classical liberals had always sought to further no longer had much resonance in the United States (or, for that matter, the United Kingdom). Given the anti-imperialist moralism which became a part of U.S. foreign policy after Wilson, attempts like the ill-fated Suez adventure of the British and the French in 1956 to prevent Nasser's nationalization of the Suez canal were scuttled by the U.S. There was no way in which anyone could thereafter stand against the new nation-states to assert their rights of national sovereignty against any purported international property rights. There was no bulwark against this disintegration of the international legal order. Most developing countries (and many European ones too) being both nationalist and dirigiste, sought to regulate, tax, or nationalize particular foreign investments on the grounds of national social utility rather than any particular antagonism to private property. This made it difficult for the U.S. to identify expropriation of foreign capital with a socialist ideology, as the nationalization of foreign oil companies in the 1960s and early 1970s by right-wing governments in the Middle East proved. This has cast a long shadow on the present.

But the U.S. did try after the Second World War, at Bretton Woods, to resurrect the three pillars on which the nineteenth-century LIEO had been built—free trade, the gold standard, and free capital mobility. But whereas the British Empire had fostered these by example, treaties, and direct and indirect imperialism, the U.S. instead created transnational institutions—the General Agreement on Tariffs and Trade followed by the World Trade Organization, the International Monetary Fund, and the World Bank.

Rather than following the correct British policy of adopting unilateral free trade and then allowing its hegemony to spread the norm, the U.S. chose the extremely acrimonious route of multi-lateral and, more recently, bilateral negotiations to reduce trade barriers.

This principle of reciprocity has long been the central tenet of U.S. trade policy, and the twentieth-century hegemon has sought to achieve free trade through reciprocal concessions in GATT and the WTO. But as the antiglobalization riots from Seattle onwards demonstrate, by perpetuating the myth that trade is a zero-sum game and that removing tariffs can only be done on the basis of reciprocity, issues of domestic policy will inevitably spill over into trade policy.

The attempt to resurrect something similar to the gold stan-dard based on a quasi-fixed exchange rate system policed by the IMF also foundered on its basic premise that while freeing trade and maintaining convertibility on the current account, the capital account could be controlled and managed by distinguishing be-tween long-term (good) and short-term (bad) capital flows. With the freeing of trade, such capital controls were shown to be ineffective as capital could be moved through the process of "leads and lags" in the current account. With the gradual and long drawn move to floating exchange rates, the need for the policeman of the Bretton Woods system—the IMF—also disappeared.

The World Bank was the instrument chosen to resurrect the international capital market which had been closed in particular to developing countries, with their defaults in the 1930s and the passage of the "Blue Sky" laws by the U.S. which forbade U.S. financial intermediaries from holding foreign government bonds. But the financial intermediation role of the Bank was soon overtaken by its role as a multilateral foreign aid agency, in part to play its part in the cold war, both by tying the "nonaligned" to the free world, and by promoting economic development. This was to be the instrument to be used to create another international development program, analogous to what the British had promoted in the nineteenth century through the propagation and enforcement of rules concerning international property rights, and through direct and indirect imperialism. As these routes were eschewed for the reasons already discussed, the only instrument available was the use of "conditionality," tied to these flows to promote the appropriate development policies in the third world, by changing state behavior. But as with sanctions to serve foreign policy goals, this ever more stringent "conditionality" has been unsuccessful. So the current development "mantra" is that "good governance is all." But now the stark choice which faces the successors of Wilsonian idealism in foreign policy also faces them in international economic policy: Can the order required for prosperity be promoted except through direct or indirect imperialism?

III

The third purpose empires served was to put a lid on ethnic conflicts. President Wilson's invoking of the principle of national self-determination, as he proclaimed the new moral Age of Nations to replace the immoral old Age of Empires, let the ethnic genie out of the bottle.

From the viewpoint of global order, the most common form of deadly conflict today is a civil war in the name of cultural self-determination. Recent research on the causes of civil wars finds that the relationship of ethno-linguistic fragmentation in a state and the risk of a civil war is an inverted U in shape. The most homogenous as well as the most fragmented are least at risk of civil war. Thus there is likely to be a bipolarity in the institutions best able to deal with ethnic diversity. One (complete fragmentation) is to be found in empires. The other (homogeneity) is surprisingly a course advocated by Keynes during the Second World War when speculating about political postwar order in Europe.

But this homogenized solution, which as Keynes recognized could involve "ethnic cleansing," has clearly been eschewed by the West—as witness its actions in Bosnia and Kosovo. This reflects the hopes of much progressive thought over the last two centuries, stemming from the Enlightenment, that transnational and "modern" forms of association such as "class" would transcend primordial forms of association such as "ethnicity" and "culture"—of which nationalism is an offshoot. But contemporary history continues to show the power of these primordial forces.

So, at least in principle, the Keynes solution seems to be in keeping with human nature. As in a globalized economy size does not matter for prosperity—demonstrated by the shining examples of the city states of Hong Kong and Singapore—cultural self-determination would also be feasible as long as there is someone to maintain a global pax.

However, the events in Bosnia and Kosovo show that in fact the United States and its allies have, rightly in my view, chosen to impose a regional pax by partially reconstructing parts of the Balkan Austro-Hungarian empire. The high representative of the UN in Bosnia and the chief administrator of Kosovo are the equivalent of British viceroys in areas of direct and political agents in those of indirect imperialism. Similarly the recent Afghan peace is underwritten by an Allied police force and another form of indirect imperialism, much as the British sought to do through their residents in Afghanistan during their imperium.

IV

But even if there is a case for Pax Americana to maintain global peace between states, international property rights, and to prevent ethnic conflicts, would it not lead, as Paul Kennedy argued in the late 1980s, to "imperial overstretch" and the nationalist backlash which has undermined past empires and which U.S. foreign policy has tolerated if not promoted?

It is apparent that, on past and current performance and future prospects, the only potential competitors to U.S. military power are the Chinese (by perhaps mid-century) and the Indians by the end of the century. Given the U.S. technological lead, these potential dates for catch-up are likely to be even later. So that for at least this century it is unlikely that U.S. military power is likely to be challenged.

One of the strengths of the U.S. is that in its public and increasingly private philosophy, racism no longer plays a part—witness that two of the leading lights dealing with foreign policy today are Afro-Americans. Moreover, the U.S. has now moved to recognizing dual citizenship, as have many other countries—with even the most nationalist like India planning to follow. With the growth of a cosmopolitan class of primarily U.S.-trained technicians and executives, culturally and often personally linked, at work in many different countries, there is already in existence the core of a global "Roman" political and economic elite—open to the talents—which could run this new U.S. imperium.

But even granted all this, will not a U.S. imperium lead to a coalition forming against it? Envy, jealousy, even hatred are the inevitable and unenviable consequence of disparities in economic and military power. But should the dominant economic and military power then actively seek to become poorer and weaker so it may be loved, or to prevent other powers "ganging up" against it in the future? Or should it instead try to use its hegemony to bring along the other great powers into a concert maintaining the global pax as the British did in the nineteenth century, recognizing that its dominance will lead both to emulation by many—the "soft power" that idealists so often talk about—but also fear and loathing among others. Preventing the latter from spilling over into global disorder has in fact been one of the essential tasks of imperial statesmanship. But to undertake it sensibly one has to recognize that one is an imperial power. "Empires come before imperialism." The nub of my case is that the U.S., like any other economically and militarily dominant powers in the past, has acquired an empire, but it is reluctant to face up to the resulting imperial responsibilities because in its domestic discourse it refuses to face up to the reality. This would involve developing a theory for the beneficent exercise of its imperial power. Wishing the empire would just go away, or can be managed by global love and compassion, is not only to bury one's head in the sand but actually to promote global disorder.

In fact, if we look at the current threats to global or regional political and economic order, there would seem to be a convergence rather than divergence in the interests of the U.S. and other potential great powers. There are clearly two major regions of the world where disorder rules. First, the vast region spanning the Islamic world in the Middle East and Central Asia, and second, the continent of Africa.

We can be brief in dealing with Africa, because (sadly) with the ending of the cold war, it does not represent a strategic challenge to any of the potential great powers we had identified earlier. Its strategic importance in the nineteenth century lay in guarding the sea lanes to India—the jewel in the British imperial crown. That reason no longer applies. Apart from justified humanitarian concerns about the plight of its people, there is little that the rest of the world has to lose or gain from engaging or disengaging from Africa. Given the dismal failure of the Western development program in Africa, based on conditional aid channeled through governments run by predatory elites, little short of costly direct imperialism is likely to provide that good governance which everyone now maintains is the prerequisite for the economic advancement of the continent.

For the U.S. and the world, the best policy towards Africa, if direct imperialism is ruled out as being too costly, is to keep markets for African goods and capital flows to Africa open, and leave it to the Africans to sort out their own problems.

The Islamic world poses a more serious challenge. In rightly trying to distinguish the direct threats posed to national and global security after September 11 from Islamists, as distinct from Islam—in no small measure to protect the substantial Muslim minorities in many Western countries—many commentators and world leaders have gone out of their way to say that, in the "war of terror," the enemy is not Islam. At one level this is true. But once one seeks to understand the reason for the rise of Islamic fundamentalism, and its seeming attraction to large numbers in Muslim countries, it is difficult to escape the conclusion that it has something to do with the nature of Islam itself.

Until the Muslim world wholeheartedly embraces modernization, recognizing that this does not involve Westernization and the giving up of its soul, there is little hope of the Islamist threat to other Muslims and the rest of the modern world being eliminated. But how is this modernization to come about?

Here we have briefly to go back to the world created in the Middle East with the dismemberment of the Ottoman empire. Apart from Egypt, Turkey, Saudi Arabia, and Iran, the rest of the states in the Middle East today are the artificial creations of the victorious powers that dismembered the Ottoman empire. Thus Iraq, instead of being—as Saddam Hussein has claimed—the successor state of Nebuchadnezzar, was put together by Britain as a unit containing Kurdish, Sunni, and Shia tribes. This artificial tribal confederation has always been brittle, and its unity has been maintained not by any national feeling but by tribal deals and most recently by terror.

The Kingdom of Saudi Arabia is also not the descendant of any ancient Arab state, but the result of a religious movement—the Wahabis (an extreme version of Islam) creating a state in central Arabia in the eighteenth century. Then oil was discovered, extracted, and exported by Western companies, and by 1960 the total Middle Eastern oil reserves were estimated to be about 60 percent of known world reserves. Given the erosion of international rules concerning property rights, and the growth of statism, the Saudi oil fields along with others in Iraq and Iran were nationalized. The Saudis were moreover protected by the U.S.

September 11 finally showed up the dangers in this Faustian pact. It concerns both money and ideology. The Saudis have maintained a tightrope act for half a century. They have balanced their alliance with the infidels and the untold riches they provide the dynasty, by maintaining what is probably the most virulent and medieval form of Islam in their own country, and using their newfound wealth to propagate it through financing mosques and Wahabi preachers around the world.

For the rest of the world, the poison being spread by this Wahabi evangelism is becoming intolerable. To see how pernicious it is, imagine what we would think if German schools just had lessons in anti-Semitism, or those in America were just teaching the young to hate blacks. But this is what the large number of madrasas funded by the Saudis, in Pakistan and many other countries around the world, are teaching. If there is to be an end to the "war of terror," this poisoning of the Muslim mind clearly has to stop.

But numerous commentators have argued that the reason why this poison is still being successfully spread is the continuing Arab-Israeli confrontation and the anger this arouses in the Arab street, which provides the Islamists with an unlimited supply of jehadis. Without going into the historical rights and wrongs of the issue— on which I have always believed the Arabs have a rightful grievance—there are two reasons why in my view this issue (despite Arab rhetoric) is merely another symptom of the failure of both the Islamic world to come to terms with modernity as well as the common tactic used by the third world to externalize its domestic problems.

The only solution to the Arab-Israeli problem, therefore, also lies in the Muslim world coming to terms with modernity. But this in turn requires that the Saudi and Iraqi direct and indirect support for the "intifada" must end. What this suggests is that the current status quo in the Middle East is untenable. The primary task of a Pax Americana must be to find ways to create a new order in the Middle East, where the cosmological beliefs are preserved but the prosperity engendered by modernity leads to the ending of the belief in jihad, thus easing the confusion in the Islamic soul which has plagued it for over a century.

It is accusingly said by many that any such rearrangement of the status quo would be an act of imperialism and would largely be motivated by the desire to control Middle Eastern oil. But far from being objectionable, imperialism is precisely what is needed to restore order in the Middle East.

This is not the occasion to discuss the mechanics of the exercise of imperial power to reorder the Middle East to allow its people and those of the world to prosper under an American pax. But there is this question: in this task of establishing a Middle Eastern pax, will the U.S. have to act alone? If one looks at a map of the Middle East, and sees the countries currently threatened by the spread of Islamist hatred, they comprise Russia, China, India, and of course embattled Israel. If the maintenance of global order in the near future therefore means countering this Islamo-fascism, clearly the U.S. is not going to find a coalition against it forming with these potential great powers. Deals will no doubt have to be cut on the side, but there is no real conflict of interests which would allow a hostile coalition to build up against the United States on this issue.

One can draw one's own conclusions. But it does seem laudable that some in the U.S. administration may at long last be taking the imperial task seriously.

V

There are those of course who still believe that moral persuasion will be enough to solve the Arab-Israeli dispute, and together with the use of sanctions bring order in the Middle East. The Europeans in particular are vociferous adherents of the Wilsonian order with their demand for multilateral action through the UN. But this is just the usual tactic of the weak: to tie Gulliver down with a million strings so that he cannot move. As in terms of military and economic power the Europeans are increasingly becoming second order powers, it is unlikely that any lack of support on their part will endanger an American pax. No doubt, as they have done for fifty years, they will continue to be free riders on whatever pax is created. So I think the fears of those who worry that an assertive America will provoke an aggressive countercoalition against itself are exaggerated.

After September 11, despite much continuing ambivalence, at long last the United States seems to be awaking from the Wilsonian dream and realizing that it has a unique responsibility—like the British in the nineteenth century—to maintain global order. But, as I have been at pains to emphasize, this implies the promotion of modernization—particularly in the Muslim world—but not Westernization. It is, however, the continuing domestic resonance of the "idealism" in its foreign policy emphasized by Woodrow Wilson which has the potential of undermining this emerging pax: by creating a backlash if the modernization which is required is conflated with Westernization.

Given its domestic homogenizing imperial tendencies, the U.S. (along with various other Western countries) is attempting to legislate its "habits of the heart" around the world—"human rights," democracy, egalitarianism, labor, and environmental standards. Its claim that it is thereby promoting universal values is unjustified.

For there is an important difference between the cosmological beliefs of what became the Christian West and the other ancient agrarian civilizations of Eurasia. Christianity has a number of distinctive features which it shares with its Semitic cousin Islam, but not entirely with its parent Judaism, and which are not to be found in any of the other great Eurasian religions. The most important is its universality. Neither the Jews nor the Hindu or Sinic civilizations had religions claiming to be universal. You could not choose to be a Hindu, Chinese, or Jew; you were born as one. This also meant that, unlike Christianity and Islam, these religions did not proselytize. Third, only the Semitic religions, being monotheistic, have also been egalitarian. Nearly all the other Eurasian religions (apart from Buddhism) believed in some form of hierarchical social order. By contrast, alone among the Eurasian civilizations, the Semitic ones (though least so the Jewish) emphasized the equality of men's souls in the eyes of their monotheistic deities. The so-called universal values being promoted by the West are no more than the culture-specific, proselytizing ethic of what remains at heart Western Christendom. Nor is there a necessary connection as the West claims between democracy and development. If democracy is to be preferred as a form of government, it is not because of its instrumental value in promoting prosperity—at times it may well not—but because it promotes a different Western value—liberty. Again, many civilizations have placed social order above this value, and again it would be imperialistic for the West to ask them to change their ways.

If the West ties its moral crusade too closely to the emerging processes of globalization and modernization, there is a danger that there will also be a backlash against the process of globalization. This potential cultural imperialism poses a greater danger to the acceptance of a new Pax Americana in developing countries, particularly in the Muslim countries, than the unfounded fears of their cultural nationalists that the modernization promoted by globalization will lead to the erosion of cherished national cultures.

My conclusions can be brief. Empires have unfairly got a bad name, not least in U.S. domestic politics. This is particularly unfortunate, as the world needs an American pax to provide both global peace and prosperity. The arguments that this is too costly have been found to be wanting. However, if instead of this pax the U.S. seeks to create an international moral order by attempting to legislate its "habits of the heart" through ethical imperialism, it is likely to breed disorder. The most urgent task in the new imperium is to bring the world of Islam into the modern world without seeking to alter its soul.

I have given reasons to believe that the United States should be able to fulfill this imperial task. But is it willing? Given the continuing resonance of Wilsonian moralism in public discourse, I am doubtful. A beginning would be the acceptance in domestic politics that the U.S. is an imperial power. The real debate about how best to use that power could then sensibly ensue.

CHARLES KRAUTHAMMER

The Unipolar Era

American global dominion is a good thing.
Preserving it requires the forthright exercise of
American power.

IN LATE 1990, shortly before the collapse of the Soviet Union, it was clear that the world we had known for half a century was disappearing. The question was what would succeed it. I suggested then that we had already entered the "unipolar moment." The gap in power between the leading nation and all the others was so unprecedented as to yield an international structure unique to modern history: unipolarity.

At the time, this thesis was generally seen as either wild optimism or simple American arrogance. The conventional wisdom was that with the demise of the Soviet empire the bipolarity of the second half of the 20th century would yield to multipolarity. The declinist school, led by Paul Kennedy, held that America, suffering from "imperial overstretch," was already in relative decline. The

Charles Krauthammer, winner of the Pulitzer Prize for commentary, is currently a columnist for Time *magazine and the* Washington Post. *This essay first appeared in the Winter 2003 issue of* The National Interest *and is reprinted by permission of the author.*

Asian enthusiasm, popularized by (among others) James Fallows, saw the second coming of the Rising Sun. The conventional wisdom was best captured by Senator Paul Tsongas: "The Cold War is over; Japan won."

They were wrong, and no one has put it more forcefully than Paul Kennedy himself in a classic recantation published earlier this year. "Nothing has ever existed like this disparity of power; nothing," he said of America's position today. "Charlemagne's empire was merely western European in its reach. The Roman empire stretched farther afield, but there was another great empire in Persia, and a larger one in China. There is, therefore, no comparison."[1] Not everyone is convinced. Samuel Huntington argued in 1999 that we had entered not a unipolar world but a "uni-multipolar world."[2] Tony Judt writes mockingly of the "loud boasts of unipolarity and hegemony" heard in Washington today.[3] But as Stephen Brooks and William Wohlforth argue in a recent review of the subject, those denying unipolarity can do so only by applying a ridiculous standard: that America be able to achieve all its goals everywhere all by itself. This is a standard not for unipolarity but for divinity. Among mortals, and in the context of the last half millennium of history, the current structure of the international system is clear: "If today's American primacy does not constitute unipolarity, then nothing ever will."[4]

A second feature of this new post–Cold War world, I ventured, would be a resurgent American isolationism. I was wrong. It turns out that the new norm for America is not post–World War I withdrawal but post–World War II engagement. In the 1990s, Pat Buchanan gave 1930s isolationism a run. He ended up carrying Palm Beach.

Finally, I suggested that a third feature of this new unipolar world would be an increase rather than a decrease in the threat of

---

[1]Paul Kennedy, "The Eagle Has Landed," *Financial Times*, February 2, 2002.

[2]Samuel P. Huntington, "The Lonely Superpower," *Foreign Affairs*, March / April 1999.

[3]Tony Judt, "Its Own Worst Enemy," *New York Review of Books*, August 15, 2002.

[4]Stephen Brooks and William Wohlforth, "American Primacy in Perspective," *Foreign Affairs*, July / August 2002.

war, and that it would come from a new source: weapons of mass destruction wielded by rogue states. This would constitute a revolution in international relations, given that in the past it was great powers who presented the principal threats to world peace.

Where are we twelve years later? The two defining features of the new post–Cold War world remain: unipolarity and rogue states with weapons of mass destruction. Indeed, these characteristics have grown even more pronounced. Contrary to expectation, the United States has not regressed to the mean; rather, its dominance has dramatically increased. And during our holiday from history in the 1990s, the rogue state/WMD problem grew more acute. Indeed, we are now on the eve of the history's first war over weapons of mass destruction.

UNIPOLARITY AFTER SEPTEMBER 11, 2001

There is little need to rehearse the acceleration of unipolarity in the 1990s. Japan, whose claim to power rested exclusively on economics, went into economic decline. Germany stagnated. The Soviet Union ceased to exist, contracting into a smaller, radically weakened Russia. The European Union turned inward toward the great project of integration and built a strong social infrastructure at the expense of military capacity. Only China grew in strength, but coming from so far behind it will be decades before it can challenge American primacy—and that assumes that its current growth continues unabated.

The result is the dominance of a single power unlike anything ever seen. Even at its height Britain could always be seriously challenged by the next greatest powers. Britain had a smaller army than the land powers of Europe, and its navy was equaled by the next two navies combined. Today, American military spending exceeds that of the next *twenty* countries combined. Its navy, air force, and space power are unrivaled. Its technology is irresistible. It is dominant by every measure: military, economic, technological, diplomatic, cultural, even linguistic, with a myriad of countries trying to fend off the inexorable march of Internet-fueled MTV English.

American dominance has not gone unnoticed. During the 1990s, it was mainly China and Russia that denounced unipolarity in their occasional joint communiqués. As the new century dawned it was on everyone's lips. A French foreign minister dubbed the United States not a superpower but a hyperpower. The dominant concern of foreign policy establishments everywhere became understanding and living with the 800-pound American gorilla.

And then September 11 *heightened* the asymmetry. It did so in three ways. First, and most obviously, it led to a demonstration of heretofore latent American military power. Kosovo, the first war ever fought and won exclusively from the air, had given a hint of America's quantum leap in military power (and the enormous gap that had developed between American and European military capabilities). But it took September 11 for the United States to unleash with concentrated fury a fuller display of its power in Afghanistan. Being a relatively pacific, commercial republic, the United States does not go around looking for demonstration wars. This one was thrust upon it. In response, America showed that at a range of 7,000 miles and with but a handful of losses, it could destroy within weeks a hardened, fanatical regime favored by geography and climate in the "graveyard of empires."

Such power might have been demonstrated earlier, but it was not. "I talked with the previous U.S. administration," said Vladimir Putin shortly after September 11, "and pointed out the bin Laden issue to them. They wrung their hands so helplessly and said, 'the Taliban are not turning him over, what can one do?' I remember I was surprised: If they are not turning him over, one has to think and do something."

Nothing was done. President Clinton and others in his administration have protested that nothing could have been done, that even the 1998 African embassy bombings were not enough to mobilize the American people to strike back seriously against terrorism. The new Bush Administration, too, did not give the prospect of mass-casualty terrorism (and the recommendations of the Hart-

Rudman Commission) the priority it deserved. Without September 11, the giant would surely have slept longer. The world would have been aware of America's size and potential, but not its ferocity or its full capacities. (Paul Kennedy's homage to American power, for example, was offered in the wake of the Afghan campaign.)

Second, September 11 demonstrated a new form of American strength. The center of its economy was struck, its aviation shut down, Congress brought to a halt, the government sent underground, the country paralyzed and fearful. Yet within days the markets reopened, the economy began its recovery, the president mobilized the nation, and a united Congress immediately underwrote a huge new worldwide campaign against terror. The Pentagon started planning the U.S. military response even as its demolished western façade still smoldered.

America had long been perceived as invulnerable. That illusion was shattered on September 11, 2001. But with a demonstration of its recuperative powers—an economy and political system so deeply rooted and fundamentally sound that it could spring back to life within days—that sense of invulnerability assumed a new character. It was transmuted from impermeability to resilience, the product of unrivaled human, technological, and political reserves.

The third effect of September 11 was to accelerate the realignment of the current great powers, such as they are, behind the United States. In 1990, America's principal ally was NATO. A decade later, its alliance base had grown to include former members of the Warsaw Pact. Some of the major powers, however, remained uncommitted. Russia and China flirted with the idea of an "anti-hegemonic alliance." Russian leaders made ostentatious visits to pieces of the old Soviet empire such as Cuba and North Korea. India and Pakistan, frozen out by the United States because of their nuclear testing, remained focused mainly on one another. But after September 11, the bystanders came calling. Pakistan made an immediate strategic decision to join the American camp. India enlisted with equal alacrity, offering the United States basing, overflight rights, and a level of cooperation unheard of during its half century of Nehruist genuflection to anti-American nonalignment. Russia's Putin, seeing both a coincidence of interests in the fight against Islamic radicalism and an opportunity to gain acceptance in the Western camp, dramatically realigned Russian foreign policy toward the United States. (Russia has already been rewarded with a larger role in NATO and tacit American recognition of Russia's interests in its "near abroad.") China remains more distant but, also having a coincidence of interests with the United States in fighting Islamic radicalism, it has cooperated with the war on terror and muted its competition with America in the Pacific.

The realignment of the fence-sitters simply accentuates the historical anomaly of American unipolarity. Our experience with hegemony historically is that it inevitably creates a counterbalancing coalition of weaker powers, most recently against Napoleonic France and Germany (twice) in the 20th century. Nature abhors a vacuum; history abhors hegemony. Yet during the first decade of American unipolarity no such counterbalancing occurred. On the contrary, the great powers lined up behind the United States, all the more so after September 11.

The American hegemon has no great power enemies, an historical oddity of the first order. Yet it does face a serious threat to its dominance, indeed to its essential security. It comes from a source even more historically odd: an archipelago of rogue states (some connected with transnational terrorists) wielding weapons of mass destruction.

The threat is not trivial. It is the single greatest danger to the United States because, for all of America's dominance, and for all of its recently demonstrated resilience, there is one thing it might not survive: decapitation. The detonation of a dozen nuclear weapons in major American cities, or the spreading of smallpox or anthrax throughout the general population, is an existential threat. It is perhaps the only realistic threat to America as a functioning hegemon, perhaps even to America as a functioning modern society.

Like unipolarity, this is historically unique. WMD are not new, nor are rogue states. Their conjunction is. We have had fifty years of experience with nuclear weapons—but in the context of bipolarity, which gave the system a predictable, if perilous, stability. We have just now entered an era in which the capacity for inflicting mass death, and thus posing a threat both to world peace and to the dominant power, resides in small, peripheral states.

What does this conjunction of unique circumstances—unipolarity and the proliferation of terrible weapons—mean for American foreign policy? That the first and most urgent task is protection from these weapons. The catalyst for this realization was again September 11. Throughout the 1990s, it had been assumed that WMD posed no emergency because traditional concepts of deterrence would hold. September 11 revealed the possibility of future WMD-armed enemies both undeterrable and potentially undetectable. The 9/11 suicide bombers were undeterrable; the author of the subsequent anthrax attacks has proven undetectable. The possible alliance of rogue states with such undeterrables and undetectables—and the possible transfer to them of weapons of mass destruction—presents a new strategic situation that demands a new strategic doctrine.

THE CRISIS OF UNIPOLARITY

Accordingly, not one but a host of new doctrines have come tumbling out since September 11. First came the with-us-or-against-us ultimatum to any state aiding, abetting, or harboring terrorists. Then, pre-emptive attack on any enemy state developing weapons of mass destruction. And now, regime change in any such state.

The boldness of these policies—or, as much of the world contends, their arrogance—is breathtaking. The American anti-terrorism ultimatum, it is said, is high-handed and permits the arbitrary application of American power everywhere. Pre-emption is said to violate traditional doctrines of just war. And regime change, as Henry Kissinger has argued, threatens 350 years of post-Westphalian international practice. Taken together, they amount to an unprecedented assertion of American freedom of action and a definitive statement of a new American unilateralism.

To be sure, these are not the first instances of American unilateralism. Before September 11, the Bush Administration had acted unilaterally, but on more minor matters, such as the Kyoto Protocol and the Biological Weapons Convention, and with less bluntness, as in its protracted negotiations with Russia over the ABM treaty. The "axis of evil" speech of January 29, however, took unilateralism to a new level. Latent resentments about American willfulness are latent no more. American dominance, which had been tolerated if not welcomed, is now producing such irritation and hostility in once friendly quarters, such as Europe, that some suggest we have arrived at the end of the opposition-free grace period that America had enjoyed during the unipolar moment.

In short, post-9/11 U.S. unilateralism has produced the first crisis of unipolarity. It revolves around the central question of the unipolar age: Who will define the hegemon's ends?

The issue is not one of style but of purpose. Secretary of Defense Donald Rumsfeld gave the classic formulation of unilateralism when he said (regarding the Afghan war and the war on terrorism, but the principle is universal), "the mission determines the coalition." We take our friends where we find them, but only in order to help us in accomplishing the mission. The mission comes first, and we decide it.

Contrast this with the classic case study of multilateralism at work: the U.S. decision in February 1991 to conclude the Gulf War. As the Iraqi army was fleeing, the first Bush Administration had to decide its final goal: the liberation of Kuwait or regime change in Iraq. It stopped at Kuwait. Why? Because, as Brent Scowcroft has explained, going further would have fractured the coalition, gone against our promises to allies, and violated the UN resolutions under which we were acting. "Had we added occupation of Iraq and removal of Saddam Hussein to those objectives," wrote Scowcroft in the *Washington Post* on October 16, 2001, " . . . our Arab allies, refusing to countenance an invasion of an Arab colleague, would have deserted us." The coalition defined the mission.

Who should define American ends today? This is a question of agency, but it leads directly to a fundamental question of policy. If the coalition—whether NATO, the wider Western alliance, *ad hoc* outfits such as the Gulf War alliance, the UN, or the "international community"—defines America's mission, we have one vision of America's role in the world. If, on the other hand, the mission defines the coalition, we have an entirely different vision.

LIBERAL INTERNATIONALISM

For many Americans, multilateralism is no pretense. On the contrary: it has become the very core of the liberal internationalist school of American foreign policy. In the October 2002 debate authorizing the use of force in Iraq, the Democratic chairman of the Senate Armed Services Committee, Carl Levin, proposed authorizing the president to act only with prior approval from the UN Security Council. Senator Edward Kennedy put it succinctly while addressing the Johns Hopkins School of Advanced International Studies on September 27, 2002: "I'm waiting for the final recommendation of the Security Council before I'm going to say how I'm going to vote."

This logic is deeply puzzling. How exactly does the Security Council confer moral authority on American action? The Security Council is a committee of great powers, heirs to the victors in the Second World War. They manage the world in their own interest. The Security Council is, on the very rare occasions when it actually works, *realpolitik* by committee. But by what logic is it a repository of international morality? How does the approval of France and Russia, acting clearly and rationally in pursuit of their own interests in Iraq (largely oil and investment), confer legitimacy on an invasion?

Yet this kind of logic utterly dominated the intervening Clinton years. The 1990s were marked by an obsession with "international legality" as expressed by this or that Security Council resolution. To take one long forgotten example: After an Iraqi provocation in February 1998, President Clinton gave a speech at the Pentagon laying the foundation for an attack on Iraq (one of many that never came). He cited as justification for the use of force the need to enforce Iraqi promises made under post–Gulf War cease-fire conditions that "the United Nations demanded—not the United States—the United Nations." Note the formulation. Here is the president of the most powerful nation on earth stopping in mid-sentence to stress the primacy of commitments made to the UN over those made to the United States.

This was not surprising from a president whose first inaugural address pledged American action when "the will and conscience of the international community is defied." Early in the Clinton years, Madeleine Albright formulated the vision of the liberal internationalist school then in power as "assertive multilateralism." Its principal diplomatic activity was the pursuit of a dizzying array of universal treaties on chemical weapons, biological weapons, nuclear testing, global environment, land mines, and the like. Its trademark was consultation: Clinton was famous for sending Secretary of State Warren Christopher on long trips (for example, through Europe on Balkan policy) or endless shuttles (uncountable pilgrimages to Damascus) to consult; he invariably returned home empty-handed and diminished. And its principal objective was good international citizenship: it was argued on myriad foreign policy issues that we could not do X because it would leave us "isolated." Thus in 1997 the Senate passed a chemical weapons convention that even some of its proponents admitted was unenforceable, largely because of the argument that everyone else had signed it and that failure to ratify would leave us isolated. Isolation, in and of itself, was seen as a diminished and even morally suspect condition.

A lesson in isolation occurred during the 1997 negotiations in Oslo over the land mine treaty. One of the rare holdouts, interestingly enough, was Finland. Finding himself scolded by his neighbors for opposing the land mine ban, the Finnish prime minister noted tartly that this was a "very convenient" pose for the "other Nordic countries" who "want Finland to be their land mine."

In many parts of the world, a thin line of American GIs is the land mine. The main reason we oppose the land mine treaty is that we need them in the Korean DMZ. We man the lines there. Sweden and France and Canada do not have to worry about a North Korean invasion killing thousands of their soldiers. As the unipolar power and thus guarantor of peace in places where Swedes do not tread, we need weapons that others do not. Being uniquely situated in the world, we cannot afford the empty platitudes of allies not quite candid enough to admit that they live under the umbrella of American power. That often leaves us "isolated."

Multilateralism is the liberal internationalist's means of saving us from this shameful condition. But the point of the multilateralist imperative is not merely psychological. It has a clear and coherent geopolitical objective. It is a means that defines the ends. Its means—internationalism (the moral, legal, and strategic primacy of international institutions over national interests) and legalism (the belief that the sinews of stability are laws, treaties, and binding international contracts)—are in service to a larger vision: remaking the international system in the image of domestic civil society. The multilateralist imperative seeks to establish an international order based not on sovereignty and power but on interdependence—a new order that, as Secretary of State Cordell Hull said upon returning from the Moscow Conference of 1943, abolishes the "need for spheres of influence, for alliances, for balance of power."

Liberal internationalism seeks through multilateralism to transcend power politics, narrow national interest, and, ultimately, the nation-state itself. The nation-state is seen as some kind of archaic residue of an anarchic past, an affront to the vision of a domesticated international arena. This is why liberal thinkers embrace the erosion of sovereignty promised by the new information technologies and the easy movement of capital across borders. They welcome the decline of sovereignty as the road to the new globalism of a norm-driven, legally bound international system broken to the mold of domestic society.

The greatest sovereign, of course, is the American superpower, which is why liberal internationalists feel such acute discomfort with American dominance. To achieve their vision, America too—America especially—must be domesticated. Their project is thus to restrain America by building an entangling web of interdependence, tying down Gulliver with myriad strings that diminish his overweening power. Who, after all, was the ABM treaty or a land mine treaty going to restrain? North Korea?

This liberal internationalist vision—the multilateral handcuffing of American power—is the dominant view in Europe. That is to be expected, given Europe's weakness and America's power. But it is a mistake to see this as only a European view. The idea of a new international community with self-governing institutions and self-enforcing norms—the vision that requires the domestication of American power—is the view of the Democratic Party in the United States and of a large part of the American foreign policy establishment. They spent the last decade in power fashioning precisely those multilateral ties to restrain the American Gulliver and remake him into a tame international citizen. The multilateralist project is to use—indeed, to use up—current American dominance to create a new international system in which new norms of legalism and interdependence rule in America's place—in short, a system that is no longer unipolar.

REALISM AND THE NEW UNILATERALISM

The basic division between the two major foreign policy schools in America centers on the question of what is, and what should be, the fundamental basis of international relations: paper or power. Liberal internationalism envisions a world order that, like domestic society, is governed by laws and not men. Realists see this vision as hopelessly utopian. The history of paper treaties—from the pre-war Kellogg-Briand Pact and Munich to the post–Cold War Oslo accords and the 1994 Agreed Framework with North Korea—is a history of naiveté and cynicism, a combination both toxic and volatile that invariably ends badly. Trade agreements with Canada are one thing. Pieces of parchment to which existential enemies affix a signature are quite another. They are worse than worthless because they give a false sense of security and breed complacency. For the realist, the ultimate determinant of the most basic elements of international life—security, stability, and peace—is power.

Which is why a realist would hardly forfeit the current unipolarity for the vain promise of goo-goo one-worldism. Nor, however, should a realist want to forfeit unipolarity for the familiarity of traditional multipolarity. Multipolarity is inherently fluid and unpredictable. Europe practiced multipolarity for centuries and found it so unstable and bloody, culminating in 1914 in the catastrophic collapse of delicately balanced alliance systems, that Europe sought its permanent abolition in political and economic union. Having abjured multipolarity for the region, it is odd in the extreme to then prefer multipolarity for the world.

Less can be said about the destiny of unipolarity. It is too new. Yet we do have the history of the last decade, our only modern experience with unipolarity, and it was a decade of unusual stability among all major powers. It would be foolish to project from just a ten-year experience, but that experience does call into question the basis for the claims that unipolarity is intrinsically unstable or impossible to sustain in a mass democracy.

I would argue that unipolarity, managed benignly, is far more likely to keep the peace. Benignity is, of course, in the eye of the beholder. But the American claim to benignity is not mere self-congratulation. We have a track record. Consider one of history's rare controlled experiments. In the 1940s, lines were drawn through three peoples—Germans, Koreans, and Chinese—one side closely bound to the United States, the other to its adversary. It turned into a controlled experiment because both states in the divided lands shared a common culture. Fifty years later the results are in. Does anyone doubt the superiority, both moral and material, of West Germany vs. East Germany, South Korea vs. North Korea, and Taiwan vs. China?

Benignity is also manifest in the way others welcome our power. It is the reason, for example, that the Pacific Rim countries are loath to see our military presence diminished: they know that the United States is not an imperial power with a desire to rule other countries—which is why they so readily accept it as a balancer. It is the reason, too, why Europe, so seized with complaints about American high-handedness, nonetheless reacts with alarm to the occasional suggestion that America might withdraw its military presence. America came, but it did not come to rule. Unlike other hegemons and would-be hegemons, it does not entertain a grand vision of a new world. No Thousand Year Reich. No New Soviet Man. It has no great desire to remake human nature, to conquer for the extraction of natural resources, or to rule for the simple pleasure of dominion. Indeed, America is the first hegemonic power in history to be obsessed with "exit strategies." It could not wait to get out of Haiti and Somalia; it would get out of Kosovo and Bosnia today if it could. Its principal aim is to maintain the stability and relative tranquility of the current international system by enforcing, maintaining, and extending the current peace.

The form of realism that I am arguing for—call it the new unilateralism—is clear in its determination to self-consciously and confidently deploy American power in pursuit of those global ends. Note: global ends. There is a form of unilateralism that is devoted only to narrow American self-interest and it has a name, too: it is called isolationism. Critics of the new unilateralism often confuse it with isolationism because both are prepared to unashamedly exercise American power. But isolationists oppose America acting as a unipolar power not because they disagree with the unilateral means, but because they deem the ends far too broad. Isolationists would abandon the larger world and use American power exclusively for the narrowest of American interests: manning Fortress America by defending the American homeland and putting up barriers to trade and immigration.

The new unilateralism defines American interests far beyond narrow self-defense. In particular, it identifies two other major interests, both global: extending the peace by advancing democracy and preserving the peace by acting as balancer of last resort. Britain was the balancer in Europe, joining the weaker coalition against the stronger to create equilibrium. America's unique global power allows it to be the balancer in every region. We balanced

Iraq by supporting its weaker neighbors in the Gulf War. We balance China by supporting the ring of smaller states at its periphery (from South Korea to Taiwan, even to Vietnam). Our role in the Balkans was essentially to create a microbalance: to support the weaker Bosnian Muslims against their more dominant neighbors, and subsequently to support the weaker Albanian Kosovars against the Serbs.

Of course, both of these tasks often advance American national interests as well. The promotion of democracy multiplies the number of nations likely to be friendly to the United States, and regional equilibria produce stability that benefits a commercial republic like the United States. America's (intended) exertions on behalf of pre-emptive non-proliferation, too, are clearly in the interest of both the United States and the international system as a whole.

Critics find this paradoxical: acting unilaterally but for global ends. Why paradoxical? One can hardly argue that depriving Saddam (and potentially, terrorists) of weapons of mass destruction is not a global end. Unilateralism may be required to pursue this end. We may be left isolated in so doing, but we would be acting nevertheless in the name of global interests—larger than narrow American self-interest and larger, too, than the narrowly perceived self-interest of smaller, weaker powers (even great powers) that dare not confront the rising danger.

What is the essence of that larger interest? Most broadly defined, it is maintaining a stable, open, and functioning unipolar system. Liberal internationalists disdain that goal as too selfish, as it makes paramount the preservation of both American power and independence. Isolationists reject the goal as too selfless, for defining American interests too globally and thus too generously.

A third critique comes from what might be called pragmatic realists, who see the new unilateralism I have outlined as hubristic, and whose objections are practical. They are prepared to engage in a pragmatic multilateralism. They value great power concert. They seek Security Council support not because it confers any moral authority, but because it spreads risk. In their view, a single hegemon risks far more violent resentment than would a power that consistently acts as *primus inter pares*, sharing rule-making functions with others.

I have my doubts. The United States made an extraordinary effort in the Gulf War to get UN support, share decision-making, assemble a coalition, and, as we have seen, deny itself the fruits of victory in order to honor coalition goals. Did that diminish the anti-American feeling in the region? Did it garner support for subsequent Iraq policy dictated by the original acquiescence to the coalition?

The attacks of September 11 were planned during the Clinton Administration, an administration that made a fetish of consultation and did its utmost to subordinate American hegemony and smother unipolarity. The resentments were hardly assuaged. Why? Because the extremist rage against the United States is engendered by the very structure of the international system, not by the details of our management of it.

Pragmatic realists also value international support in the interest of sharing burdens, on the theory that sharing decision-making enlists others in our own hegemonic enterprise and makes things less costly. If you are too vigorous in asserting yourself in the short-term, they argue, you are likely to injure yourself in the long-term when you encounter problems that require the full cooperation of other partners, such as counter-terrorism.

If the concern about the new unilateralism is that American assertiveness be judiciously rationed, and that one needs to think long-term, it is hard to disagree. One does not go it alone or dictate terms on every issue. On some issues such as membership in and support of the WTO, where the long-term benefit both to the American national interest and global interests is demonstrable, one willingly constricts sovereignty. Trade agreements are easy calls, however, free trade being perhaps the only mathematically provable political good. Others require great skepticism. The Kyoto Protocol, for example, would have harmed the American economy while doing nothing for the global environment. (Increased emissions from China, India, and Third World countries exempt from its provisions would have more than made up for American cuts.) Kyoto failed on its merits, but was nonetheless pushed because the rest of the world supported it. The same case was made for the chemical and biological weapons treaties—sure, they are useless or worse, but why not give in there in order to build goodwill for future needs? But appeasing multilateralism does not assuage it; appeasement merely legitimizes it. Repeated acquiescence to provisions that America deems injurious reinforces the notion that legitimacy derives from international consensus, thus undermining America's future freedom of action—and thus contradicting the pragmatic realists' own goals.

America must be guided by its independent judgment, both about its own interest and about the global interest. Especially on matters of national security, war-making, and the deployment of power, America should neither defer nor contract out decision-making, particularly when the concessions involve permanent structural constrictions such as those imposed by an International Criminal Court. Prudence, yes. No need to act the superpower in East Timor or Bosnia. But there is a need to do so in Afghanistan and in Iraq. No need to act the superpower on steel tariffs. But there is a need to do so on missile defense.

The prudent exercise of power allows, indeed calls for, occasional concessions on non-vital issues if only to maintain psychological goodwill. Arrogance and gratuitous high-handedness are counterproductive. But we should not delude ourselves as to what psychological goodwill buys. Countries will cooperate with us, first, out of their own self-interest and, second, out of the need and desire to cultivate good relations with the world's superpower. Warm and fuzzy feelings are a distant third. Take counterterrorism. After the attack on the *U.S.S. Cole*, Yemen did everything it could to stymie the American investigation. It lifted not a finger to suppress terrorism. This was under an American administration that was obsessively accommodating and multilateralist. Today, under the most unilateralist of administrations, Yemen has decided to assist in the war on terrorism. This was not a result of a sudden attack of goodwill toward America. It was a result of the war in

Afghanistan, which concentrated the mind of heretofore recalcitrant states like Yemen on the costs of non-cooperation with the United States. Coalitions are not made by superpowers going begging hat in hand. They are made by asserting a position and inviting others to join. What "pragmatic" realists often fail to realize is that unilateralism is the high road to multilateralism. When George Bush senior said of the Iraqi invasion of Kuwait, "this will not stand," and made it clear that he was prepared to act alone if necessary, that declaration—and the credibility of American determination to act unilaterally—in and of itself created a coalition. Hafez al-Asad did not join out of feelings of goodwill. He joined because no one wants to be left at the dock when the hegemon is sailing.

Unilateralism does not mean seeking to act alone. One acts in concert with others if possible. Unilateralism simply means that one does not allow oneself to be hostage to others. No unilateralist would, say, reject Security Council support for an attack on Iraq. The nontrivial question that separates unilateralism from multilateralism—and that tests the "pragmatic realists"—is this: What do you do if, at the end of the day, the Security Council refuses to back you? Do you allow yourself to be dictated to on issues of vital national and international security?

When I first proposed the unipolar model in 1990, I suggested that we should accept both its burdens and opportunities and that, if America did not wreck its economy, unipolarity could last thirty or forty years. That seemed bold at the time. Today, it seems rather modest. The unipolar moment has become the unipolar era. It remains true, however, that its durability will be decided at home. It will depend largely on whether it is welcomed by Americans or seen as a burden to be shed—either because we are too good for the world (the isolationist critique) or because we are not worthy of it (the liberal internationalist critique).

The new unilateralism argues explicitly and unashamedly for maintaining unipolarity, for sustaining America's unrivaled dominance for the foreseeable future. It could be a long future, assuming we successfully manage the single greatest threat, namely, weapons of mass destruction in the hands of rogue states. This in itself will require the aggressive and confident application of unipolar power rather than falling back, as we did in the 1990s, on paralyzing multilateralism. The future of the unipolar era hinges on whether America is governed by those who wish to retain, augment, and use unipolarity to advance not just American but global ends, or whether America is governed by those who wish to give it up—either by allowing unipolarity to decay as they retreat to Fortress America, or by passing on the burden by gradually transferring power to multilateral institutions as heirs to American hegemony. The challenge to unipolarity is not from the outside but from the inside. The choice is ours. To impiously paraphrase Benjamin Franklin: History has given you an empire, if you will keep it.

DAVID NORTH

America's Drive for
World Domination

*Under the administration of George W. Bush,
American imperialism has become a criminal
enterprise.*

ON SEPTEMBER 17, 2002, the Bush administration published
its "National Security Strategy of the United States of America."
This important document advances the political and theoretical
justification for a colossal escalation of American militarism. It asserts as the guiding policy of the United States the right to use
military force anywhere in the world, at any time it chooses,
against any country it believes to be, or it believes may at some
point become, a threat to American interests. No other country in
modern history, not even Nazi Germany at the height of Hitler's
madness, has asserted such a sweeping claim to global hegemony—or, to put it more bluntly, world domination—as is now
being made by the United States.

*David North chairs the editorial board of World Socialist Web Site (www.wsws.org)
where this essay was posted on October 4, 2002. It appears here by permission of the
World Socialist Web Site.*

The message of this document, stripped of its cynical euphemisms and calculated evasions, is unmistakably clear: the United States government asserts the right to bomb, invade and destroy whatever country it chooses. It refuses to respect as a matter of international law the sovereignty of any other country, and reserves the right to get rid of any regime, in any part of the world, that is, appears to be, or might some day become, hostile to what the United States considers to be its vital interests. Its threats are directed, in the short term, against so-called "failed states"—that is, former colonies and impoverished Third World countries ravaged by the predatory policies of imperialism. But larger competitors of the United States, whom the document refers to, in a revival of pre–World War II imperialist jargon, as "Great Powers," are by no means out of the gun sights of the Bush administration. The wars against small and defenseless states that the United States is now preparing—first of all against Iraq—will prove to be the preparation for military onslaughts against more formidable targets.

The document begins by boasting that "The United States possesses unprecedented—and unequaled—strength and influence in the world." It declares with breathtaking arrogance that "The U.S. national security strategy will be based on a distinctly American internationalism that reflects the union of *our values* and *our national interests*." This formula is so striking that it should be committed to memory: American Values + American Interests = A Distinctly American Internationalism. It is indeed a very distinct sort of internationalism that proclaims what's good for America is good for the world. As President Bush asserts in the introduction of the document, America's values "are right and true for every person, in every society. . . ."

These values are none other than a collection of the banal nostrums of the American plutocracy. They include "respect for private property"; "pro-growth legal and regulatory policies to encourage business investment, innovation, and entrepreneurial activity"; "tax policies—particularly lower marginal tax rates—that improve incentives for work and investment"; "strong financial systems that allow capital to be put to its most efficient use"; and "sound fiscal policies to support business activity." The document then declares that "The lessons of history are clear: market economies, not command-and-control economies with the heavy hand of government, are the best way to promote prosperity and reduce poverty. Policies that further strengthen market incentives and market institutions are relevant for all economies—industrialized countries, emerging markets, and the developing world."

All these right-wing platitudes are asserted in the midst of a deepening world economic crisis, in which entire continents are suffering the consequences of market economics that have shattered whatever once existed of their social infrastructures and reduced billions of people to conditions that defy description. One decade after the dismantling of the USSR and the restoration of capitalism, the death rate of Russia exceeds its birthrate. South America, a laboratory where the International Monetary Fund has gleefully practiced its anti-social experiments, is in a state of economic disintegration. In Southern Africa, a substantial portion of the population is infected with the HIV virus.

These catastrophic conditions are the product of the capitalist system and the rule of the market. The strategic document acknowledges in passing that "half of the human race lives on less than $2 a day," but, as to be expected, the prescription drawn up by the Bush administration is the more intensive application of the economic policies that are responsible for the misery that exists all over the world.

Defining its idea of a "distinctly American internationalism," the document states that "While the United States will constantly strive to enlist the support of the international community, we will not hesitate to act alone. . . ." In another passage, the document warns that the United States "will take the actions necessary to ensure that our efforts to meet our global security commitments and protect Americans are not impaired by the potential for investigations, inquiry, or prosecution by the International Criminal Court (ICC), whose jurisdiction does not extend to Americans and which we do not accept." In other words, the actions of the leaders of the

United States will not be restrained by the conventions of international law.

The essential claim asserted in this document is the right of the United States to take unilateral military action against another country without offering credible evidence that it is acting to prevent a clear and verifiable threat of attack. This assertion of all-encompassing powers to resort to violence whenever it decides to do so is justified with loosely constructed language that cannot withstand even a cursory analysis: "We must be prepared to stop *rogue states and their terrorist clients before they are able to threaten or use weapons of mass destruction* against the United States and our allies and friends."

Who defines what a "rogue state" is? Is it any state that challenges, directly or indirectly, American interests? A list of all those countries that the Bush administration considers to be "rogue states," not to mention potential "rogue states," is a very long one.

The assertion of the right to take military action against "rogue states and their terrorist clients *before* they are able to threaten or use weapons of mass destruction" can only mean that the United States claims the right to attack whatever state it identifies as a *potential* threat. Although a state may not, at present, pose a threat to the United States—though it may not even be planning, let alone actively preparing to attack the U.S.—it may still find itself a legitimate target if Washington identifies it as a potential or embryonic danger.

A definition of "threat" that requires no overt action against the United States, but merely the potential to pose a danger at some point in the future, would place virtually every country in the world on the list of possible targets for an American attack. This is not an exaggeration. The document speaks not only of "enemies," but also of "potential adversaries," and warns them not to pursue "a military build-up in hopes of surpassing, or equaling, the power of the United States." It directly warns China against attempting to acquire "advanced military capabilities," asserting that by doing so "China is following an outdated path that, in the end, will hamper its own pursuit of national greatness"—that is, it will call upon itself a preemptive military response by the United States.

While the report tells China that the pursuit of "advanced military capabilities" means following "an outdated path," it proclaims hypocritically just two pages later that "It is time to reaffirm the essential role of American military strength. We must build and maintain our defenses beyond challenge." And this project entails a vast expansion of America's military presence throughout the world. "To contend with uncertainty and to meet the many security challenges we face, the United States will require bases and stations within and beyond Western Europe and Northeast Asia, as well as temporary access arrangements for the long-distance deployment of U.S. forces."

The document asserts repeatedly that the new doctrine of preemptive strikes against existing and/or potential threats, and the abandonment of the previous doctrine of deterrence, is a necessary response to the events of September 11, 2001, when the United States suddenly confronted a new, unprecedented, and unimagined danger. "The nature of the Cold War threat," the report asserts, "required the United States ... to emphasize deterrence of the enemy's use of force, producing a grim strategy of mutual assured destruction. With the collapse of the Soviet Union and the end of the Cold War, our security environment has undergone profound transformation." Somewhat later, the document describes the Soviet Union as "a generally status quo, risk-adverse adversary. Deterrence was an effective defense."

Those unfamiliar with the history of the Cold War would hardly imagine that the authors of this strategic document—who now describe the USSR in almost nostalgic terms as a "status quo, risk-averse adversary" against whom a gentlemanly and polite deterrence was effective—are more or less the same people who, as recently as the 1980s, were describing the Soviet Union as the "focus of evil" against whom the United States had to prepare for all-out war. The present defense secretary, Donald Rumsfeld, was closely associated with the right-wing Committee for the Present Danger, formed in the 1970s, which was bitterly opposed to arms control agreements with the Soviet Union. This organization demanded a massive military build-up against the USSR, and argued that it was possible for the United States to wage and win a nuclear war against the Soviet Union. The Reagan administration's sponsorship of the Strategic Defense Initiative (SDI), known as "Star Wars," arose from the demand of extreme right-wing elements in the Republican Party—among whom are now to be found the principal *dramatis personae* who direct the policies of the Bush administration, especially Dick Cheney, Donald Rumsfeld, and Paul Wolfowitz—for the development of technology that would make it possible for the United States to consider the use of nuclear weapons against the USSR to be a viable military option.

Here we come to the historical falsification and political deception that underlie the Bush administration's National Security Strategy—the claim that the policies outlined in the report are essentially a response to the events of September 11, determined and shaped by the inescapable military obligations imposed upon the United States by the threat of Al Qaeda and other terrorist organizations. Far from being an exceptional response to the events of September 11, 2001, the plan for world domination outlined in the National Security Strategy of the Bush administration has been in development for more than a decade.

The origins of Bush's National Security Strategy unveiled in September 2002 can be dated back to the dissolution of the Soviet Union in December 1991. This had for the United States the most far-reaching significance. For nearly three-quarters of a century, the fate of American imperialism and the Soviet Union were inextricably linked. The October Revolution that brought the Bolshevik Party to power followed by only a few months the April 1917 entry of the United States into World War I. Thus, from the earliest days of its emergence as the principal imperialist power, the United States confronted the reality of a workers' state that proclaimed the advent of a new historical epoch of world socialist revolution.

Though it emerged from World War II as the leader of world

capitalism, the United States was not in a position to organize the world as it saw fit.

In the end, the self-dissolution of the Soviet Union in 1991 created for American imperialism an unprecedented historical opportunity. For the first time it could operate in an international environment in which there did not exist any significant restraints—military or political—on the use of force to achieve its aims. From this point on, internal discussions on the strategic aims of the United States were taken over by the most vicious and reactionary tendencies.

The demise of the USSR, they declared, created for the United States the opportunity to establish an unchallengeable global hegemony. The task of the United States was to exploit what right-wing columnist Charles Krauthammer referred to in 1991 as a "unipolar moment" to establish an absolutely dominant global position. The United States, argued Krauthammer, should not hesitate to use military power to get whatever it wanted. The Europeans and Japanese should be treated with contempt, and compelled to recognize that they had to approach the United States as supplicants. While it might be politically advisable for U.S. leaders to pay lip service to multilateralism, that policy was, in reality, dead. The time had come for the United States to exercise its power unilaterally, "unashamedly laying down the rules of world order and being prepared to enforce them."[1]

The first Bush administration responded to the demise of the USSR by initiating a full-scale review of U.S. military strategy. Its overriding objectives were to exploit aggressively the power vacuum left by the dissolution of the Soviet Union, and, by so doing, establish a geopolitical stranglehold that would prevent any country from emerging as a credible competitor of the United States. The key to this project was to be the use of military power to intimidate and, if necessary, smash any enemy or adversary, existing or potential. In 1992, Defense Secretary Richard Cheney and then-General Colin Powell called for the implementation of vastly

[1]Charles Krauthammer, "The Unipolar Moment," *Foreign Affairs*, vol. 70, no. 1, 1991, p. 33.

expanded operational objectives for U.S. military forces. They stipulated that the military should be able to complete one major war in 100 days and two in less than 180 days.

The election of Bill Clinton did not produce any significant change in the increasingly aggressive attitude of American military planners. Under the slogan, "Shaping the World Through Engagement," the 1990s saw the emergence of a political consensus within both the Democratic and Republican parties that saw military power as the principal means by which the United States would secure long-term global dominance.

This insistence on the decisive role of military power arises not from the strength but rather the underlying weakness of American capitalism. In essence, militarism is symptomatic of economic and social decline. As it loses, and with good reason, confidence in the economic strength of American capitalism vis-à-vis its major international rivals, and grows increasingly fearful about fissures within the domestic social structure, the ruling elite views military power as the means by which it can counteract all the troubling negative tendencies. As Thomas Friedman of the *New York Times* wrote in March 1999, "The hidden hand of the market will never work without a hidden fist—McDonald's cannot flourish without a McDonnell Douglas, the builder of the F-15. And the hidden fist that keeps the world safe for Silicon Valley's technologies is called the United States Army, Air Force, Navy and Marine Corps. . . . Without America on duty, there will be no America On Line."

The issue of Iraq has played a central role in high-level discussions on America's strategic ambitions. In a sense, the first war against Iraq occurred just a few months too early for American imperialism. In January–February 1991, with the fate of the USSR still uncertain, the Bush administration considered it too risky to overstep the boundaries of the UN mandate and attempt unilaterally to overthrow the regime of Saddam Hussein. But almost from the moment the war had come to a close, there was a sense within powerful sections of the ruling elite that an immense opportunity had been missed. Within the context of the new strategic aim to prevent the emergence of any power or combination of powers that might challenge American domination, the conquest of Iraq came to be seen as a crucial strategic objective. In countless documents produced by right-wing strategists, it was openly argued that the overthrow of the regime of Saddam Hussein would provide the United States with strategic control over oil, the supremely critical resource that is essential to the economies of its potential economic and military rivals in Europe and Japan.

Except in the American mass media, where discussion of this sensitive issue is virtually taboo, it is widely recognized all over the world that oil, not so-called weapons of mass destruction, is the central preoccupation of the United States. While the war in Afghanistan provided the opportunity for the establishment of new American military bases in Central Asia—which is believed to hold the second largest reserves of petroleum in the world—the conquest of Iraq would immediately place the second largest reserve of crude oil in the Persian Gulf region under the control of the United States. To quote the ineffable Thomas Friedman, "[H]aving broken Iraq, we own Iraq."

The Bush administration, whose leading personnel consists of people like Cheney who honed their criminal skills as oil industry executives, looks at the Persian Gulf as the potential jewel in the crown of an emerging American empire. If domination of that region were combined with effective control of the oil and natural gas reserves that will be eventually pumped out of Central Asia, the leaders of American imperialism believe that they will have achieved the long-term strategic hegemony that has eluded the United States for so long. This vision of a world dominion, secured through control of strategic global resources, is a reactionary fantasy that has found an enthusiastic audience among broad sections of the Establishment. The frame of mind that prevails within America's political and financial aristocracy is reflected in a new book by Robert Kaplan, entitled *Warrior Politics: Why Leadership Demands a Pagan Ethos*. In a typical passage, he declares:

> The more successful our foreign policy, the more leverage America will have in the world. Thus, the more likely that

future historians will look back on the twenty-first-century United States as an empire as well as a republic, however different from that of Rome and every other empire throughout history. For as the decades and the centuries march on, and the United States has had a hundred presidents, or 150 even, instead of forty-three, and they appear in long lists like the rulers of bygone empires—Roman, Byzantine, Ottoman—the comparison with antiquity may grow rather than diminish. Rome, in particular, is a model for hegemonic power, using various means to encourage a modicum of order in a disorderly world. . . .[2]

This drivel is of interest only as a sort of bizarre cultural phenomenon—an example of the delusionary state of mind within a ruling elite that has lost all sense of history and of contemporary reality, not to mention common decency.

It does not seem to occur to Mr. Kaplan that to the extent that the United States seeks to implement these fantasies, it will encounter opposition: first of all, from those who are the immediate targets of American depredations—the masses in the countries targeted for conquest. There is also the opposition of America's imperialist rivals in Europe and Japan, who simply cannot accept a situation that threatens them with economic strangulation. It is precisely the growing fears over the implications of America's long-term strategic aims—the establishment of global domination—that found expression in the increasingly open opposition to US plans for war in Iraq. A likely consequence of a U.S. war against Iraq will be an enormous intensification of inter-imperialist conflicts—principally between the United States and its major economic and geopolitical competitors. The stage will be set for World War III.

So far, in discussing the reasons for the drive of the United States for war, we have concentrated on the global geo-strategic

---

[2]Robert Kaplan, *Warrior Politics: Why Leadership Demands a Pagan Ethos* (New York, 2002), p. 153.

and economic motivations. But there is yet another crucial factor in the political equation—that is, the increasingly explosive state of social relations in the United States and the threat that this poses to capitalist rule.

Throughout the past decade U.S. policy experts have expressed concern over growing signs of a decay of social cohesion. Samuel Huntington, who is best known for his book *The Clash of Civilizations*, warned several years ago that the end of the Cold War had deprived the U.S. government of a cause that could foster mass support for the state. There did not seem to exist, he wrote, any genuine sense of national interests that commanded mass support. The problem noted by Huntington, however, is not primarily ideological. It is rooted in increasingly irreconcilable social conflicts within American society. It is becoming ever more difficult to mask the massive social inequality that presently characterizes American society. The concentration of extraordinary levels of personal wealth among a very small percentage of the population has far-reaching social implications, no matter how vigorously the mass media glorifies the rich and their lifestyles.

The erosion of democratic norms and the ever-more-apparent dysfunctional state of American politics are objective consequences of social polarization. In the year 2000, for the first time since the immediate aftermath of the Civil War, it was not possible to arrive at a democratic resolution of the election. In the end, the financial plutocracy handpicked the president.

The United States is beset by social problems for which the existing political setup has no answers. Indeed, it is unable to even address them. The existing two-party system, whose personnel are utterly dependent on the financial support of the plutocracy, is thoroughly unrepresentative of the general population. How else can one explain the fact that the deep unease and ambivalence felt by millions of Americans toward the drive toward war find virtually no articulation in the political establishment? Rather, the political establishment, whose constituencies are different fractions of the richest two percent of the population, is absolutely incapable of giving voice to the concerns and interests of the broad masses.

The current economic crisis has profoundly deepened the estrangement between the working class and the ruling class. The ongoing exposures of the criminality of the corporate elite threaten to transform the economic crisis—which is, in itself, of a fairly serious character—into a general crisis of class rule. To no small extent, the Bush administration hopes that dramatic successes overseas will somehow distract the people from the domestic crisis. But history provides many examples of the catastrophes that befell reactionary regimes that played with war to keep domestic problems at bay. Governments that prescribe war as a medication for a failing domestic economy and intensifying social conflict may suffer all sorts of unforeseen side effects—of which revolution may prove to be the most serious.

The drive of the Bush administration toward war confronts every concerned individual with political and, I might add, moral questions of the greatest magnitude. Let me emphasize: The policies of the Bush administration are not merely mistaken. They are criminal. Those responsible for these policies are not misguided individuals. They are political criminals. But the criminality of their policy flows from the essentially criminal character of American imperialism—which strives to shore up a faltering capitalist system through a policy of plunder and mass murder. There is really no essential difference between the methods employed by the ruling elite within the United States and those it uses internationally.

II

The Nature of American Empire

PETER BENDER

The New Rome

*America's quest for security impels it, like
Rome, to expand and to dominate.*

WHEN ONE COMPARES the American and Roman paths to
world power, one notes a similarity distinguishing them from that
of other great world empires. The American and Roman empires
were not the creation of one great conqueror such as Alexander,
Genghis Khan, or Napoleon, whose empires grew quickly but
then rapidly fell apart. Rome's and America's power increased
slowly and steadily until each grew into a superpower that could
no longer be resisted and was seen by many as a salvation. Whoever found themselves in a difficult situation called on Rome or
Washington for assistance. Restricting itself to the "island" described by its borders appeared to be less and less practical, yet
only extraordinary challenges led to engagement beyond the protective seas; and only existential threats, real or imagined, would

*Peter Bender, a student of ancient history, has been a journalist and lecturer on post-
war history at the Universities of Berlin and Rostock. He is currently writing a book
that expands on the themes of this essay. The present essay, translated from German
by Andrew I. Port, is an abridged version of an article appearing in the Winter 2003
issue of* Orbis. *It appears here by permission of that journal.*

lead to long-term commitments in other countries and on other continents.

The decisive struggles that made world powers of both (America vs. the Soviet Union, Rome vs. Carthage) were essentially duels. In each case, the foes had sunk their teeth so deeply into one other that they no longer had complete control over their own decisions. "We are both caught in an unholy and dangerous cycle," President Kennedy observed, "in which suspicion on the one side engenders suspicion on the other, and in which new weapons lead again to new defensive weapons." Rome and America both expanded in order to achieve security. Like concentric circles, each circle in need of security demanded the occupation of the next larger circle. The Romans made their way around the Mediterranean, driven from one challenge to their security to the next. The struggles against Hitler, Stalin, Mao, and Japan brought the Americans to Europe and East Asia; the Americans soon wound up all over the globe, driven from one attempt at containment to the next. The boundaries between security and power politics gradually blurred. The Romans and Americans both eventually found themselves in a geographical and political position that they had not originally desired, but which they then gladly accepted and firmly maintained. Neither power, it would seem, corresponds to the distorted picture painted by their enemies or to the ideal portrait depicted by their admirers. They were neither world conquerors nor unwilling world powers.

SPECIAL TRAITS

Almost all states have security concerns and commercial interests, but not all become world powers. Only certain special characteristics can explain why a Latin state under Etruscan rule and why thirteen English colonies were able to reach the highest peak of power. In the American case, one first thinks of its democratic constitution, which not only released great stores of energy but also gave its citizens opportunities that proved beneficial to the state itself. The Roman state was able to function with its unwritten constitution in a way that a state seldom functions. In the decisive century between 264 and 168 BCE, it both developed and was able to focus energies that allowed Rome to survive the most difficult of times. Even if one is skeptical of Livius' pious histories or of jingoist flagwaving in the United States, one can still recognize a genuine constitutional patriotism on the part of both Romans and Americans.

The steady immigration of especially active, entrepreneurial, and powerful individuals provided a permanent source of energy for the United States. Thomas Jefferson believed early on that rapid population increase would eventually encompass the entire northern continent, and perhaps the southern one as well. The Romans, for their part, created a masterpiece unmatched by anyone else in antiquity. Rome the city-state grew into an Italian territorial power—and eventually a territorial state—through incorporations, the extension of civic rights, the founding of colonies, and the creation of "eternal" alliances. No matter how different the paths they took and the forms they ultimately created, Americans and Romans provided their states with a broad-based population, in the absence of which their economic and military expansion would have been well-nigh unimaginable.

But expansion required personal qualities as well. Regardless of how problematic "folk-based" psychological categories are, one can only understand America by focusing on its unmatched economic dynamism; Rome's secret of success was its political genius. But what unites both are their untamed energy, their refusal to be content with half measures, their determination to carry something out to its logical conclusion, and their conviction that anything can be achieved quickly if one only invests enough energy. The Americans at times had difficulty sustaining the conflict with the Soviet Union because there was no end in sight; Polybios, who came to know Rome intimately during the second century BCE, criticized the Romans for wanting "to achieve everything by force" and thinking that "anything they have set their hearts on can be achieved."

Americans and Romans aimed, wherever possible, for victory—

and not for a negotiated peace; "unconditional surrender" was the equivalent of the *deditio*, according to which "the Romans rule over all, the vanquished nothing." Both claimed the unlimited right to render their enemies permanently harmless. The Japanese constitution, which was written by Americans, declares that Japan renounces "forever" the "sovereign right" to make war. Using the terminology of the Nuremberg Trials, the German Basic Law forbids the Federal Republic from preparing an offensive war. After the Second Punic War, Carthage was allowed to wage war only with Roman permission, and after the Second Macedonian War, Philip was only permitted to travel north in order to fight against the barbarians.

Finally, in perhaps the most important similarity, Romans and Americans both developed that sense for power in the absence of which one could not become a world power in the first place. The logic of security for their respective "islands" led each to demand to rule beyond their "islands." They became protective lords after each act of assistance provided to other states; in effect, they offered protection and gained control. The protected were mistaken when they assumed that they could use Rome or America to their own ends without suffering a partial loss of sovereignty. With increasing power grew the consciousness of power and the willingness to use it, as when Rome demanded that Antiochos IV abort his campaign for the conquest of Egypt. The Roman senator sent to tell Antiochos this drew a circle around him with a stick and told him he could only leave the circle once he gave the senator his answer. After brief hesitation, Antiochos promised to comply with Rome's demand.

American senators and diplomats certainly don't go to such extremes, but one hears echoes of Antiochos and Egypt when they publicly exhort, warn, censure, and lecture, and when they make known almost everywhere they go that disobedience will lead to certain consequences. The conviction of the Romans that they had a calling to rule the world—already recognizable beginning in the middle of the first century BCE—engendered a high degree of single-minded self-certainty. Americans act in the unswerving belief that their country has a world mission: if it's good for America, then it must be good for the entire world. William Fulbright's dictum about the "arrogance of power" had its corollary in the *superbia* of which Rome was accused by both friends and foes alike.

GLOBAL IMPERIUM

When power is no longer limited by an adversarial power, power politics and the sense of one's own power reaches its greatest heights. After the battle of Pydna, which marked the final victory over Macedonia in 168 BCE, no other state in the entire Mediterranean was in a position to challenge Rome. Since the dissolution of the Soviet Union, the United States no longer has an enemy that must be feared. Rome and America both became the only world powers in their time, a situation unparalleled in world history except perhaps by China during certain epochs. Seriously endangered by no one, superior to all, almost always the more powerful in every relationship, hated by many, solicited by just as many for protection, even from friends less loved than used, but only accountable to itself—being the only world power creates a sense of giddiness. It allows for almost complete arbitrariness, but also calls for the greatest responsibility. No regime or nation can bear such a situation without undergoing changes and perhaps suffering damage.

World powers without rivals are mainly concerned with making sure that no future rivals appear on the horizon. In Cicero's words, the Romans fought against some enemies in order to ensure Rome's existence (*uter esset*) and against others for power (*uter imperaret*). According to one definition of American national interests in 1996, two things had to be prevented above all: first, an attack against America with atomic, biological, or chemical weapons; and second, the creation of a hostile hegemonic power in Europe or Asia. The securing of one's own existence is the first requirement of all states; the second, however—the securing of one's own rule—is an imperative peculiar to dominant world powers.

Rome was always concerned with making sure that defeated

enemies never rose again; this goal was accomplished with increasing brutality after the victory at Pydna. Macedonia was divided into quarters, the kingdom (which had produced an Alexander) dissolved, the last king incarcerated, 150,000 Epirotes enslaved, and 2,000 Greek hostages deported to Italy. Later, in the year 146, Rome flattened Carthage and brought about the destruction and enslavement of Corinth, the richest city in Greece. Future policy was aimed at making sure that everyone else remained small; those that managed to become even a little larger were reduced again in size. But even the status of being a satellite state became unbearable for some; as a result, kings bequeathed their kingdoms to the Romans. Roman policies offered a prime example of the high-handed behavior of a state no longer inhibited by anything: destroying foes that no longer present any threat (Carthage became the victim of a historical complex) and punishing diplomatic insults as if they were a form of lèse-majesté (the Roman envoy had been booed in Corinth). Rome strove for the maintenance and extension of its power solely for power's sake: the small and medium-sized powers in the East posed not even the smallest of threats to Italy's security.

Washington's policies have also become gradually more stringent since the Soviet Union ceased to exist. America may not become as brutal as Rome—an essential distinction for those affected—yet its increasing high-handedness as well as its primary goal of preventing the appearance of a rival nevertheless remind one of Rome. It relies on the other former Soviet republics, especially Ukraine, in order to place restrictions on Russia; it penetrates economically into the oil-rich regions of Central Asia, where it promotes non-Russian interests. It places limits on Russia in the West and extends its power over Europe by accepting the former Soviet satellites into NATO. It maintains its political and military position against China in Japan and South Korea and enjoys the fact that its presence is generally desired in most of these countries because it helps create stability.

Prior to 9/11/01, power had also become a means to an end for the Americans. They no longer armed in order to frighten an enemy, but rather in order to assure that their military strength remained unrivaled. They maintained military bases throughout the world as if "world communism" still had to be contained. They spoke of a global order for which they supposedly had to provide, but to which they failed to adhere; instead, they laid claim to a privileged position above all other states in the world. They refused to join an international court of justice by arguing that they had special global responsibilities. Even before 1990 they ignored the United Nations, their own creation, when it came to minor disputes; they have done so since even when it came to war and peace, such as in the case of Yugoslavia. They shunt aside that which goes against their own interests or wishes: global humanitarian and ecological agreements just as much as disarmament treaties vital to world peace.

AMERICA AFTER 9/11/01

All of that appeared to change after the 9/11/01 attacks on America. In order to find and punish those involved in the attacks and put a stop to terrorism, the United States sought the assistance of its allies and the benevolent patience of other countries. As a result, the world experienced a more conciliatory America. The United States sought understanding, took into consideration Russian and Chinese interests and concerns, and continually assured the Islamic world that it was not fighting against its religion but only against terrorists. Even the authority of the UN, which Washington had ignored in the past, was solicited or invoked.

It is questionable whether the post-9/11 attitude marks a fundamental change. Current circumstances need to be taken into account. How will America behave when the fear of terror disappears or tapers off? Nobody can confidently answer that question. But historical experience suggests reason for doubt. Power can only be effectively and lastingly limited by an equal counterpower—and regardless of its awful and frightening effect, terrorism does not have the strength to change the habits of the world's first state or its understanding of its own interests. America's power will only be restricted when a multipolar world develops in which other states gradually become more powerful.

Meanwhile, America will continue to use and demonstrate its superiority. No superior state manages to exercise more than enlightened power. A country that has nothing to fear does what suits itself best; its domestic policy determines its foreign policy. Caesar conquered Gaul in order to assert himself against his enemies in Rome. He who feels secure allows himself to wage civil war for fifty-two years, from Marius and Sulla to Octavianus and Antonius. Democratic America has transformed civil war into election campaigns; along the way, foreign policy is simply forgotten during certain periods, regardless of what may be going on in the world.

World powers without rivals are a class unto themselves. They do not accept anyone as an equal, and are quick to call loyal followers friends, or *amicus populi Romani*. They no longer know any foes, just rebels, terrorists, and rogue states. They no longer fight, merely punish. They no longer wage wars but merely create peace. They are honestly outraged when vassals fail to act like vassals. But world powers enjoy no real periods of rest even when they no longer have any rivals. Because they are the only ones whose power allows for the hope that problems will be solved, they are continually called upon and can seldom allow themselves to reject the requests, wishes, calls for aid, and demands that they use their power to provide for peace. If they fail to respond, their credibility becomes endangered, and, in consequence, their power as well. Yet involvement runs counter to their desires. One detects feelings of ambivalence in Rome as well as in Washington: on the one hand, one would like to remain undisturbed by quarrels among lesser powers, but on the other, one wants to maintain control.

PROSPECTS

Long-lasting power is not only based on legionnaires, interventions, and investments. Culture must play a role as well, as it did in the case of both Rome and America. That this is so suggests an-

other similarity. For a long time, both Rome and America remained dependent on their forefathers: *"Graecia capta Romam
cepit,"* in Horace's words—Greece, which had been conquered by
sword, conquered Rome in turn with its spirit. Both Romans and
Americans felt a mixture of awe and disdain for their models. The
Roman aristocrats had spoken Greek since the second century
BCE, but felt condescension toward the minor political quarrels
that characterized relations among the "little Greeks." The latter
may have been able to sculpt better statues out of marble, but the
Romans, for their part, had mastered the art of ruling the world.
Up to the 1930s Americans went to Europe to become acquainted
with traditional culture and the newest trends; today, they can only
look on with frustration at the confusion of states that has brought
about two great wars and which remains unable to deal effectively
with minor trouble spots on its own continent.

The Romans and Americans gradually emancipated themselves
from their models, creating their own literature, arts, and sciences.
They not only became independent but also came to set standards
in some areas. And the more powerful they became, the more attractive their power became for intellectuals. In the end, the Romans Romanized the world, to the extent that it did not remain
Greek; today the Americans have Americanized a good portion of
the world and are trying to do so in the rest as well. They are a
world power not only because they can reach every place on the
globe militarily, but also because they have already done so with
the products of their mass culture.

But world powers do not remain world powers for eternity.
There are three main reasons for their eventual downfall: new
states or coalitions of states that become more powerful than they,
overextension of their own power, and internal decay. Beginning
in the middle of the fourth century, Rome faced both an invasion
by primarily Germanic peoples and the challenge of a new major
power, the Persian Sassanid Empire; the defensive struggle
launched on almost all of its borders exceeded its human and material resources. But all of that first occurred after Rome had been
the sole world power for almost a half-millennium.

There will not be a single power or coalition of powers that could endanger America's imperial position, at least for the next two to three decades. Only China has the capacity, ambition, and desire to modernize necessary to challenge America's leading position—but only if it first overcomes its immense internal difficulties. The danger for the United States lies less in the increasing strength of other states than in a reduction of its own power. Prescient individuals already warned against the overcommitment of the 1960s. And even before 9/11/01, America was facing the insurmountable challenge of having more foreign interests and responsibilities than it could effectively master. The war against terrorism has expanded U.S. power for the time being, but it can also weaken the United States in the long run. Maintaining a huge defense budget to ensure its military predominance, coupled with a multi-front global struggle that threatens to increase both the number and tenacity of its enemies, may possibly become too great a challenge even for such a strong and rich land.

Overextension is one danger, exhaustion the other. The axiomatic phrase "conditions like in ancient Rome" refers to the decline of those customs that had made Rome great in the first place: a commitment to serving the *res publica* instead of pursuing personal interests, moderation instead of luxury, military discipline instead of softness. In short, it signifies the loss of power through the loss of old virtues. Even Richard Nixon wandered at night among the columns of the Lincoln Memorial and the National Archives thinking about the glory that was Greece and the grandeur that was Rome—of which nothing tangible remains today except for the columns. But, he thought, America had the vitality, strength, and health to avoid succumbing to the decadence that had destroyed the ancients. Less optimistically, Zbigniew Brzezinski later spoke of "personal hedonism" and a "dramatic decline in values," observing "parallels with the decline" of earlier "imperial systems," including the Roman one.

For all their decadence, the Romans created an empire that lasted four to five centuries, but they were only able to do so by changing their constitution. The Roman Republic ended as Rome became the Roman Empire; the aristocratic city-state could not effectively deal with ruling the world. Then the Augustinian monarchy could not survive the Germanic invasions (which began under Marc Aurel); the defense of the imperial borders called for forces and means that only the coercive state of late antiquity was still able to muster. Can the United States remain a republic if it rules an empire?

What is America today? The sole world power, surpassing and dominating all other states, or an empire in a form fit for the times? Rome ruled by forging the *orbis terrarum*, the world at that time, into a single state; America rules by indirectly steering the world with as much soft power as possible and as much hard power as necessary.

Ultimately, there can be no American "world state," nor will there be an American renunciation of world power. One cannot foretell the exact path the United States will seek or whether it will remain the democracy it currently is. It is helpful, in this respect, to consider what differentiates the United States from the empire of antiquity. The Romans were able to rule their geographically limited world. The Americans have to deal with the entire globe: in some areas they have the say, in others they can only exert their influence. Their client states are also stronger: France is no Bithynia, Germany no Pergamon, and Japan no Rhodos. Rome remained a sole great power for a very long time; America, on the other hand, expects a multipolar world in the foreseeable future, one shared by China, India, and perhaps Europe and even Russia again. Compared to the Pax Romana, the Pax Americana not only has far less reach but also less of a chance to exist.

In the middle of the second century BCE, Polybios wondered whether Rome's empire was a blessing or a curse for humanity. It was both, first a curse and then a blessing. Up until the imperial period, Rome's policies toward its provinces and client states proved thoroughly destructive; they had no aim, were not guided by morals, and meant centuries of misery for those subjected. Augustus' re-formation of the state first led to the realization that power also meant responsibility. The violent pre-Augustan peace metamorphosed into a peace that dispensed blessings. The first, and even more so the second, century of the common era was one of the happiest epochs in world history.

The Americans are—and were—hardly less inhibited than the Romans when it comes to using their military might. But they seldom act in as irresponsible a fashion as the Roman Republic did for a long time. America truly wants to bring the world peace, freedom, and welfare, as it claims—as long as this accords with its own interests. A democracy builds in greater restraint and self-control than an aristocracy or monarchy. Hardly a single annexation or act of violence by the United States took place without the government's first having to overcome strong domestic opposition or without later being regretted. But this cannot be the last word on the subject, for we have only experienced the United States as a world power for a half-century and as the sole world power for a mere twelve years. The containment of the Soviet Union now stands as one of its great achievements. What remains to be seen is the meaning of America's notion of a new world order and what it will mean in terms of gain and loss for humanity. We will only be able to determine this in hindsight—that is, once America is no longer the sole world power.

ANDREW J. BACEVICH

New Rome, New Jerusalem

The wellsprings of American empire are to be
found in America's self-identity.

NO LONGER FODDER for accusations and denials, American imperialism has of late become a proposition to be considered on its
merits. In leading organs of opinion, such as *The New York Times*
and *The Washington Post*, the notion that the United States today
presides over a global imperium has achieved something like respectability.

This is a highly salutary development. For only by introducing
the idea of empire into the mainstream of public discourse does it
become possible to address matters far more pressing than mulling
over the semantic distinctions between empire and hegemony and
"global leadership." What precisely is the nature of the Pax Americana? What is its purpose? What are the challenges and pitfalls
that await the United States in the management of its domain?
What are the likely costs of empire, moral as well as material, and

*Andrew J. Bacevich is professor of international relations at Boston University and
the author of* American Empire: The Realities and Consequences of U.S.
Diplomacy *(2002). This essay appeared in the Summer 2002 issue of* The Wilson
Quarterly *and is reprinted by permission.*

who will pay them? These are the questions that are now beginning to find a place on the agenda of U.S. foreign policy.

As befits a nation founded on the conviction of its own uniqueness, the American empire is like no other in history. Indeed, the peculiar American approach to empire offers a striking affirmation of American exceptionalism. For starters, that approach eschews direct rule over subject peoples. Apart from a handful of possessions left over from a brief, anomalous land grab in 1898, we have no colonies. We prefer access and influence to ownership. Ours is an informal empire, composed not of satellites or fiefdoms but of nominally coequal states. In presiding over this empire, we prefer to exercise our authority indirectly, as often as not through intermediary institutions in which the United States enjoys the predominant role but does not wield outright control (e.g., the North Atlantic Treaty Organization, the United Nations Security Council, the International Monetary Fund, and the World Bank).

Although we enjoy unassailable military supremacy and are by no means averse to using force, we prefer seduction to coercion. Rather than impose our will by the sword, we count on the allure of the "American way of life" to win over doubters and subvert adversaries. In the imperium's most valued precincts, deference to Washington tends to be rendered voluntarily. Thus, postwar Europe, viewing the United States as both protector and agent of economic revival, actively pursued American dominion, thereby laying the basis for an "empire by invitation" that persists even though European prosperity has long since been restored and threats to Europe's security have all but disappeared. An analogous situation prevails in the Pacific, where Japan and other states, more than able to defend themselves, willingly conform to an American-ordered security regime.

Imperial powers are all alike in their shared devotion to order. Imperial powers differ from one another in the values they purport to inculcate across their realm. To the extent that the empires of Spain, France, and Great Britain defined their purpose (at least in part) as spreading the benefits of Western civilization, the present-day Pax Americana qualifies as their historical successor. But whereas those earlier imperial ventures specialized in converting pagans or enlightening savages, the ultimate value and the ultimate aspiration of the American imperium is freedom. Per Thomas Jefferson, ours is an "empire of liberty."

From the outset, Americans self-consciously viewed the United States as an enterprise imbued with a providential significance extending far beyond the nation's boundaries. America was no sooner created than it became, in the words of the poet Philip Freneau, "a New Jerusalem sent down from heaven." But the salvation this earthly Zion promised was freedom, not eternal life. Recall George Washington's first inaugural address, in 1789: "The preservation of the sacred fire of liberty," he declared, had been "intrusted to the hands of the American people." The imperative in Washington's day not to promulgate the sacred fire but simply to keep it from being extinguished reflected a realistic appraisal of the young republic's standing among the nations of the world. For the moment, it lacked the capacity to do more than model freedom.

Over the course of the next 200 years, that would change. By the time the Berlin Wall fell in 1989, effectively bringing to a close a century of epic ideological struggle, the New Jerusalem had ascended to a category of its own among the world's powers. The United States was dominant politically, economically, culturally, and, above all, militarily. In effect, the New Jerusalem had become the New Rome, an identity that did not supplant America's founding purpose but pointed toward its fulfillment—and the fulfillment of history itself. To President Bill Clinton, the moment signified that "the fullness of time" was at hand. Thomas Paine's claim that Americans had it in their power "to begin the world over again" no longer seemed preposterous. Salvation beckoned. In Reinhold Niebuhr's evocative phrase, the United States stood poised to complete its mission of "tutoring mankind on its pilgrimage to perfection."

Early Americans saw the task of tutoring mankind as a directive from on high; later Americans shouldered the burden out of a profound sense of self-interest. Despite the frequent allusions to liberty in describing that pilgrimage's final destination and in justifying the use of American power, the architects of U.S. policy in the 20th century never viewed empire as an exercise in altruism. Rather, at least from the time of Woodrow Wilson, they concluded that only by protecting and promoting the freedom of others could Americans fully guarantee their nation's own well-being. The two were inextricably linked.

In the eyes of Wilson and his heirs, to distinguish between American ideals (assumed to be universal) and American interests (increasingly global in scope) was to make a distinction without a difference. It was a plain fact that successive crusades to advance those ideals—against German militarism in 1917, fascism and Japanese imperialism in 1941, and communism after World War II—resulted in the United States' accruing unprecedented power. Once the smoke had cleared, the plain fact defined international politics: one nation with its own particular sense of how the world should operate stood like a colossus astride the globe.

Not surprisingly, Americans viewed the distribution of power as a sort of cosmic judgment, an affirmation that the United States was (in a phrase favored by politicians in the 1990s) on "the right side of history." American preeminence offered one measure of humanity's progress toward freedom, democracy, and world peace. Those few who persisted in thinking otherwise—in American parlance, "rogue regimes"—marked themselves not only as enemies of the United States but as enemies of freedom itself.

The barbarous events of September 11 revealed that the pilgrimage to perfection was far from over. But not for a moment did they cause American political leaders to question the project's feasibility. If anything, September 11 reinforced their determination to complete the journey. In offering his own explanation for the attack on the World Trade Center and the Pentagon, George W. Bush refused to countenance even the possibility that an assault on symbols of American economic and military power might have anything to do with how the United States employed its power. He chose instead to frame the issue at hand in terms of freedom. Why do they hate us? "They hate our freedoms," Bush explained.

Thus did the president skillfully deflect attention from the consequences of empire.

September 11 became the occasion for a new war, far wider in scope than any of the piddling military interventions that had kept American soldiers marching hither and yon during the preceding decade. In many quarters, that conflict has been described as the equivalent of another world war. The description is apt. As the multifaceted U.S. military campaign continues to unfold, it has become clear that the Bush administration does not intend simply to punish those who perpetrated the attacks on New York and Washington or to preclude the recurrence of any such incidents. America's actual war aims are far more ambitious. The United States seeks to root out terror around the globe. It seeks also to render radical Islam and the nations that make up the "axis of evil" incapable of threatening the international order.

But there is more still: the Bush administration has used the war on terror as an occasion for conducting what is, in effect, a referendum on U.S. global primacy. In this cause, as President Bush has emphasized, all must declare their allegiance: nations either align themselves with the United States or they cast their lot with the terrorists—and, by implication, can expect to share their fate. As a final byproduct of September 11, the administration has seized the opportunity to promulgate a new Bush Doctrine, incorporating such novel concepts as "anticipatory self-defense" and "preemptive deterrence." Through the Bush Doctrine, the United States—now combining, in the words of Stanley Hoffmann, the roles of "high-noon sheriff and proselytizing missionary"—lays claim to wider prerogatives for employing force to reorder the world.

In short, the conflict joined after September 11 may well qualify as a war *against* terror and *against* those who "hate our freedoms." But it is no less genuinely a conflict waged *on behalf of* the American imperium, a war in which, to fulfill its destiny as the New Jerusalem, the United States, as never before, is prepared to exert its authority as the New Rome.

Thus, when the president vowed in December 2001 that

"America will lead the world to peace," he was not simply resurrecting some windy Wilsonian platitude. He was affirming the nation's fundamental strategic purpose and modus operandi. The United States will "lead"—meaning that it will persevere in its efforts to refashion the international order, employing for that purpose the preeminent power it acquired during the century of its ascendancy (which it has no intention of relinquishing in the century just begun). And it will do so with an eye toward achieving lasting "peace"—meaning an orderly world, conducive to American enterprise, friendly to American values, and perpetuating America's status as sole superpower. This was the aim of U.S. policy prior to September 11; it remains the aim of the Bush administration today.

How widespread is support for this imperial enterprise? Despite the tendency of American statesmen from Wilson's day to our own to resort to coded language whenever addressing questions of power, the project is not some conspiracy hatched by members of the elite and then foisted on an unsuspecting citizenry. The image of the United States leading the world to peace (properly understood) commands broad assent in virtually all segments of American society. A fringe of intellectuals, activists, and self-described radicals might take umbrage at the prospect of a world remade in America's image and policed by American power, but out on the hustings the notion plays well—so long, at least, as the required exertions are not too taxing. The fact is that Americans like being number one, and since the end of the Cold War have come to accept that status as their due. Besides, someone has to run the world. Who else can do the job?

What are the empire's prospects? In some respects, the qualities that have contributed to the nation's success in other endeavors may serve the United States well in this one. Compared with the citizens of Britain in the age of Victoria or of Rome during the time of the Caesars, Americans wear their imperial mantle lightly. They go about the business of empire with a singular lack of pretense. Although Washington, D.C., has come to exude the self-importance of an imperial capital, those who live beyond its orbit have, thus far at least, developed only a limited appetite for pomp, privilege, and display. We are unlikely to deplete our treasury erecting pyramids or other monuments to our own ostensible greatness. In matters of taste, American sensibilities tend to be popular rather than aristocratic. Our excesses derive from our enthusiasms—frequently vulgar, typically transitory—rather than from any of the crippling French diseases: exaggerated self-regard, intellectual bloat, cynicism, and envy. All things considered, America's imperial ethos is pragmatic and without ostentation, evidence, perhaps, that the nation's rise to great-power status has not yet fully expunged its republican origins. Above all, measured against societies elsewhere in the developed world, American society today seems remarkably vigorous and retains an astonishing capacity to adapt, to recover, and to reinvent itself.

That said, when it comes to sustaining the Pax Americana, the United States faces several challenges.

First, no one is really in charge. Ours is an empire without an emperor. Although in times of crisis Americans instinctively look to the top for leadership—a phenomenon that greatly benefited George W. Bush after September 11—the ability of any president to direct the affairs of the American imperium is limited, in both degree and duration. Though he is routinely described as the most powerful man in the world, the president of the United States in fact enjoys limited authority and freedom of action. The system of government codified by the Constitution places a premium on separation and balance among the three branches that vie with one another in Washington, but also between the federal government and agencies at the state and local levels. Hardly less significant is the impact of other participants in the political free-for-all—parties, interest groups, lobbies, entrenched bureaucracies, and the media—that on any given issue can oblige the chief executive to dance to their tune. The notion of an "imperial presidency" is a fiction, and for that Americans can be grateful. But the fact remains that the nation's political system is not optimally configured for the management of empire.

Second, although popular support for the empire is real, it is, in all likelihood, highly contingent. The heirs of the so-called greatest generation have little stomach for sacrifice. They expect the benefits of empire to outweigh the burdens and responsibilities, and to do so decisively. The garden-variety obligations of imperial policing—for example, keeping peace in the Balkans or securing a U.S. foothold in Central Asia—are not causes that inspire average Americans to hurry down to their local recruiter's office. To put it bluntly, such causes are not the kind that large numbers of Americans are willing to die for.

In this sense, the empire's point of greatest vulnerability is not the prospect of China's becoming a rival superpower or of new terrorist networks' supplanting Al Qaeda—those developments we can handle—but rather the questionable willingness of the American people to foot the imperial bill. Sensitive to the limits of popular support—as vividly demonstrated after a single night's action in Mogadishu in 1993—policymakers over the past decade have exerted themselves mightily to pass that bill off to others. In the process, they have devised imaginative techniques for ensuring that when blood spills, it won't be American blood. Hence the tendency to rely on high-tech weapons launched from beyond the enemy's reach, on proxies to handle any dirty work on the ground, or, as a last resort, on a cadre of elite professional soldiers who are themselves increasingly detached from civilian society.

Over the past decade, this effort to maintain the American empire on the cheap has (with the notable exception of September 11) enjoyed remarkable success. Whether policymakers can sustain this success indefinitely remains an open question, especially when each victory gained with apparent ease—Bosnia, Kosovo, Afghanistan—only reinforces popular expectations that the next operation will also be neat, tidy, and virtually fault-free.

The third challenge facing the American imperium concerns freedom itself. For if peace (and U.S. security) requires that the world be free as Americans define freedom, then the specifics of that definition complicate the management of empire in ways that thus far have received inadequate attention.

Here's the catch: as Americans continuously reinvent themselves and their society, they also reinvent—and in so doing, radi-cally transform—what they mean by freedom. They mean not just independence, or even democracy and the rule of law. Freedom as Americans understand it today encompasses at least two other broad imperatives: maximizing opportunities for the creation of wealth and removing whatever impediments remain to confine the sovereign self. Freedom has come to mean treating the market and market values as sacrosanct (the economic agenda of the Right) and celebrating individual autonomy (the cultural agenda of the Left).

Without question, adherence to the principles of free enter-prise offers the most efficient means for generating wealth. With-out question, too, organizing society around such principles undermines other sources of authority. And that prospect mobi-lizes in opposition to the United States those in traditional and, es-pecially, religious societies who are unwilling to abandon the old order.

The implications of shedding the last constraints on the indi-vidual loom even larger. The contemporary pursuit of freedom has put into play beliefs, arrangements, and institutions that were once viewed as fundamental and unalterable. Gender, sexuality, identity, the definition of marriage and family, and the origins, meaning, sa-credness, and malleability of life—in American society, they are all now being reexamined to accommodate the claims of freedom.

Some view this as an intoxicating prospect. Others see it as the basis for a domestic culture war. In either case, pursuant to their present-day understanding of what freedom entails, Americans have embarked on an effort to reengineer the human person, reorder basic human relationships, and reconstruct human institu-tions that have existed for millennia.

To render a summary judgment on this project is not yet possi-ble. But surely it is possible to appreciate that some in the world liken it to stepping off a moral precipice and view the New Jerusalem with trepidation. Their fears, and the resistance to which fear gives birth, all but guarantee that the legions of the New Rome will have their hands full for some time to come.

JEDEDIAH PURDY

Universal Nation

Not blood and conquest but a flair for innova-
tion and a genius for popular culture define
America's empire.

ON SEPTEMBER 11, 2001, it was said, the United States was vi-
olently inducted into membership of the rest of the world. Some
commentators have noted with satisfaction that at last U.S. deci-
sion-makers can now appreciate the experience of—depending on
their sympathies—Israelis, Belgraders, Nicaraguans, or the residents of Baghdad. Kinder commentators reflected that terrorism
has long been a fact of life in Britain, India, Turkey, and elsewhere, and that Americans would have had to lose the illusion of
invulnerability sooner or later—if perhaps not so suddenly and
horribly.

But the response to the attacks was just as much a reminder
that Americans are not alone in believing themselves special.
Americans in countries wracked by violence much more severe
than New York's described outpourings of sympathy even from or-

Jedediah Purdy is the author, most recently, of Being America: Liberty, Commerce, and Violence in an American World. *This essay first appeared in the mag-*
azine Prospect *in October 2002 and is reprinted by permission.*

dinarily chary hosts. The "World Trade Center" was no hubristic misnomer. The twin towers that burned and collapsed stood not just on an island along one edge of North America but in the homeland of the global imagination. They represented power, boundless possibility, and a curious kind of innocence. Yet as the United States leads the world's countries into a campaign against Islamist terrorism, the country still awaits a reckoning on its place in the world. For the fact is that this conflict takes place in a world deeply marked by new forms of American power and by new resentments against the United States itself. The more a newly aggressive and focused U.S. foreign policy disregards these resentments in favor of Cold War–vintage verities, the less likely it is to succeed.

For several years now, there have been worldwide rumblings about an alleged American empire. *Frontline*, an Indian weekly magazine, called a 1999 cover article on U.S. foreign policy, "Ways of Imperialism." A South African journalist writes of living in "the outer provinces of the empire," and an Arab scholar refers matter-of-factly and without venom to Egypt's incorporation into "the American imperium." The French, with special insistence, lament that "we are being globalized by the Americans." These are not the voices of the far left, residues of the Cold War, or the mouth-pieces of governments nursing grudges. They express a perception that the U.S. writ reaches everywhere—not to govern the world but to set the terms on which the governance of the next century will take place.

Here is what they have in mind. American economists supervise the policies of poor nations in debt to the IMF, and the U.S. economy every year presses its ethic of entrepreneurship and creative destruction deeper into Europe, East Asia, and India. American academics draft constitutions for new governments in Africa and central Asia, and Americans from financier George Soros's Open Society Institute fund efforts to create local civil society. English is the world's second language: 350 million people are native speakers, but more than a billion have learned enough to strike a bargain or argue about a basketball game. American culture is the other global second language—a shared patois whose vocabulary includes Michael Jordan's face, the ragged beats of hip-hop music, and *Baywatch*, the world's most popular television program. Immigrants arrive in U.S. airports having already lived much of their imaginary lives between New York and Los Angeles. What are we to call this, other than empire?

To the American ear, talk of an American empire sounds foreign. Empire means conquest, the apogee of Old World wickedness. It is to Americans what oriental despotism was to the European imagination in the 19th century—the cruel expression of a degenerate civilization. The Spanish conquest of South America, with its slaughters and wholesale enslavement: that was empire. So too was the carving up of Africa by the European powers and the British Raj in South Asia. Those bloody, domineering episodes, Americans insist, have nothing to do with us.

There is surely a question here. Those who have attempted to explain America's special position in today's world have pressed into service the unsatisfactory term "soft power." American influence, they argue, does not rely on American armies but on economic might and cultural allure.

Can soft power really be imperial power? It was so in Rome, the great empire of the West. The Roman Empire ruled not by terror but by extending the system of Roman law and, by degrees, the privilege and discipline of Roman citizenship across its vast tracts. What law did not accomplish, culture did: Roman fashions and especially the Latin language spread throughout the Western empire. Roman citizens might have a local language and local loyalties, but they were also members, by law and culture, of a universal imperium. They shared in a commerce that knitted together all the Roman regions. The empire's authority began in the sword, but it settled in the mind, the tongue, and even the soul. This made it an ideal of order and power long after its government had disintegrated. Rome led with the sword only when necessary, where a primitive people such as the Britons or the Iberians could not be mollified by more subtle means. Rome's governors often preferred indirect rule through pliant local monarchies, alliances with formally independent cities and the Germanic tribes that retained much of their traditional internal governance.

Allowing others' energy to flow to one's own purposes is always more fruitful than putting up with sullen resistance. "It was," Montesquieu wrote in his history of Rome, "a slow way of conquering." Through new loyalties and gradual shifts in power, an ally "became a subject people without anyone being able to say when its subjection began." Anyone who has watched the IMF huddle with his country's leaders or seen the arrival of a new multiplex must have an inkling of Montesquieu's meaning. Soft power is not a new reality but a new word for power's most efficient form. It is hardly surprising that empire should change its forms in 2,000 years. In a time when wealth comes from control of markets and ideas, sovereignty over territory is neither necessary nor sufficient for greatness. In a world of demanding citizens and discontented national populations, territory can be as much an impediment as a boon: witness Russia's ethnic conflicts and China's terrified dance with its poor regions and huge minority populations. Any sensible emperor would want what Rome achieved, without the landmass: an empire where all markets lead to Rome, but the roads can be closed on command.

Americans do not perceive this condition as empire, because they have always been inclined to believe that they are the world's universal nation. Unlike the French and certain 19th-century Germans, they do not possess a theory of why this should be so; they simply cannot imagine that it could be otherwise. Americans believe, somewhere below the level of articulation, that every human being is born an American, and that their upbringing in different cultures is an unfortunate but reversible accident.

This idea has a history, now mainly forgotten, that is as old as European settlement in North America. The first English settlers, members of radical Protestant sects, famously envisioned the new continent as "a city on a hill," shining the light of its inspiration on the world. Thomas Jefferson, the author of the Declaration of Independence and a great muse of American democracy, wrote that in the new country men might at last feel universal law in their hearts, so that the code of law books would become superfluous. For Jefferson, the movement of the law from outward codes to inward conviction repeated the transformation from the Old Testament's elaborate strictures to the New Testament's stress on conscience. Wherever one looked, Americans were anointing themselves the homeland of universal law.

The U.S. also became the homeland of the distinctly modern form of liberty: free self-expression, whether of conscience or whim. The 18th and 19th centuries were full of pessimism about what the fall of aristocracy and the rise of mass culture would mean for human character. The heralds of the new society, such as Adam Smith and Alexis de Tocqueville, accepted that greater equality would come at the price of cultural mediocrity and intellectual and spiritual sluggishness. In response, the American prophets of the 19th century announced that the end of aristocracy and other hierarchies freed men to look into their own souls and find there as much grace, dignity, and harmony as the courtly refinements of the old order had ever achieved. In the vision of Emerson and Whitman, the U.S. would become the world's "first nation of men," the first people whose national life would be the unfolding of individuality.

The Americans took this idea from the European ideal of the romantic artist, the unconventional young man of passionate, sincere, and incorrigible feeling. In the new world, however, the idea of self-expression found its home in the free market. The hero of American individuality was not the artist but the inventor, the pioneer, and, above all, the entrepreneur. Americans look to the market for the finest uses of modern freedom. It is there that we find our heroes, our nobility, and even our saints.

So, when Americans see their version of the market economy spreading through the world, they do not see other forms of life giving way, other civilizations being transformed. The advance of what Europeans are sometimes polite enough to call "the Anglo-Saxon model" of capitalism is to Americans just the progress of modern life. And when they learn that *Baywatch* is the most popular program in Indonesia, it does not cross their minds that this might give a new inflection to that Islamic civilization's idea of feminine beauty, erotic satisfaction, or the good life. Of course the world is adopting our market. Of course the world loves *Baywatch*. These are the natural human desires that have been inhibited for so long by awkward European politics and the heavy weight of the black chador. At last the rest of the world is becoming fully human.

This American attitude—one might call it parochial universalism—has found further comfort in the discipline of economics. In its recently ascendant neo-classical form, economics forms the cornerstone of U.S. market-individualism: nearly unlimited power of contract, a state that serves mainly to enforce private bargains and makes them axioms of the first universally valid science of human behavior. In the U.S., economics has expanded its reign to become the most respectable vocabulary for discussions of public policy, legal reasoning, and even intimate relations. Whatever their other merits, the IMF and the World Trade Organization both reflect the global ascendance of the same version of economic logic. The American and American-trained economists who guide these institutions believe, in the foreground of their minds, that they are applying science, and in the background that they are bringing a retrograde world into full humanity. The suspicion that they are also helping to remake humanity in the image of one nation is buried very deeply indeed.

It is for all of these reasons that Americans tend to think of "globalization" as a natural process that affects everyone in more or less the same way—like global warming, only with less human responsibility. Thomas Friedman, a *New York Times* writer who has become America's official interpreter of globalization, likes to compare the process to the dawn: there is no escaping it, objecting to it is futile unto madness, and it shines on the just and the unjust alike. The idea that other countries are "being globalized by the Americans" seems preposterous.

We must not forget that the rest of the world gives every sign of wanting American prosperity, American entertainment, American styles, and the American language. Pretending that global change is some crude kind of hegemony, not really so different from conquest, would be intellectually criminal—especially after 11th September's stark reminder of the difference between metaphoric and actual violence. But, as the Romans understood, power over desire and loyalty can be the most important kind, and does deserve closer examination.

The U.S. exercises two special kinds of power that have nothing to do with blood and conquest. The first might be called Microsoft power. The real reason Microsoft is ubiquitous is not that it forces its operating system on computer users but that its very ubiquity creates enormous advantages for a new buyer who chooses it over a different system. If everyone else has one sort of stove and you choose another, you lose nothing. But if you choose a different operating system, you cannot trade files, transfer documents, or sit down at nearly any terminal confident that you can manipulate its programs. Microsoft is the vocabulary that gives people access to global flows of communication, information, and commerce. Choosing it is impeccably rational, but it also creates resentment: the chooser knows there are other ways of doing the same tasks, but they have been marginalized. Economists call the advantages of a big information system "network effects." Microsoft power is the power of big networks to stay big because they create the language in which people access each other.

The so-called "language" of Microsoft is one thing; English is another. It is the world's second language because it is to the tongue what Microsoft is to the screen: the way people reach each other across distances of geography and civilization. So also are the trade rules of the WTO—a set of common terms that open up the world's places to each other. The world is full of networks that people have every reason to join—but to which, in a real sense, they also have no alternative. These networks are American, in origin and in idiom. Such a regime can remain invisible to Americans while its power is always and everywhere inescapable to the rest of the world.

If Microsoft power directs free choices in a way that still feels coercive, *Baywatch* power works more directly on the desires that well up beneath choice. American entertainment is everywhere, and its culture industry has a century's history of understanding the lowest common denominator of entertainment for a mass audience. In 1999, 72 percent of television drama exported worldwide came from the U.S.. A teenager in Delhi can know the arc of the Nike swoosh and the curves of a *Baywatch* model—and in some sense want them both. (A certain humility of analysis is in order here. We do not, after all, know quite how the *Baywatch* sensibility mingles with preexisting ones. Nor do we know exactly how many people in the developing world watch American soaps, but the best guess is a lot.)

Still, where it reaches, *Baywatch* power invites a special kind of resentment. On the one hand, what you desire becomes a part of you. You move towards it of your own eager will. On the other hand, this desire is still manifestly foreign to much of the world. It is one's own, and yet it is not. Such power shapes appetites and guides tongues. It directs the eye to its image of beauty and convictions to its idea of justice. You cannot easily drive out what you have invited in. You cannot escape what has become a part of you. If you resent it, your resentment becomes more insistent as it grows less effective.

It is an article of contemporary faith that empire is an altogether bad thing. In the last word, this may prove true, although it is worth remembering that other times have found it neither obvious nor likely. It is much more certain that there is no virtue in ignoring empire when it in fact exists.

On reflection, the staggering thing about American empire—if that term is the right one—may turn out to be its generosity. Other countries have sapped the resources of subject economies. The U.S. submitted to partners, such as Taiwan and Japan, sometimes to the point of national embarrassment—recall the sale of New York's Rockefeller Center to the Japanese. The U.S. government also ties itself to the same mast as other countries in the WTO. One can debate the wisdom of neo-liberalism and point to such glaring contradictions as America's vast and persistent agricultural subsidies, but the overall impression is that the U.S. is trying to play fair.

The same is true in the cultural realm. From Spanish conversions at swordpoint to Macaulay's brown-skinned Englishmen, modern empires have put their stamps on subject populations. Not so Americans. Although it is obscured by the rhetorical silliness that surrounds it, a real openness and tolerance is one of the great achievements of American civilization. Notionally at least, we welcome the world's variety and do not set out to remake it. The unhappy irony is that, in our faith that being American is humankind's natural condition, we have difficulty appreciating the intense attachment that people may feel to a very different nationality, language, or social order.

The U.S. offers—no, the U.S. is—one picture of the world's future. It is a tolerant, pleasurable world, where no tie or tradition constrains the individual too much and few convictions move a person to violence. The military mobilization now under way is explicitly in defense of that future—a world with more comfort and less capacity to imagine the need for war. Some version of it is probably the fairest and finest world that modernity makes possible. But it is very different from the fractured and transitional world that billions of people inhabit. A people constitutionally unsuited to empire could prove either the best or the least suited to bringing this new world about. For the time being, they are the awkward sole contenders, and our only peaceful future.

DAVID MARQUAND

Playground Bully

*History summons the United States to assume
the responsibilities exercised by Britain at the
apex of its power. But Washington's overbearing approach to statecraft suggests that it is ill-
suited for the role of benign hegemon.*

AN EXTRAORDINARY EXPERIMENT has dominated world history since the fall of communism: the construction of a global
market unsupported by a global state. Except in France, the political elites of the West insist, with breathtaking insouciance, that
this experiment is necessary, inevitable, and benign. In truth, it is
much more hazardous than they appreciate. Historically, states
came before markets. Adam Smith may have been right that a
propensity to "truck, barter and exchange" is fundamental to
human nature. But, as the history of his own country showed, that
propensity could not be fully realized until a powerful and imper-
sonal state, with the will and capacity to enforce contracts, keep
the peace, and dismantle traditional obstacles to the operation of

*David Marquand is former principal of Mansfield College, Oxford. This essay first
appeared in the October 21, 2002, issue of* The New Statesman *and is reprinted by
permission.*

market forces, had come into existence. National markets were created by nation states; the states concerned were then sustained by the wealth that national markets brought in their train.

To be sure, the 19th century saw an experiment in stateless globalization presaging the one through which we are now living. As far back as 1847, Marx and Engels proclaimed the "universal interdependence of nations" in the Communist Manifesto. They were premature but, by the late 19th century, a global market, more complete than anything seen until our own day, was unmistakably in being. It, too, had developed without the help of a global state. The surrogate for such a state—the architect and linchpin of the global market—was Great Britain, the world's first global hegemon. The Royal Navy policed the world's sea lanes, opening markets in distant continents and keeping them open. The world's trade was conducted in sterling and largely carried in British ships. The gold standard, operated by the Bank of England, ensured currency stability across the globe. Britain was overwhelmingly the world's chief creditor nation, earning vast sums from overseas investments and exporting capital on a huge scale. Her formal empire was the biggest in human history. It was buttressed by an informal one: the economic ties that bound Buenos Aires to London were as strong as those that bound Brisbane and Bombay; the British ideal of gentlemanly capitalism flourished as vigorously in Hamburg as in Huddersfield, in Cambridge, Massachusetts, as in Cambridge, England.

But Britain's days as a hegemon were numbered, and the global market she had brought into being came to a bad end. The dynamic continental powers that triumphed in the American Civil War and the Franco-Prussian war—the U.S. and imperial Germany—challenged her politically, economically, and, in the German case, militarily. By the turn of the 19th and 20th centuries, far-sighted intellectuals and politicians, from Alfred Milner and Joseph Chamberlain on the right to Sidney Webb and Ramsay MacDonald on the left, were beginning to suspect that she was no longer strong enough to bear the burdens of hegemony. Their suspicions turned out to be only too well founded. In the 1920s,

British political and economic elites made heroic, self-lacerating efforts to repair the damage that the First World War had inflicted on the global system and to put Britain back on her hegemonic perch. But when the national government was forced off the gold standard in 1931, the game was up. The global system collapsed, with disastrous consequences for the entire world.

Will history repeat itself? Or will we learn from it to shape a more enduring, multilateral, civic version of globalization, based on law, negotiation, and political participation rather than on the power of an inevitably self-interested and temporary hegemon? These questions reverberated through the anguished debates that followed the atrocities of September 11, 2001, and will do so again as other incidents of terror occur. They hovered over the Johannesburg Earth Summit, and they haunted the United Nations Security Council and the feverish diplomatic maneuvers aimed at disarming Iraq.

At first sight, the omens are not encouraging. So far, the globalization of our day has been a repeat performance of that of the 19th century, with a hegemonic America playing Britain's old role as linchpin of the global system. True, Britain was never the world's only superpower as the United States now is. She was supreme at sea but never on land. British governments always had to reckon with the great powers of the European mainland, even in the decades following the defeat of Napoleon I. And 19th-century Britain's prudent, gentlemanly capitalism could hardly have been more different from the profligate and distinctly un-gentlemanly capitalism of present-day America.

Yet the similarities between Britain's global role a hundred years ago and America's today are more striking than the differences. Today's global market is an essentially American construct, underpinned by American power and shaped by American interests. American cruise missiles are today's equivalent of the guns of the Royal Navy. The so-called "Washington consensus" constrains lesser nations as tightly as the gold standard used to do.

For most Europeans (though not for Russians exposed to the ravages of kleptocratic mafia capitalism, or for Palestinians exposed to illegal Jewish colonization on the West Bank) the results have been, on the whole, acceptable. But recent events have called this version of globalization into question. Enduring hegemony comes with a price tag. The elites that run the hegemonic power need the self-discipline and imagination to subordinate the short-term interests of their own country to the long-term requirements of the global system (knowing that it is in their country's long-term interest to do so). With occasional exceptions, this was spectacularly true of the elites that ran 19th-century Britain; and it was only slightly less true of the elites that shaped American policy during and after the Second World War.

But the United States of Roosevelt, Acheson, Marshall, and Truman is now a distant memory. Today the United States wants hegemony on the cheap. As the balance of internal power shifts from the Atlantic seaboard to the south and west, the political forces that shape American policy are becoming more parochial, more shortsighted, more impatient with external constraints and more contemptuous of the rest of the world. A raw, provincial brutalism pervades the Bush administration. Bush and his political allies are indifferent to the long-term health of the global system. What matters to them is that narrowly defined American national interests should prevail in the shortest of short terms. If American steelworkers want protection, then to hell with free trade. If European leaders demur at America's tenderness to Ariel Sharon, that only proves that Europeans are anti-Semitic wimps.

This was the real meaning of Bush's campaign for "regime change" in Iraq. By any reckoning a loathsome figure, Saddam Hussein was equally loathsome when Britain and the United States supplied him with arms. Nuclear proliferation in the Middle East is an undoubted danger, but few Americans complained when Israel joined the nuclear club. The truth was that Bush's lust for battle had little to do with the character of Saddam's rule or with nuclear proliferation as such. The point of the exercise was to prove that, despite the humiliation of 11 September and the disappointing longueurs of the war against terrorism, the United States remained invincible.

In this, Bush proved himself to be a mirror image of Osama bin Laden. Bin Laden wanted to show the world, and the Islamic world in particular, that the United States was not invulnerable, that a handful of martyrs could strike at America's heart and that Muslim states therefore had no need to crawl to Washington. He succeeded beyond his wildest dreams, and the Afghanistan war did not undo the effect.

Bush in turn sought a reverse demonstration. He was not deterred by the risks of regime change in Iraq: the implosion of the Iraqi state, with a Kurdish revolt in the north and a Shiite turn to Iran in the south; further damage to America's appalling image in the Muslim world; and the danger of an anti-American backlash in Europe. He acted on Machiavelli's precept that a wise prince would rather be feared than loved. As Khrushchev once said of West Berlin, Saddam had become a bone sticking in America's throat. Toppling him became an end in itself. Success in that regard would prove that there are no limits to American power; that the U.S. can and will dictate the terms on which globalization continues. If lesser nations squeal, so be it.

Yet there is a paradox in all this, which may account for the increasingly hysterical quality of Bush's rhetoric. Hegemonial globalization on the 19th-century British and present-day American model is no longer the only kind on offer. Tentatively, and sometimes confusingly, a different approach has started to challenge it; and Bushite brutalism has given the challenge an extra edge of moral passion. This second approach stresses interdependence, dialogue, and law, rather than hegemony. One of its most striking examples is the emergence of an embryonic global legal system, manifested most clearly in the effort to bring General Pinochet to book, in the trial of Slobodan Milosevic, and in the establishment of the International Criminal Court in the teeth of American hostility.

Perhaps more significant for the long term are the faint beginnings of a stateless or borderless politics. Increasingly, non-state associations and social movements of all kinds—women's groups, think tanks, networks of local authorities, anti-capitalist protesters, human rights campaigners, non-governmental organizations, and, on a different level, multinational corporations, employers' associations, and trade unions—seek to structure public debate and to influence public policy on a global as well as a national level. Their activities transcend national boundaries and elude the essentially national political categories we have inherited from the great thinkers of the past, but they are no less political for that. Meanwhile, notions of global citizenship—usually vaguely defined, often mutually contradictory, but nevertheless strongly held—are steadily gaining currency.

There is still no global polity, still less a global government. The nation state has not suddenly become obsolete. It is still overwhelmingly the most important focus for political allegiance and the chief site of political conflict. Yet we are at least beginning to see the emergence of a global civil society or public space. This space is extraordinarily difficult to map. Its contours and boundaries change all the time. In the language of the American political scientist Joseph Nye, it has more to do with "soft" power than with "hard," and the ebbs and flows of soft power are inherently unpredictable. But this global civil society exists, and it is growing. Potentially, at least, it offers a civilized, multilateral alternative to the brutal, hegemonial globalization favored in present-day Washington.

Which approach will prevail? The only certainty is that the hegemonial approach cannot do so. The rest of the world will not tolerate American hegemony forever. Its tolerance is already wearing thin, as the German electorate's response to Gerhard Schroeder's election campaign in 2002 showed. If they had a chance to do so, the British and French electorates would almost certainly follow where the Germans have led. China, the world's next superpower, is keeping her own counsel. The same is true of India, the next but one. To the extent that they defer to Washington, they do so for reasons of national *realpolitik*, not out of enthusiasm for the United States or its hegemonial role. Russia can probably be bribed to follow the American lead, but the price will be high.

America's overwhelming preponderance will come to an end sooner or later, just as Britain's did. But the Bushites' aim is to freeze the global political economy in its present shape, to ensure that the United States is forever invulnerable and invincible, and, to that end, to remake the rest of the world in the image of American-style democracy and the American version of capitalism. In short, the Bush administration intends to turn Francis Fukuyama's preposterous vision of "the end of history" into a reality. It cannot be done. The American model is specific to the United States, the product of a unique (and very short) history to which the rest of the world offers no parallel. The notion that it can be transplanted in the ancient soil of China and India, or even in the somewhat less ancient soil of Europe, betrays a mixture of arrogance and parochialism that would be comic if the likely consequences were not so tragic.

American predominance will sooner or later be challenged by the rising superpowers of east and south Asia, just as Britain's predominance was challenged by Germany and the United States itself a hundred years ago. They may well be joined by a phoenix-like Eurasian successor to impoverished and IMF-battered Russia. Sadly, multilateral globalization through law and politics may not be the wave of the future. Another possibility is a new version of the shifting balance of power that led to the First World War, the demise of the Victorian global market, and the economic disasters of the 1920s and 1930s. That is the real nightmare for our time.

The choice between these futures will not be made in or by Europe, but Europe will have a crucial part to play. It will not be an easy one. Fawning on the Americans, as virtually all postwar British governments have done, does no service to anyone, least of all to the Americans themselves. President Bush has become the playground bully of the West. The only way to stop him is to stand up to him. Blairite sweet talk does more harm than good. Members of the American hard right see it as a sign of weakness and, like all bullies, they despise the weak. De Gaulle's proud intransigence is a better model than Churchill's sentimental Atlanticism for the federalizing Europe that is slowly beginning to emerge from the quagmire of confederalism.

Yet simplistic anti-Americanism is equally dangerous. The civic, law-based model of globalization, which offers the only alternative to the bankrupt hegemonial model, cannot come into being without American participation. This won't happen under Bush, but Bush is not the United States. (Apart from any other considerations, he actually lost the presidential election.) So Europe has a testing hand to play. It needs the courage to tell the Americans when they are wrong, coupled with the imagination to appeal to the best in the American tradition, which has by no means disappeared. Above all, it needs the self-discipline and political creativity to put its own civic house in order.

JAMES CHACE

In Search of Absolute Security

*America's empire is a byproduct of American
anxieties.*

WHO WOULD NOW DENY that America is an imperial power?
The American response to the attack on the World Trade Center
and the Pentagon was swift and merciless. Thousands of troops
swept down upon Afghanistan in an effort to capture or kill the
terrorists and their protectors. The Afghan war as such lasted only
a few weeks. The continuing search to root out terrorists worldwide and those who harbor them has no end point. As the usually
cautious secretary of state, Colin Powell, echoing the president,
declared in February 2002 at the World Economic Forum in New
York, the United States will "go after terrorism wherever it threatens free men and women," even if that means taking "evil regimes"
head on.

American military power is awesome—on land, on the seas,

*James Chace is the Paul W. Williams Professor of Government and Public Law at
Bard College. He is the author, among other books, of* Acheson: The Secretary of
State Who Created the American World. *This essay first appeared as "Imperial
America and the Common Interest" in the Spring 2002 issue of* World Policy Jour-
nal *and is reprinted by permission of the publisher.*

and in the air. President George W. Bush has called for a defense budget that will reach $451 billion in 2007. We now spend more for defense than the next 15 industrialized countries combined, or 40 percent of what the rest of the world spends. Moreover, despite America's commitment to such a bloated military budget, our economic strength is such that America can afford to do so. Of course this means that public spending on health care and education will almost certainly suffer. There has been no outcry, however, for cutting military spending, especially in the wake of the September 11 attacks.

During the recent global recession, the economic weight of the United States was such that Europe, its only potential economic rival, could not act as a locomotive to pull the world out of its economic doldrums. With the apparent American recovery this spring, the likelihood is for a general global recovery, America leading the way.

What therefore is the nature of this American imperium? How did it come about? And what should its role be in the twenty-first century?

Almost two decades ago, the historian Arthur Schlesinger, Jr., referred to America's empire as an "informal" one, not colonial in the traditional sense of using military forces and colonial administrators to run territory acquired and occupied by the imperial power, often against the wishes of the locals. Rather, in Schlesinger's words, it was one "richly equipped with imperial paraphernalia: troops, ships, planes, bases, proconsuls, local collaborators, all spread wide around the luckless planet."[1]

What I propose to do is to discuss the growth and reach of the American imperium not by emphasizing its economic dimension—for example, that the United States expanded in order to seek and secure markets—but rather by showing that its expansion came about primarily because Americans wanted to feel safe. Even as the United States has quite clearly become an economic giant,

[1]Arthur Schlesinger, Jr., "America and Empire," in *The Cycles of American History* (Boston, 1986), p. 141.

whose prosperity fuels global prosperity and whose economic travails infect even such economic leviathans as the European Union, the growth of the American empire has come about not so much through a search for economic well-being as through a quest for absolute security, that is to say, invulnerability.

Although U.S. political and military leaders want to ensure the interest and security of the state, which has also meant promoting trade and foreign investment, there is also a peculiarly American cast of mind that has linked this quest for absolute security to American exceptionalism. In essence, this was the belief that America was a great experiment, fraught with risk but animated by the conviction—as John Winthrop, the first governor of Massachusetts, famously described it in 1630 aboard a ship off the New England coast—that America should be "as a city upon a hill," the eyes of all people upon us, and if we should fail to make this city a beacon of hope and decency, and "deal falsely with our God," we should be cursed.

At times this has given Americans a messianic mission to redeem the world, as Woodrow Wilson believed; at other times even the founders of the nation, who preferred to see the United States as a model for all mankind, believed that the infant American republic was "a rising empire." "Extend the sphere," wrote James Madison in the 1780s, evoking the image of an "extended republic" as "one great, respectable, and flourishing empire."[2]

While the United States expanded, seeking new territories by intimidation and treaty, as in the acquisition of Florida in 1819, or by military action, as in the Mexican War of 1846, it coupled its quest for absolute security with a belief in its own moral superiority, seeing itself as either an example for the world or a crusader for an empire of liberty. With this heritage, can America today find common ground with other great powers, such as the European Union, China, Russia, Japan, and India, seeking areas of shared interest that will prevent a balance of power being organized against us?

[2]Cited in Schlesinger, *Cycles of American History*, p. 129.

SOLITUDE, NOT ISOLATION

Since the earliest days of the Republic, the United States has sought to ensure the territorial integrity of the nation without the assistance of outside powers. Of course, Americans have on occasion also found it in their interest to follow George Washington's advice to "safely trust to temporary alliances for extraordinary emergencies." This was notably true with the treaty of alliance with France, signed in 1778, without which America could not have won its independence at the time. But in 1800, the treaty with France was abrogated. The United States henceforth remained free from any long-term alliance until the founding of NATO in 1949.

As a whole, though eager to cooperate with other nations in economic matters, America has been singularly unwilling to allow others to dictate policy in questions of national safety. This unilateral approach to security has carried with it an implicit message that allies can inhibit America's freedom of action and thus undermine its security. For this reason, America has never shied away from employing force unilaterally—either in defense of its own borders or in foreign regions viewed as vital—in response to perceived threats to the security of the state.

To be sure, the American nation has gone to war for a variety of specific reasons: to expand territory and seek markets for economic gain; in response to affronts to the national honor—as in Jefferson's military and naval actions against the Barbary pirates from 1801 to 1805; when attacked; and to play out the nation's role as promoter of democratic values. Moreover, the overarching response to the American need for safety and well-being—from the assertion of the Monroe Doctrine to the current war on terrorism—has been to take unilateral action as the surest way to achieve national security. The Monroe Doctrine, which declared that the United States would not permit any foreign power to intervene in the Western Hemisphere, was echoed by Grover Cleveland, who insisted that Great Britain accept American arbitration in a dispute between Britain and Venezuela in 1895. William McKinley's taking of the Philippines in the Spanish-American War, and Woodrow Wilson's military interventions in Mexico in 1914 and 1916, continued this policy.

This is not to say that all American political leaders believed absolute security was an immediately attainable goal. But for well over two centuries this aspiration has been seen as central to an effective American foreign policy—and never more so than at the outset of the twenty-first century, with the terrorist attacks against New York's World Trade Center and the Pentagon.

Political leaders have only two basic tools at their disposal when enforcing the national interest—diplomacy and force. But diplomatic negotiation implies compromise. Absolute security, however, cannot be negotiated; it can only be won. Achieving invulnerability in this manner is a lonely task.

The American reluctance to use diplomatic means before resorting to military force as a way of ensuring national security cannot be viewed as isolationism. Despite the popular myth to the contrary, the United States has never been isolationist. Even in the period between the two world wars, America was isolationist only toward Europe, and even there international naval reductions agreements were signed between the United States and the European nations; in the Western Hemisphere, especially in Central America and the Caribbean, the United States was openly interventionist; and in East Asia and the Western Pacific it played an active role.

THE MARGIN OF SAFETY

To be sure, most American leaders have fully appreciated the large measure of safety from external threats—what has been called "free security"—that America's geographical position offered and may have also contributed to the belief that absolute security could be achieved. As Thomas Jefferson said, the fact that the United States was "separated by nature and a wide ocean from the exterminating havoc of one quarter of the globe" was a blessing to the cause of American security. Today, the development of missiles has reduced the margin of safety the oceans once provided. But even before the air age, no American leader, including Jefferson, has ever been prepared to see the nation's safety rely on that blessing alone. Military interventions—not only in the Western Hemisphere but in all parts of the world—have been viewed as necessary to safeguard the American people.

Until the First World War, real or perceived threats to the nation's security were physical. For example, our activist foreign policy in the early and late nineteenth century centered on our continued anxiety over British meddling in the Western Hemisphere following the War of 1812. But that policy did not disappear when the presumed British threat clearly evaporated after 1895. At the turn of that century, with the closing of the continental frontier, American leaders feared that such rising naval powers as Germany and Japan threatened access to foreign markets in East Asia.

In the years immediately before and after the First World War, however, radical ideologies of the left and right gravely affected the American perception of security. Threats from anarchism, communism, and fascism, while not purely territorial, were nonetheless seen as perils that could undermine the strength and even the physical safety of the American commonwealth by promoting internal dissent and civil strife. These threats were countered by American presidents, most notably Woodrow Wilson, not only by curbing civil liberties at home but also by exporting American liberal democracy—more often than not imposed by American troops—to Latin America, Europe, and Asia.

Traditional territorial fears thus merged with ideological threats in determining America's international behavior. During the Second World War, and the Cold War that followed it, these anxieties prompted the adoption of internationalist policies unprecedented in their global scope, and the expansion of American power worldwide. Beginning with the Reagan presidency, and now seen as a legacy of the Cold War, the need for a universal response to both physical and ideological threats has finally resulted in a

National Missile Defense program that takes our historic quest for absolute security into a new realm—outer space.

Since the time of the American Revolution, however, there have also been American leaders who have warned us that the goal of absolute security was, in Alexander Hamilton's words, a "deceitful dream," one based on false confidence in American moral exceptionalism and on exaggerated fears that the United States, because of its democratic government and its wealth of natural resources, had been targeted for attack by foreign powers. But Hamilton's words were largely disregarded by later generations. To understand why his words went unheeded, one has to understand the roots of America's exceptionalism, its belief in itself as divinely guided, its mission to build here as elsewhere Winthrop's city on the hill.

THE MISSIONARY IMPULSE

Except for Hamilton's warning that Americans were no exception "from the imperfection, weaknesses and evils incident to society in every shape," the critique of American perfectibility came not in political discourse but in the writings of the classic American novelists, notably Nathaniel Hawthorne and Herman Melville. They knew that this vision of an untrammeled world that could be made over into an idealized American image was dangerously simplistic; on the contrary, everything is impure, even the brave new world of America, and everything is limited, even American possibilities.

Melville, whose masterpiece, *Moby Dick*, was dedicated to Hawthorne, at first seemed to be the quintessential American optimist, the man of action. "We are the pioneers of the world," he wrote in *White Jacket*, "the advance guard set out through the wilderness of untried things to break a path in the New World." But later his tales darkened. In "Benito Cereno," he wrote the story of an American sea captain, Amasa Delano, who comes upon a drifting Spanish slave ship and, innocently, boards it to help. What he does not realize is that the captain, Benito Cereno, has been taken captive by the slaves, who have revolted and seized the ship. When Delano himself is threatened by the slaves, he asks, bewildered, "But who would want to kill Amasa Delano?" Unwittingly, he had been drawn into the evils of the Old World. Experience, in the guise of the Spanish sea captain, is akin to corruption; the revolt of the slaves is like a rush from darkness into light. Yet, paradoxically, that revolt threatened the enlightened American's life.

In his story "The Birthmark," Hawthorne describes a single blemish that disturbs the beauty of the wife of the scientist Aylmer. The mark itself is in the shape of a small red hand against her pale skin, a symbol of the wife's liability to "sin, sorrow, decay, and death." These very characteristics are, of course, the sign of mortality. But Aylmer cannot accept them. In attempting to enforce man's control over nature, he gives his wife a potion he has invented to remove the flaw. The experiment appears to succeed, for the birthmark fades away. Her beauty is perfect. But she is dead. Thus, the quest for perfection ends in death.

A literature tending to subvert the extraordinary freedom of action Americans had in pursuing their country's exceptional destiny was disregarded—except when read as tales of adventure and gothic mystery. Throughout the nineteenth century and much of the twentieth, the U.S. government seldom admitted anything less than a moral vision of the world, in which Americans, virtuous and right, sought perfection on a continent whose vast natural resources seemed to promise autarky and, more important, invulnerability. Moreover, U.S. foreign policy was singularly successful. It ensured American security from the Atlantic to the Pacific, and seemed bent on removing all direct threats to the new republic.

At the same time, the expansionists of the nineteenth century generally saw America as an exemplar of freedom in the tradition of John Winthrop. John Quincy Adams, arguably the greatest secretary of state prior to the twentieth century, cautioned us not to go abroad "in search of monsters to destroy," but to be "the well-wisher to the freedom and independence of all . . . the champion and vindicator only of our own." He warned America not to enlist under other banners than her own, "were they even the banners of foreign independence." Should America do so, the "fundamental maxims of her policy would insensibly change from *liberty* to *force*. . . . She might become the dictatress of the world. She would no longer be the ruler of her own spirit."

By the time of the First World War, however, Woodrow Wilson picked up the crusader strand in American exceptionalism and became the very personification of the democratic mission, a man who believed that only by interfering in the affairs of other nations could the United States wage its campaign of self-determination for all peoples. Unable to compromise with his domestic opponents over the issue of American participation in the League of Nations, Wilson remained convinced of the unique mission of the United States. In his last speech, made in 1919, when he was urging ratification of the league by the Senate, he spoke of the American soldiers who had died crusading for a new world of democratic nations: "I wish some men in public life who are now opposing the settlement for which these men died . . . could feel the moral obligation that rests upon us not to go back on those boys, but to see the thing through, to see it through to the end and make good their redemption of the world. For nothing less depends on this decision, nothing less than the liberation and salvation of the world." As we know, the Senate refused to ratify the league.

It was not until the election of Franklin Delano Roosevelt that the United States found a president who combined the idealistic aspirations of the Founders to create a republic of virtue and their realistic appraisal of the need to seek *temporary* alliances to ensure America's security. Like Hamilton, Roosevelt counseled against the dangers of exceptionalism: "Perfectionism, no less than isolationism or imperialism or power politics, may obstruct the paths to international peace." Like Hamilton's, his warnings were largely disregarded as the Cold War came to dominate the American political scene.

Indeed, throughout the decades of the Cold War, the idea of America as a crusader, as a force for freedom, seems to have become engraved on the national consciousness. But spreading freedom, or making the world safe for democracy, if it is to be America's peculiar destiny, is likely to be a lonely task. America's allies have not generally shared its missionary zeal. More than they have cared to admit, they have agreed with General Charles de Gaulle's view that America, in its turn, would cloak its will to power in the raiment of idealism.

THE AMERICAN CONSCIENCE

Nonetheless, American foreign policy is likely to be most successful when accompanied by strong moral values. These values can be expressed not only by creating a domestic polity that aspires to John Quincy Adams's model that America act as an exemplar of freedom and democracy, but also by embracing by word *and* deed the international institutions that respond to our deepest values. That quintessential realist Walter Lippmann, after the Kennedy administration's misguided attempt to overthrow Cuba's Fidel Castro at the Bay of Pigs, wrote: "A policy is bound to fail which deliberately violates our pledges and our principles, our treaties and our laws." He reminded Americans that "the American conscience is a reality. It will make hesitant and ineffectual, even if it does not prevent, an un-American policy."[3]

Which brings us to the present condition of the United States—an imperial power the like of which has not been seen in the West since ancient Rome. Not only has President Bush embarked on a worldwide crusade to eradicate terrorism, but he hopes through these vast endeavors to bring about a great and durable peace.

In modern times after each major war, the peacemakers have searched for a way to achieve such a lasting peace. Although the Cold War lasted almost half a century, the victors—in this case, the United States and the Western allies—did not come up with a new approach to the perennial problem of keeping nations and

[3]Walter Lippmann, "Today and Tomorrow," *New York Herald Tribune*, May 9, 1961.

peoples from homicidal conflict. Even suggestions for improving the work of the United Nations in this respect—a standing military force to prevent or quell conflict, enlargement of the Security Council to include permanent representation of such regional powers as India, Brazil, and South Africa—have gone nowhere.

The realist historian David Fromkin, author of *A Peace to End All Peace*, has written that in a world of independent states, we cannot achieve a lasting peace because there is nobody to prevent war. His warning that America is neither strong enough to govern the world nor wise enough to provide political direction for other peoples has never been more salient. With these strictures in mind, we nonetheless need to ask ourselves if there are common interests among the great powers that the United States shares that can both satisfy America's moral concerns and allay its fears for the security of the nation.

Fromkin also referred to the "common interest," which Franklin Delano Roosevelt spoke of when he met with Winston Churchill in Morocco during the Second World War, conjuring up a future in which there would be compulsory education, immunization against disease, and universal birth control. Now, more than half a century later, what seems to be developing in Europe and the United States is an increased emphasis on the moral dimension in international politics.

Surely a long-term American policy should seek to promote a sense of shared values among the most powerful nations in the world, that is, those countries which, working together, can impose a peaceful settlement on unruly regions. Such was the case in Europe during the roughly 40 years that followed the Congress of Vienna, when the Concert of Europe operated with a reasonable degree of effectiveness. This was so even while the two relatively liberal powers, Britain and France, had serious ideological differences with the three autocratic powers, Russia, Austria, and Prussia, and with each other.

Could the United States, working with the European Union, Russia, China, and Japan find enough common ground to act in the common interest by preventing major conflicts among nations?

And in those instances where violence does not arise from the ambitions of traditional nation-states, as has recently been the case, but from terrorist activities that may be linked across borders, can the present war bind together the great powers in efforts to stamp out terrorism—since the absence of terrorism is in the national interest of these same powers?

In short, even in a world that may never be ready for a global superstate or world government, does this preclude a future concert of powers that see it in their respective national interests to cooperate over a wide range of issues that afflict mankind? After all, there are treaties that are largely supported by many nations—the treaty creating the International Criminal Court, the Kyoto Protocol on halting global warming, the Comprehensive Nuclear Test-Ban Treaty, the agreements on curbing biological warfare—all of which, if ratified by the great powers, might go a long way toward realizing a new vision of the common interest.

Unfortunately, the United States has been foremost in asserting its unwillingness to sign virtually anything that might limit its sovereignty. This not only harks back to the tradition of acting alone but is also characteristic of an imperial power whose refusal to cede its authority to a supranational authority cannot be overruled by others. Despite the lip service paid to multilateralism, the Bush administration has threatened to use force against any nation that might be developing biological, chemical, and nuclear weapons that could theoretically threaten the United States. Specifically, Deputy Secretary of Defense Paul Wolfowitz has warned that a preemptive strike aimed "at prevention, not merely punishment" awaits those who oppose America's will and jeopardize its sense of security.

An evolving Bush Doctrine thus emerged in the president's State of the Union address in January 2002, when he labeled Iraq, Iran, and North Korea an "axis of evil" that he would not permit to threaten America with weapons of mass destruction. To combat such a buildup, the president said he would not "wait upon events while dangers gather," nor "stand by as peril draws closer and closer," a statement that surely implies the use of conventional forces—or even tactical nuclear weapons—in preventive strikes against missile launchers and other facilities that might be involved in the creation and production of weapons of mass destruction.

A plan to develop new types of nuclear weapons precisely for the purpose of striking targets in Iraq, Iran, North Korea, Syria, and Libya was revealed in a Pentagon report known as the Nuclear Posture Review, in which high priority is given to creating an earth-penetrating, nuclear-tipped bunker buster. Should developing such a weapon require nuclear testing, ending the voluntary moratorium on such tests that now restrains nuclear programs in such countries as Iran and North Korea, the anti-proliferation effort to curb the spread of nuclear weapons would surely be shattered. Replying to these criticisms, National Security Advisor Condoleezza Rice declared that the way to deter the proliferation of weapons of mass destruction was to be clear that this "would be met with a devastating response."

President Bush also called for the development and deployment of "effective missile defenses" to protect the nation against sudden attack. While research and deployment of a limited missile defense is clearly in the offing, it would be an historical anomaly were the United States to develop such a system and then restrict it to a limited defensive capability. If a theater defense can merge into a national defense, other nuclear powers would be right to expect the United States to deploy a comprehensive defensive missile force if this were technologically feasible.

AMERICAN MESSIANISM

In this respect, invulnerability would seem at last in sight. While disclaiming any intention of "imposing our culture," the president struck a note of American messianism by listing "nonnegotiable demands"—"the rule of law, limits on the power of the state, respect for women, private property, free speech, equal justice and religious tolerance."

Although Bush again and again referred to working closely with "our coalition" to defeat terrorism, his endorsement of the unilateral use of American power to disarm "the world's most dangerous regimes [that] threaten us with the world's most destructive weapons" is likely to make it even more difficult to find allies willing to give blanket approval to such a strategy. In the wake of the president's address, the accusation of the French foreign minister, calling Bush's worldview "simplistic" and criticizing America for "making decisions based on its own view of the world and its own interests," may have been harsh, but his criticisms were shared by other American allies. Echoing his French colleague, German foreign minister Joschka Fischer declared that the "international coalition against terror is not the foundation to carry out just anything against anybody.... All the European foreign ministers see it that way. Throwing Iran, North Korea and Iraq into one pot... Where does that lead us?"

An imperial power such as the United States may well conclude that its values are universal values. But were the United States to link its national interest—and hence its values—to a search for the common interest, the redefinition of the nation's vital interests might very well shape a different world in the twenty-first century.

REALISM AND A MORAL CONSENSUS

Of course, unless these changes are discussed and presented to the vast public in terms of interests, they are unlikely to be supported. Even Hans Morgenthau, the preeminent theorist of twentieth-century realism, argued that it was a moral consensus for moderation, rather than the balance of power, that brought about relative stability for the four decades after the Congress of Vienna. This did not mean that Morgenthau was dismissing the balance of power as a means of containing conflict, but rather that he believed stability was more likely if the balance was underpinned by a moral consensus.

Such shared values, however, seem unlikely so long as the United States, in an era of unparalleled American predominance, prefers to go it alone. Already the Bush administration has agreed to intervene in a number of countries that, in Washington's view, are either sponsors or victims of terrorism. These include—in addition to Afghanistan—Yemen, the Philippines, Georgia, and possibly Indonesia, as well as Colombia (whose decades-long conflict with leftist rebels was previously supported by the United States as part of the war on drugs; now American aid to quell the insurgency will be deemed an effort to combat terrorism). The administration is also likely to take some military action against Iraq and will apparently do so with or without allied support.

This inclination to act unilaterally, stemming from the traditional American preference to define the national interest without the constraint of allies, has only been strengthened by America's economic and military prowess. With such power undergirded by a belief in America's moral exceptionalism, the most dangerous threat to American omnipotence may very well come about as a result of the alienation of Europe and Japan, and the wariness of China and Russia. The duration of the American imperium will thus depend on our ability to seek common ends with potential rivals. In this respect we have more to fear from our own mistakes than from those enemies who are now determined to bring us down.

MARTIN WALKER

An Empire Unlike Any Other

Comparisons between the United States and the empires of Rome and Great Britain are misplaced—except as a reminder that no empire is permanent.

HAS THE UNITED STATES become the new Rome? The analogy that began as a journalist's flippant conceit more than a decade ago has flourished into a cliché. The comparison is as glib as it is plausible, and there has always been something fundamentally unsatisfactory about it. Of course it's possible to see broad resemblances to contemporary America in the policies of the ancient state. Rome established authority by exercising power. It then spread and maintained the authority through a kind of consent that took root in the widening prosperity of a pan-Mediterranean trading network sustained by Rome's naval strength, in a tolerable system of law and order, and in the seductive infiltration of Rome's language and culture.

Martin Walker is a journalist and the author of many books, among them America Reborn: A Twentieth-Century Narrative in Twenty-Six Lives *(2000) and* The Caves of Perigord *(2002), a novel. This essay, reprinted by permission of the author, first appeared in the Summer* 2002 *issue of* The Wilson Quarterly.

But the United States does not rule, and it shrinks from mastery. When, for example, in the early 1990s the government of the Philippines requested the return of Clark Air Base and the Subic Bay Naval Station, the American legions calmly folded their tents and stole away. Even important strategic assets, such as the Panama Canal, have been freely bestowed by amicable treaty. American presidents are not the victors of civil wars, nor are they acclaimed to the purple by the Praetorian Guard. They are elected (though we had best pass hastily over the parallel between the fundraising obligations of modern campaigns and the oblations of gold that secured the loyalty of the Roman legions). Moreover, America has a reasonable and accepted system for managing the succession and the institutionalized rejuvenation of power. The president, elected for a specific term, is no emperor; he is a magistrate who administers laws that he is not empowered to enact. His powers are checked and supervised by an elected legislature and restrained by courts. Above all, he does not command the power to declare war.

Rome's empire was the real thing, held down by brutal force and occupation, at least until the benefits of law and order, trade, and cultural assimilation reconciled colonized peoples to their new status. It was a single geographic bloc, as classical empires usually were, its frontiers garrisoned and its limits set by the reach and pace of marching troops and the organizing skills that ensured that imperial armies could be paid and fed. Rome was at constant war with barbarians on the northern front and with the all-too-civilized Persians to the east. It had no allies, only satellites and client states that were required to reward their protectors with the tribute that symbolized dependence. And Rome showed no magnanimity to its defeated enemies; it organized no Marshall Plans or International Monetary Fund bailouts to help them recover and join the ranks of the civilized world. Carthage was destroyed and salt plowed into its fields to render them forever barren. Of his fellow Romans' approach to pacification, the historian Tacitus said, "They make a wasteland and call it peace."

The historically flawed identification of America with Rome, which has now entered the language and the thinking of senior aides in the White House and the State Department, can foster some dangerously misleading habits of mind. European friends complain of an alarming tendency of the United States to act alone and treat allies with disdain. In 2001, French foreign minister Hubert Védrine, who coined the term *hyperpuissance* (hyperpower) to define America's current preeminence, told a seminar of senior French diplomats in Paris that France would "pursue our efforts toward a humane and controlled globalization, even if the new high-handed American unilateralism doesn't help matters." Chris Patten, the European Union's external affairs commissioner, has complained that the success of the United States in Afghanistan "has perhaps reinforced some dangerous instincts: that the projection of military power is the only basis of security; that the United States can rely on no one but itself; and that allies may be useful as an optional extra."

The troubling habits of mind are not simply a consequence of the attacks of September 11, or even of the arrival of the current Bush administration. Triumphalist rhetoric characterized the United States during the Clinton years as, in Secretary of State Madeleine Albright's arresting phrase, "the indispensable nation," endowed with the capacity "to see further" than lesser powers. But the Clinton administration believed in collective international action. The Bush team, by contrast, applauded the refusal of the Republican-controlled Congress to ratify the Comprehensive Test Ban Treaty or accept American adhesion to the procedures of an international criminal court. The same Congress demanded a reduction in America's dues to the United Nations and held back payments until the country got its way. America's friends were outraged that the nation gave priority to domestic political interests. They thought less of America because they expected so much more of America: They presumed that the United States would keep its global responsibilities paramount and be governed always by Thomas Jefferson's "decent respect for the opinions of mankind." But such was not the disposition of the Washington where the Roman analogy had encouraged a frankly imperial ambition.

But can there be an American empire without an emperor? Indeed, how great a sprawl of meaning can the term empire usefully sustain—when it is already overburdened by having to encompass the vast differences among the Macedonian, Carthaginian, Roman, Persian, Ottoman, Carolingian, Mongol, Incan, Mogul, British, and Russian variants, to name but a few? Just as every unhappy family is, for Tolstoy, unhappy after its own fashion, so every empire is imperial in its own distinctive way. There are land empires and oceanic empires. There are empires such as the Ottoman, based on a common religious faith, and there are religiously tolerant, pagan, or even largely secular empires, such as Rome became in its grandest centuries. There are short-lived empires, based, like that of Alexander the Great, upon raw military power. And there are empires that thrive for centuries, usually because, like Rome and Carthage, they achieve a commercial prosperity that can enlist the allegiance of far-flung economic elites, or because they establish a professional civil service, an imperial governing class.

Such bureaucracies, whether the mandarinate of China or the Indian Civil Service or the staff of the Vatican, have much to offer. They embody the prospect of predictable if not reasonable governance, some form of justice, the stability that allows trade to flourish, and, above all, the likelihood of continuity. Although Germany and Japan after 1945 enjoyed a fleeting exercise of administrative benefits by the occupying U.S. forces, Washington has bred and trained no imperial bureaucracy. Successive presidents have preferred to swallow the embarrassment of having South American dictatorships and feudal sheikdoms as allies rather than be accused of meddling in the affairs of other nations. This squeamishness about interfering with other governments is a telling instance of the difference between the United States and classic empires.

In its current more-than-imperial reach and quasi-imperial authority, the United States is very different from the real empire of Rome and slightly different from the British Empire. Imagine a gauge of imperial character on which Rome scores 10. Britain might then score between 4 and 8, depending on the temporal and geographic circumstances of the measurement. Various characteristics of the United States in 2002 would score between 2 and 7: high numbers for its military power, commercial dominance, and cultural influence; low for the extent of its rule and for its preferring free allies to client states.

The British Empire seems to have more in common with contemporary America (beyond the importance of their shared language, legal systems, and naval traditions) than either of the two has with classical Rome. The matter is complicated because there were two British Empires, and the differences between them must be understood before any attempt is made to define what is and is not imperial about America's current hegemony. The first British Empire, which ended with the loss of half the North American colonies, was frankly mercantilist. The second, which was accumulated in fits and starts, was far more imperial in style and governance. But it was already being dismantled when it achieved its greatest extent, after the First World War (the League of Nations granted Britain the mandate to run the former German colonies in Africa and to be principal custodian of what had been the Ottoman Empire).

This second British Empire was always controversial. In 1877, the past and future Liberal prime minister William Gladstone claimed that it drained the economy and managed "to compromise British character in the judgment of the impartial world." Queen Victoria bridled at the "overbearing and offensive behavior" of the Indian Civil Service in "trying to trample on the people and continually reminding them and making them feel that they are a conquered people." Historians still pick their way through the varied motivations behind the empire: missionary zeal and commercial greed, high strategic concerns and low political ambitions, an honest faith in human improvement and a determination to force China to import Indian opium. As Cambridge University historian J. R. Seeley observed in 1883, "We seem to have conquered and peopled half the world in a fit of absence of mind."

For the seafaring British, the imperial project began as a commercial venture: North America was explored, exploited, and turned into a profitable enterprise by the Hudson's Bay Company.

But Britain came relatively late to formal rule over its far-flung possessions. The first empire—a strange mix of crown lands, semi-feudal estates, free ports, penal colonies, and vast tracts for religious dissidents—was forced by the requirements of war with the French and the Indians to adopt a formal system of rule. This empire came to an end at Yorktown in 1781 largely because London belatedly wanted to tax the colonists as if they really were subjects of the Crown.

Britain's nonrule of India continued for 75 years after its first empire crumbled at Yorktown. India was conquered, pillaged, and increasingly ruled by the Honorable East India Company, which was an independent commercial operation until 1773, when the Crown assumed partial control after financial disappointments. As Adam Smith noted in his *Wealth of Nations*, "Under the present system of management Great Britain derives nothing but loss from the dominion which she assumes over her colonies." The Indian Mutiny of 1856 revealed the limitations of this system, and the Crown then took over, not entirely willingly, a going financial concern. Lord Palmerston, then the prime minister, defined British ambitions as "trade without rule where possible, trade with rule where necessary." Rule was expensive, cumbersome, and problematic, and equivalent commercial benefits could be obtained far more cheaply. A British subject at the head of Chinese customs, for example, might favor British interests and discourage rivals, without the unnecessary expense of a British garrison.

Britain exercised a similarly oblique sway in the Middle East. After defaulting on loans and being visited by a French and British fleet in 1876, Egypt accepted the installation of Anglo-French controllers over its national finances. Although the powers of the British grew, and the French were squeezed out, the Egyptian monarchy, government, and army all remained in place. That proved a model for British influence throughout the Persian Gulf: advisers at the sheikh's right hand held the trump card of a British fleet offshore. In parts of the world where there was little to attract British colonists and a reasonably effective local government was in place, the British preferred to rule through that government.

Where there was no such local government to co-opt, as appeared to be the case in much of Africa, the British installed full imperial rule through their own law courts, schools, and district governors. The Islamic world proved far more resistant to British sway than did either Africa or Asia because the Christian missionaries, whose schools engaged in a subtle indoctrination, were made most unwelcome.

Reluctant to finance the large standing armies characteristic of the Continental great powers, the British cultivated an oceanic enterprise through trade and their excellent Royal Navy. They avoided the trap that snared many land empires, which overextended themselves and had to defend ever-wider frontiers. Sea power allowed the British Empire to rule by something very close to bluff. Until the South African War (1899–1902) and the demands of the trenches of the First World War, there were never more than 150,000 troops in the entire British Army—a smaller number than today's Pentagon routinely stations overseas (almost 100,000 in Europe, 25,000 in the Persian Gulf, 37,000 in Korea, and another 20,000 in Japan). At its peacetime Victorian peak in 1897, the British Empire rested on the bayonets of 55 battalions of infantry stationed abroad—about 40,000 troops. The locally recruited sepoys of the Indian Army brought the total number of British imperial forces in 1897 to 356,000—slightly larger than the size of the Roman Army at the time of the Emperor Trajan in the early second century A.D., the period of Rome's greatest extent.

There were always far more British troops stationed in Ireland than in India, and as Rudyard Kipling suggested in "The Green Flag," his tale of Irish heroism in imperial service, more Irish and Scottish than English troops in India. As Rome had done, the British Raj defended itself with auxiliary forces recruited from the ruled. And yet, having successfully devised the concept of empire on the cheap, the British fell into a technology trap: when sail gave way to steam, carefully spaced coaling stations defined the route to India. The British showed little interest in the Middle East until the building of the Suez Canal in the 1870s required a British strategic presence along the route to the jewel in the imperial crown. Even then, the "imperial" presence was legally less than met the eye. Egypt retained its king, its army, and its customs, while Britain pulled the strings. Throughout the Persian Gulf region, British advisers saw to it that British interests were paramount, without the expense of imperial rule. The Bank of Persia, for example, was founded and run by Englishmen. When the emirs of Aden proved unwilling to build the lighthouses British navigation required in the Red Sea, the P & O Steamship Company built and manned its own on Dardalus Reef.

The erection of that lighthouse out of commercial self-interest was also an act with altruistic implications, and in that respect it sheds light on the current debate about the nature of the American imperium. The British Empire defined its role in terms of a wider good, akin to *la mission civilisatrice* of its French contemporary. Again, the oceanic character of the British imperial project is central. Once its freebooters and licensed pirates had seized command of the Caribbean and North American waters from the Spaniards in the 16th century, the British found it in their commercial interest to suppress piracy; they did so by enacting what became the first enforced international law. In the 19th century, motivated in part by guilt over previous profits, the British ordered the Royal Navy to suppress the slave trade.

The construction of lighthouses and the suppression of piracy and the slave trade gave some meaning to the usually self-serving British claim to be defending the freedom of the seas. For a trading nation such as Britain, peaceful and safely navigable waters were useful, but they also benefited others. Under the benign rule of Britannia, the seas became a common good for all seafarers. And under the guns of the Royal Navy, sovereign states that borrowed money (usually from the City of London) and refused to pay found themselves required to do so. British troops would be landed to seize the ports, control the customs operations, and impose duties and tariffs, as happened in Egypt, until the debt was repaid. If the property of British citizens suffered in local riots, there was retaliation: when, for example, Athenian warehouses belonging to Don Pacifico, a Jewish merchant who was a British subject of Gibraltar, were damaged, the British fleet bombarded the Greek port of Piraeus until proper compensation was paid. It was in defense of this high-handed action before Parliament that Lord Palmerston made the clearest correlation between the empires of Britain and Rome: "As the Roman, in days of old, held himself free from indignity, when he could say '*Civis Romanus sum*,' so also a British subject, in whatever land he may be, shall feel confident that the watchful eye and the strong arm of England will protect him against injustice and wrong."

Freedom of the seas, the defense of property rights, and the ability to enforce commercial contracts were the essential building blocks of that surge of economic growth and prosperity that marked the Victorian Age. British investors financed the railroads that opened the American West, the pampas of Argentina, and the gold mines of South Africa. Vessels were launched from the shipyards of the rivers Clyde and Tyne and Humber, powered by the coal fields of Wales and Durham, and insured by Lloyd's of London. The Reuters news service informed all customers—in English, which was also the language of navigation—of the price of commodity X at port Y in the universal currency of the gold sovereign as produced at London's Royal Mint. The ships, the coal, the insurance, and the gold coins were available, like the seas, to all comers, just as the British market was in those days of free trade, when Britain was the exporting and importing customer of first and last resort.

The parallels are clear between the role of the British Empire in fostering the first great wave of globalization in the 19th century and that of the United States in promoting the second in the latter half of the 20th century. But does that make the United States, as ruler of the waves, guarantor of global finance, prime foreign investor, and leading importer, an empire? It certainly makes the United States, for all the universal benefits its broadly benign hegemony has brought, as unpopular as Britain once was. "No people are so disliked out of their own country," noted the American traveler Robert Laird Collier of the British during a visit to their homeland in the 1880s. "They assume superiority. As a nation they are intensely selfish and arrogant."

Collier sounds mild by comparison with the Indian novelist Arunhati Roy, who wrote the following in Britain's *Guardian* in September 2001: "What is Osama bin Laden? He's America's family secret. He is the American president's dark doppelgänger. The savage twin of all that purports to be beautiful and civilized. He has been sculpted from the spare rib of a world laid to waste by America's foreign policy: its gunboat diplomacy, its nuclear arsenal, its vulgarly stated policy of 'full-spectrum dominance,' its chilling disregard for non-American lives, its barbarous military interventions, its support for despotic and dictatorial regimes, its merciless economic agenda that has munched through the economies of poor countries like a cloud of locusts. Its marauding multinationals who are taking over the air we breathe, the ground we stand on, the water we drink, the thoughts we think."

So the charge of imperialism stumbles forth again, and comes loaded with a wider postmodern meaning, at least on best-seller lists, in universities, and among radical groups who regard globalization as the new focus of unjust imperial authority. The success of *Empire* (2001), a sprawling and grandiose book from Harvard University Press about the power structures of the global economy, testifies both to a resurgent concern with imperialism and to the controversial implications of the current extraordinary role of the United States, the sole superpower. The authors of *Empire* are Michael Hardt, a professor of literature at Duke University, and Antonio Negri, an Italian revolutionary theorist and professor at the University of Padua who is serving a prison term on charges of practicing what he preached with the Red Brigades. They attempt to resuscitate Lenin's imploded theory of imperialism as the last resort of capitalism: "What used to be conflict or competition among several imperialist powers has in important respects been replaced by the idea of a single power that overdetermines them all, structures them in a unitary way, and treats them under one common notion of right that is decidedly post-colonial and post-imperialist."

Empire, despite its flaws, deserves to be taken seriously, if only because among the anti-globalization militants who mobilize against World Bank or Group of Eight or World Trade Organization summits, it is hailed as the *Das Kapital* of the 21st century. The book's argument is confused, sometimes suggesting that the United States is the new single empire, and sometimes suggesting that, beyond any petty definitions of nationality, the new dispensation is "empire as system"—though a system highly congenial to American interests. Countries such as Britain, France, and Japan have built vast corporations with a global reach, but they operate within an economic system of which the United States is the financial linchpin and military guarantor.

This free-trading, free-market, American-dominated empire, Hardt and Negri contend, has become an all-encompassing presence, a form of cultural hegemony (to use Antonio Gramsci's phrase) that influences the consciousness of all who live under it. Although the argument is rather subtler than that the empire has developed Disney World and friendly clowns at McDonald's to lure the infant who will become the future consumer, a cardinal feature of this new American predominance is indeed its allure, in addition to its power. Joseph S. Nye, dean of the Kennedy School of Government at Harvard University, calls this characteristic "soft power," the power to make others want the things America wants. It's a force much easier to wield than hard, military power. The process is hardly new. Indian schoolboys under the Raj grew up dreaming of playing cricket at Lord's Ground in London, and African and Arab children in the French Empire were brought up with a history textbook that represented their forebears as "our ancestors, the Gauls."

But France and Britain, like Rome before them, lost their empires. And there is no guarantee that America's current superiority will endure. Despite its military dominance, America may not be able to maintain the political will, supply the financial means, and guarantee the technological monopolies to sustain its lonely eminence indefinitely. Regional challengers, ever more likely to be nuclear armed, already have the muscle to perturb and distract—and may someday have the power to deter or even attack—the United States. To manage what is likely to become a turbulent political environment, the United States should look beyond the simplistic image of itself as the modern Rome. Its choices for a sustainable grand strategy in the 21st century might better be defined by two other models from classical times, Athens and Sparta. Which does America wish to be?

Athens would be the more congenial model for a free-trading, self-indulgent democracy with a strong naval tradition and a robust belief in the merits and survivability of its own civilization. But there is much in the American political and military culture that leans to the fortress mentality and uncompromising attitudes of Sparta. America as Sparta would be introspective, defensive, protectionist, and unilateralist. It would prefer clients and satellites to allies that might someday challenge its primacy. It would seek to maintain military superiority at all costs and be suspicious of the erosions of national sovereignty that might result from cooperation with other states. America as Athens would join allies and partners in collaborative ventures with a common purpose, such as global warming treaties and international legal structures. It would be extrovert and open, encourage the growth of democracies and trading partners, and help to build a world where all can enjoy freedom and dream of prosperity.

Put in those terms, the choice for America makes itself. And yet, the choice ultimately may not matter. Athens and Sparta each flourished in its turn and then faded, just as the Roman, British, and Soviet empires did—indeed, as every empire has done. What remains after empires fade is neither their weapons nor their wealth. Rather, they leave behind the ideas and the arts and the sciences that seem to flourish best amid the great stability of empires. We now remember Athens for its gifts of philosophy, mathematics, drama, and democracy, just as we acknowledge the inheritance from Britain of the King James Bible and Shakespeare, a free press and jury trials, and the magnificent defiance that saved the world in 1940. Whatever its fate, America, too, will live on—for its Constitution and its movies and its having placed the first man on the moon.

VICTOR DAVIS HANSON

What Empire?

*Those who depict the United States as an impe-
rial power are simply wrong.*

IT HAS BECOME POPULAR of late to talk of the American "empire." In Europe particularly there are comparisons of George W.
Bush to Caesar—and worse—and evocations of all sorts of preten-
tious political science jargon like "hegemon," "imperium," and
"subject states," along with neologisms like "hyperpower" and
"overdogs." But if we really are imperial, we rule over a very funny
sort of empire.

We do not send out proconsuls to preside over client states,
which in turn impose taxes on coerced subjects to pay for the legions. Instead American bases are predicated on contractual obligations—costly to us and profitable to their hosts. We do not see
any lucre in Korea, but instead accept the risk of losing almost

---

*Victor Davis Hanson is Professor of Classics at California State University at Fresno,
a research fellow at the Hoover Institute, and the author of more than eighty scholarly
articles and editorials on classical and military history and contemporary culture. His
most recent books include* An Autumn of War, Carnage and Culture, *and* The
Soul of Battle. *This essay first appeared as a web posting on NROnline and is
reprinted in revised form by permission.*

40,000 of our youth to ensure that Kias can flood our shores and that shaggy students can protest outside our embassy in Seoul.

In this odd postmodern world, even North Korea does not object strenuously to our troops on the DMZ, who serve as hostages of sorts to their saber rattling. North and South alike *both* seem to think that the purpose of American troops is mostly to die in the first hours of battle. That prospect gives Pyongyang leverage in its antebellum threats and offers a complacent Seoul assurances that we will intervene en masse to prevent South Korea from being overrun. The only thing American that is invading North Korea is free wheat, rice, and diesel fuel. In sum, our more abstract reasons for stationing troops overseas in the post–Cold War—secure global trade, safe sea lanes, and consensual government—would leave the Roman Senate singularly unimpressed.

Athenians, Romans, Ottomans, and the British wanted land, colonies, treasure, and grabbed all they could get when they could. The United States hasn't annexed anyone's soil since the Spanish-American War—a checkered period in American history that still makes us, not them, out as villains in our own history books. Britain talked about a mercantile system, and so did Napoleon—more modern ways to emulate the slanted commerce that in antiquity used to drain colonies and subject states in order to enrich Athens or Rome. America instead runs vast trade deficits with everyone, from protectionist Japanese and Koreans (our "clients") and Europeans (our "allies") to communist China (our "competitor") and Russia (our "former enemy").

Most Americans are far more interested in carving up the Nevada desert for monster homes than in getting their hands on Karachi or the Amazon basin. Puerto Ricans are free to vote themselves independence anytime they wish. In California, Mexican citizens here illegally already receive in-state tuition waivers not extended to American citizens from other states, and are now agitating to receive driver's licenses. Activists on both sides of the border talk of a "Mexifornia" or "Republica del Norte" that will soon arise from the policy of a de facto open border between Mexico and California. Indeed, illegal Mexican aliens enjoy more civil rights in the southwestern United States than do legal American residents in Mexico. A genuinely imperialist power rarely seeks to weaken the very idea of sovereignty on its own borders.

Imperial powers order and subjects obey. But in our case, we offer the Turks strategic guarantees, political support—and money—for their allegiance. Before we can invade Iraq—which we fear has both terrorist liaisons and weapons of mass destruction to facilitate deadly attacks against our homeland in the aftermath of September 11—we extend debt relief to Egypt, some $15 billion in aid to Turkey, and advanced munitions for the Gulf States. France and Russia ponder about going along with us in the U.N.—but only if we ensure them the traffic of oil and security for outstanding accounts. In fact, both Germany and France vent a virulent anti-Americanism even as they continue to expect the protection of the American military. Pakistan illegally obtained nuclear weapons yet still gets American-funded debt relief that ruined dot-coms could only dream of. For his part, the king of Jordan reels in more aid than our own bankrupt municipalities. In 1991 we had in our hands all the oil of Kuwait—and easily could have scooped up Iraq's as well—and instead handed the wells back to the rightful owners. In contrast—to recall what a real empire does to a rebellious client—the Romans razed the Great Temple at Jerusalem and sold the booty off to build the Coliseum.

If acrimony and invective arise, it's usually one-way: Europeans, Arabs, and South Americans all say worse things about us than we do about them, not privately and in hurt, but publicly and proudly. To read Mexican newspapers George Bush, not Saddam Hussein, is the real threat to world peace. Vicente Fox boasts that soon our presidente will see the light and essentially create a zone libre that all but dissolves traditional borders. But for a Central American alien the hard part is not breaking into the massive gates of imperial America but first getting through Mexico's militarized southern border.

Boasting that you hate Americans—or calling our supposed imperator "moron" or "Hitler"—won't get you censured by our Senate or earn a tongue-lashing from our president. Instead it is more likely to earn ten minutes on CNN. We are considered haughty by Berlin not because we send a Germanicus with four legions across the Rhine but because Mr. Bush snubs Gerhard Schroeder by not phoning him as frequently as the German press would like. Imperial powers, whether in Gaul or India, expect deference and embrace a pomp and circumstance that reflects such pretensions; American diplomats in contrast are bombarded with visa applications and pelted with insults. Few dared kill a Roman consul, an Ottoman Bey, or a Russian KGB operative; in the last two decades dozens of the American diplomatic corps have been murdered with relative impunity. Israel went into Lebanon when a single Israeli diplomat was wounded by a PLO terrorist; American statesmen and their employees have been shot down in the Sudan, Jordan, Lebanon, and Greece without exacting serious reprisals.

Empires usually have contenders that check their power and through rivalry drive their ambitions. Athens worried about Sparta and Persia. Rome found its limits when it butted up against Germany and Parthia. The Ottomans never succeeded in bullying the Venetians or the Spanish. Britain worried about France and Spain at sea and Germans by land. In contrast, restraint on American unipower comes not from China, Russia, or the European Union but from the American electorate itself—whose reluctant worries are chronicled by weekly polls that politicians ignore at their peril. We the people, not some foreign power, prevent the political class in Washington from making the United States a real empire.

The internationalist left worries about multinational corporations and imperial aggrandizement; the nationalist right fears we are no longer a republic and thus are spending too much cash on foreigners and not on our own. Together they vie for the hearts and minds of Americans, most of whom have no idea where or why our troops are abroad. Unlike Englishmen who expressed great pride in the Raj, Americans would gladly see those troops come home from Europe, Japan, and South Korea.

The Athenian *ekklesia*, the Roman senate, and the British Parliament alike were eager for empire and reflected the energy of their people. In contrast, America went to war late and reluctantly in World Wars I and II—and never finished the job in either Korea or Vietnam. We were more than happy to shed the Philippines after promoting democracy there, and really have had no desire to return. If Chancellor Schroeder sent U.S. troops stationed in Germany packing, American polls would show relief, not anger. Isolationism, parochialism, and self-absorption loom larger as aspects of the American character than does any desire for overseas adventurism. Critics may bash the United States for "overreaching," but our military and political elites worry more about coaxing a reluctant populace to act than about constraining a blood-drunk rabble.

The desire of a young Roman quaestor or the British Victorians was to go abroad, shine in battle, and come home laden with spoils. They wanted to be feared, not liked. American suburbanites, inner-city residents, and rural townspeople all will fret because a French opportunist or a Saudi autocrat says that we are acting inappropriately. Polls show support for American unilateralism only on the condition that the UN sanctions it. Roman imperialists had names like Magnus, Britannicus, and Africanus; the British anointed their returning proconsuls as Rangers, Masters, Governors, Grandees, Sirs, and Lords. In contrast, retired American diplomats, CIA operatives, or generals are lucky if they can melt away in anonymity into the Virginia suburbs without a subpoena, media exposé, or lawsuit. Proconsuls were given entire provinces; for our part, ex-president Jimmy Carter advises us to disarm and criticizes a sitting president in a time of war. Meanwhile, Bill Clinton in the post-9/11 climate tours the globe apologizing for everything from the Crusades to chattel slavery, and is more likely to bite his lip than shake his finger when his country is blamed abroad. Proud internationalists emeriti like Dr. Henry Kissinger receive not triumphal processions but find themselves the objects of scurrilous books and endless writs.

Most empires chafe at the cost of their rule and complain that the expense is near suicidal. Athens raised the Aegean tribute often and found itself nearly broke after only the fifth year of the Peloponnesian War. The story of the Roman Empire is one of shrinking legions, a debased currency, and a chronically bankrupt imperial treasury. Even before World War I, the Raj had drained England. In contrast America today spends less of its GNP on defense than it did during the last five decades. And most of our military outlays go to training, salaries, and retirements—moneys that support, educate, and help people rather than simply stockpile weapons and hone killers. The remarkable fact is not that we have twelve massive $5 billion aircraft carriers but that we could easily build and maintain twenty more yet choose not to do so. So our military is enormous not because of our skewed priorities of guns over butter but simply because the vast size of the present-day American economy allows more soldiers and weapons with a 4 percent GNP investment than most other countries could field with 50 percent.

Empires create a culture of pride and pomp, and foster a rhetoric of superiority. Pericles, Virgil, and Kipling all talked and wrote of the grandeur of imperial domain. How odd then that what America's literary pantheon—Norman Mailer, Gore Vidal, Susan Sontag, and Alice Walker—said about 9/11 would either nauseate or bewilder most Americans. Our most popular icon of the moment seems to be Michael Moore; both his book *Stupid White Men* and film *Bowling for Columbine* sell both at home and worldwide solely on the premise that the United States is a very sick nation.

Pericles could showcase his Parthenon from the tribute of empire; Rome wanted the prestige of *Pax Romana* and *Mare Nostrum*; the Sultan thought Europe should submit to Allah; and the Queen could boast that the sun never set on British shores. Our imperial aims? We are happy enough if the Japanese can get their oil from Libya safely and their Toyotas to Los Angeles without fear; or if China can be coaxed into sending us more cheap Reeboks and in turn fewer pirated CDs. The problem we have is not unilaterally intervening for profit but resisting the entreaties of Kuwaitis, Bosnians, Kosovars, Somalis, and Rwandans to come in and save them from dictators, famine, and mass murderers. Americans have no desire to convert the world to Christianity; in fact, we welcome

Muslims to worship freely—something impossible for Western infidels in many Islamic countries.

Our bases dot the globe to keep the sea lanes open, thugs and murderers under wraps, and terrorists away from European, Japanese, and American globalists who profit mightily by blanketing the world with everything from antibiotics and contact lenses to BMWs and Jennifer Lopez—in other words, to keep the world safe and prosperous enough for Noam Chomsky to garner a lot of money and tenure from a defense-contracting MIT, for Barbra Streisand to make millions from overpriced tickets, for Edward Said's endowed chair to withstand Wall Street downturns, and for Jesse Jackson to take off safely on his jet-fuel-powered, tax-free junkets.

Why then does the world hate a country that uses its power to keep the peace rather than rule with brutality and exploitation? Resentment, jealousy, and envy of the proud and powerful are often cited as the very human and age-old motives that prompt states irrationally to slur and libel—just as individuals do against their betters. The current hegira for the world's nations is to Washington not Paris, Berlin, or London, and that weighs heavily on proud and once strong peoples. No doubt Thucydides would agree. But there are other more subtle factors involved that explain the peculiar present angst against America—and why the French or Germans say worse things about free Americans who once saved them than they do about Soviets who wanted to kill them. Mr. Vladimir Putin, the ex-KGB officer who not long ago wished to enslave West Germany, is now more warmly welcomed in Berlin than is Donald Rumsfeld, the former U.S. representative to NATO and current secretary of defense.

Observers like to see an empire suffer and pay a price for its influence. That way they think purported imperial sway is at least earned. Athenians died all over the Mediterranean, from Egypt to Sicily; their annual burial ceremony was the occasion for the best of Hellenic panegyric. The list of British disasters from the Crimea and Afghanistan to Zululand and Khartoum was the stuff of Victorian poetry. But since Vietnam, Americans have done pretty much what they wanted to in the Persian Gulf, Panama, Haiti, Grenada, Serbia, and Afghanistan, with less than an aggregate of 200 lost to enemy fire—a combat imbalance never seen in the annals of warfare. So not only can Americans defeat their adversaries, but they don't even die doing it. Shouldn't—as our critics insist—we at least have some body bags?

Yet does such an imbalance create a culture of triumphalism and awe? Just the opposite. We erect no statues for veterans of Grenada or Serbia. Instead the theme of postwar American memorials has not been the grand struggle but rather the sorrow of it all—the Wall which draws thousands to the mall in Washington is, after all, a world away from Pericles' Funeral Oration or Trajan's column.

Imperial intervention is also supposed to be synonymous with exploitation. Thus the Athenians killed, enslaved, exacted, and robbed on Samos, Scione, and Melos. No one thought Rome was going into Numidia or Gaul—one million killed, another million enslaved—to implant local democracy. Nor did the British move into 17th-century India with an eye toward organizing indigenous elections. But the United States overthrew Manuel Noriega, Slobodan Milosevic, and Mullah Omar—fascists all—to put in their places elected leaders, not legates or local clients who put a lid on national liberation, collect tribute, and do as they are told. Instead of the much-rumored "pipeline" that we supposedly coveted in Afghanistan, we are paying tens of millions to build a road and bridges so that Afghan trucks won't break their axles. Americans in Haiti or Somalia were trying to feed, not kill, people. They bombed Belgrade for 77 days but have been serving as peacekeepers and humanitarians in the former Yugoslavia for seven years.

In that regard, America's impact abroad is more revolutionary than imperial. Its crass culture abroad—rap music, Big Macs, Star Wars, Pepsi, and *Beverly Hillbillies* reruns—does not reflect the tastes and values of either an Oxbridge elite or landed Roman aristocrats. We are not Ottomans with a labyrinth of laws designed to insulate our society from foreign corruption and competition. That informality and openness explains why *Le Monde* or a Spanish deputy minister may libel us, even as millions of semi-literate Mexicans, unfree Arabs, and oppressed southeast Asians are dying to get here to partake of our free economy and dynamic culture. It is one thing to mobilize against grasping, wealthy white people who want your copper, bananas, or rubber—quite another when your own youth want what black, brown, yellow, and white middle-class Americans alike have to offer.

We so-called imperialists don't wear pith helmets but rather baggy jeans and backwards baseball caps. Michael Jordan is our emissary abroad, not a Lord Chelmsford. Having failed to formulate an ideology as alluring as the kinetic American strain of Western culture, Muslim fundamentalists, European socialists, and Chinese Communists bash us as grasping imperialists rather than admit their own inability to respond to the yearnings of their own people.

Much, then, of what we read about the evils of United States imperialism is written by post-heroic and bored elites, apparatchiks, snooty intellectuals, and coffeehouse hacks, whose freedom and security are a given but whose rarified tastes or rigid ideologies are endangered by the juggernaut of American popular culture. In contrast, plain folk want American-style freedom and material things first—and cynicism, skepticism, irony, and nihilism second.

Should the day come when Washington charges all host countries for our troops and appropriates Persian Gulf oil fields, and when epic poems about noble missions of the 101st Airborne replace pop music on our radio stations, then perhaps we should worry about the rise of empire and an imperial culture.

Critiques of the United States based on class, race, nationality, or taste have all failed to explicate, much less stop, the American cultural monstrosity. With African-Americans Condoleezza Rice and Colin Powell steering U.S. foreign policy the United States promises $15 billion in AIDS assistance for Africa—only to have Nelson Mandela condemn America two days later. Forecasts of bankrupting defense expenditures and imperial overstretch are the stuff of the faculty lounge; billions may be spent abroad, but the economy is now measured in trillions. Neither Freud nor Marx is of much help in explaining the popular spread of American influence since our culture tends to destroy hierarchy and privilege—if we can gauge correctly the angst of imams and patriarchs in the Islamic world, traditionalists in Europe, and communist grandees from China to Cuba. And real knowledge of past empires that might allow judicious analogies is beyond the grasp of popular critics, who instead deductively start with the a priori assumption we are Rome—and then make "facts" fit where they must.

Add that all up, and our exasperated critics are left with little apart from empty jargon of legions and gunboats.

III

Imperial Strategies

JOHN MILBANK

Sovereignty, Empire, Capital, and Terror

> For the nation-state, globalization poses an
> unprecedented challenge; an imperial "war on
> terror" is America's response.

CONCERNING the immediate aftermath of the events of September 11, the initial question one should ask is exactly why there was outrage on such a gigantic scale? After all, however unusual and shocking this event may have been, people are killed in large numbers all the time, by terror, politics, and economic oppression. Within a matter of days after the attack on the World Trade Center, the United States already may have killed more people in response to the attacks than died in them, through increased and tightened sanctions in the Near East which bring pressure on governments through the deliberate terrorization of civilian populations. So why this unprecedented outrage?

One must here ignore the pieties about the dreadfulness of

John Milbank is Frances Myers Ball Professor of Philosophical Theology at the University of Virginia. A longer version of this essay, reprinted here by permission of the South Atlantic Quarterly, first appeared in the Spring 2002 issue of that journal.

terrorism. The West and Israel itself engage in or covertly support many acts of terror all over the globe, and indeed terrorism has only arisen as a tactic of minority resistance in imitation of the new late-nineteenth- and twentieth-century deployment of unabashed physical and psychological terror against civilians as a primary instrument of war in contradiction to all traditional Christian teaching and even practice, up to a certain point. (These horrific new tactics were arguably first taken up during the American Civil War.) The terrorism seen here as being uniquely evil is the terrorism that assumes a power that is supposed to belong to states alone. I am not saying that the people who blew up the World Trade Center buildings were anarchists. But their *mode of action* threatens the very idea of the state. So that is my first answer.

But answer two is that there was a hidden glee in the official outrage on the part at least of some, though certainly not of others. The attack seemed to give an opportunity to do things that some factions in the West have wanted for a long time. What are these things? An assault on so-called rogue states; a continuous war against "terrorists" everywhere; a policing of world markets to ensure that free-market exchange processes are not exploited by the enemies of capitalism. But, above all, the attack provided an opportunity to reinscribe state sovereignty.

The modern secular state rests on no substantive values. It lacks full legitimacy even of the sort that Saint Paul ascribed to the "powers that be," because it exists mainly to uphold the market system, which is an ordering of a substantively anarchic (and therefore not divinely appointed in Saint Paul's sense) competition between wills to power—the idol of "liberty," which we are supposed to worship. This liberty is dubious, since it is impossible to choose at all unless one is swayed one way or another by an influence: hence a supposedly "pure" free choice will only be a cover for the operation of hidden and uniform influences. People who fondly imagine themselves the subjects of their "own" choices entirely will, in reality, be the most manipulated subjects and the most incapable of being influenced by goodness and beauty. This is why, in the affluent Anglo-Saxon West today, there is so much pervasively monotonous ugliness and tawdriness that belies its wealth, as well as why there are so many people adopting (literally) the sing-song accent of self-righteous complacency and vacuous uniformity, with its rising lilt of a feigned questioning at the end of every phrase. This intonation implies that any overassertion is an impolite infringement on the freedom of the other, and yet at the same time its merely rhetorical interrogation suggests that the personal preference it conveys is unchallengeable, since it belongs within the total set of formally correct exchange transactions. Pure liberty is pure power—whose other name is evil.

The nation-state itself creams off and piles up this pure power in the name of a people. Every modern state therefore is inherently semiracist because it proclaims the supreme interest of a discrete populace, defined by legacy as well as territory. This semiracist holding together of a people requires an exterior—a potential enemy. The occasional emergency of war is crucial for the (one must add, modern) state's legitimacy. But globalization puts the modern state into crisis. There is now the prospect of no more exterior, no more real foes. Sovereign power is consequently threatened. If it remains merely domestic, it will wither away in the face of multiple loyalties. If it exports itself and drives toward the global state, then it still needs an enemy who is other. Without an external enemy, the enemy must now be internal, lurking everywhere. Without the possibility of the occasional emergency of war, there must be perpetual war against an internal danger. Globalization inevitably evokes its own shadow: the irruptive challenge of suppressed singularity, which when all other resources are lost to it, can still make the symbolic gesture of sacrificial death (suicidal self-sacrifice or the sacrificial murder of others; the two being often combined, as on September 11). A monotonous totality both requires this opposition and tends to provoke its unexpected instance.

Because of its history of expanding frontiers—its internal wars against native Americans, African Americans, British loyalists, Spaniards in the South and West, the dissenting Confederate states, southern and Central America, dealers in alcohol and drugs, and Communists in the 1950s—the United States has in a sense been long preparing for this new sort of global conflict. As Michael Hardt and Antonio Negri have argued in their *Empire*, American neo-Roman imperialism works by a constant subsumption and inclusion of "others," such that difference is apparently welcomed, yet actually subordinated to an unremitting uniformity. Now all comes to be within the unrestricted one world market.

This contrasts with older European imperialism, which held the other at a subordinated distance, permitting its otherness even while subordinating it for the sake of an exploitation of natural and human resources. Such nuances are often overlooked in pseudo-left-wing American "postcolonial" discourses, which actually assist the ideology of the American Right by implying the original "innocence" of the United States as a once-colonized nation and its natural solidarity with all the colonized.

These implications tend to conceal the fact that American neo-colonialism is yet more insidious than the older variety. It does not attend to cultural difference; it pursues no substantive goals of the political and social good (however deluded the ones of old empire may often have been) and seeks instead both for pure economic exploitation and for the absolute imposition of American signifiers. Under French and British colonial law, child labor was banned; now within the "American Empire," but of course with total European connivance, it is everywhere rife.

But what we now see is a fearful extension of American Republican Imperialism, in terms of a logic that is impeccably Machiavellian. The unity of the republic, snatched by fate out of time for the sake of its own negative freedom (and the negative freedom of its citizens insofar as this is maintained through their absolute submission to the republic) can only be secured through constant re-unification in the face of a threat to this freedom. Given that the republic is isolationist and has no interest other than its own freedom, it is not able to mediate with the other, even in an old-European hierarchical fashion. Instead, it can only withstand by subsuming, by expanding at least its frontiers of cultural reach. Commentators who have tended to think that Bush was jolted out of isolationism by the catastrophe miss the point that isolation and hysterical expansion are two halves of the American Republican dialectic.

Moreover, the American sense that what is isolated and expanded is unquestionably the *acme* of human political achievement, frozen forever in an ideal constitution, disallows the self-denying ordinances, the sense of temporariness, of passing expediency, and of fearful desire to avoid *hubris*. Unlike Rudyard Kipling in his poem "Recessional," American imperialism never supposes that the Captains and the Kings must one day depart.

This is why, in an emergency that tends to release the unspoken truth, there has been so much apparently insane language concerning "infinite" processes: an infinite war, infinite justice, infinite retribution—sustained in George W. Bush's terrifying address to Congress shortly after the September 11 attack. There he declared, for the first time perhaps since Hitler's announcement of the Third Reich, a kind of state of perpetual emergency. He announced a new sort of war without aims or a foreseeable end, often to be fought in secret. Those not with the United States and Britain in the war were declared to be against them and allied with terrorists. This is potentially a license for totalitarianism, and already, for the sake of fighting a vague conflict explicitly projected to last almost forever, it has become unquestionable that basic legal procedures and respect for people's privacy should be suspended.

The existence of a state of emergency was witnessed in the statement by Donald Rumsfeld (about which many of his colleagues exhibited understandable unease) that non-Afghan Taliban should be "*either* killed or taken prisoner." This was more or less a license to the Northern Alliance to kill these people like dogs, on the very dubious assumption that they were somehow implicated in the attack on the Twin Towers. Of course even if they had been, the proper response would be to arrest and try them; yet implicit in Rumsfeld's statement was an exceptional suspension of all normal legality: *both* the norms of criminal legality *and* the norms of military legality. Because one is dealing with a threat to sovereignty as such, law as such no longer applies, since the merely formal, decisionistic basis of law in a state that exists mainly to undergird the market cannot appeal to a natural equity beyond itself. Without the state, there is, for the modern outlook, no good and evil, and therefore against the enemies of the state, neither morality nor law applies. They are neither warriors for another power (or an internal counterpolitics), whom one must respect as individuals, nor transgressors of the law whom one must respect as malefactors deserving punishment and the instigation of repentance.

No, they have sunk beneath humanity, as Dick Cheney later confirmed. Captured "terrorists" he declared "don't deserve to be treated as criminals. They don't deserve the same guarantees and safeguards that would be used for an American citizen going through the normal judicial process." This exclusionary logic has been impeccably realized in the confinement of Al-Qaeda suspects in animal cages exposed to the elements in Cuba. This stark denial of the *imago dei* for "terrorist suspects" tends to expose the concealed racist basis of the usual talk of "human rights." This "universal" notion was originally invoked by the West in order to intervene in the internal affairs of nonwhite countries, from Turkey in the case of the Armenian massacre onward. But as soon as the white West is threatened, it becomes clear that rights are things that archetypally belong to "American citizens" under "normal," which means local and not at all universal, circumstances. This is all a very far cry from Harry Truman in 1945, who insisted, against Churchill's unreflecting proposal to shoot the Nazis in a corner, that "this would not sit easily on the American conscience."

The suspension of all norms of legality is further confirmed by the stipulation that future secret executions of those covertly convicted of terrorism can be watched by the relatives of victims of September 11. Here one is confronted with the purest barbarism: in the past, or in the Islamic present, public executions possess at least the primitive rationale of visible justice and warning, while unwitnessed modern execution exposes a certain proper shame and hesitancy on the part of the state, but *selectively* witnessed executions obliterate the line between punishment and vengeance, since all that matters here is the death of the other power threatening "domestic" power and lives.

II

Such emergency measures are not really being proposed because of the unique character of terrorism, but rather because of the perception of a new threat to sovereignty and capital. A perpetual war against terrorism can be seen as an effort to resolve the crisis of state sovereignty in the face of globalization. Since in a real sense both the Western and the different Islamic state forms face the same crisis, one can go further and say that both terrorism and counterterrorism, which will quickly become commingled and indistinguishable, are attempts to resolve this crisis. To see globalization on one side and anti-globalization on the other is too simple.

But there is also another aspect to the crisis of globalization—the economic rather than political. The West, especially the United States, has expanded its economic hegemony since the end of the cold war. Once there was no longer any need to pander to third world regimes in order to counter Soviet influence, the United States, mostly supported by Europe, proceeded to set up economic structures that operated entirely in its own interests, with the result that global inequality has vastly increased as well as environmental damage, which is sometimes the direct result of U.S. intervention, as in Colombia at the present moment. These structures have included the liberalization of markets and the removal of all inhibitions on stock exchange speculation, as well as the scandalous patenting of genetically altered (and thereby probably contaminated) crops allied to the outlawing of the natural varieties produced, particularly in South America.

But now these hegemonic economic structures show signs of impending implosion: supply has been outrunning demand; computer technology has been overinvested; Western interests in older manufacturing have been possibly rashly sold off; and domestic shares and economically crucial information have gotten into the hands of people who are potential enemies. The United States and Europe are consequently faced with a need to implement more internal regulation—but also with the specter of having already let things slip beyond their control.

The assumption prior to this new turn has been that the market and freedom simply line up with Western dominance. Now, however, we are beginning to see how a small number of hostile, politically motivated investors can reap devastating effects. September 11 was a kind of chiasmus—a crossing over and reversal. During the 1990s, Western power became more and more abstracted and virtual in character: dominating the pathetically real and material lives of people in the South. Now suddenly the West was reduced to the Paleolithic. We saw that the abstract was still partly stored in two fragile standing totems with less resilience even than Neolithic standing stones. This still-fixed capital was simply knocked over. But meanwhile, in the face of the failure of Western information to stop this catastrophe, the terrorists, whoever they are, were manipulating information in order to seize the maximum abstract advantage.

Given the sheer convenience of war and military emergency to forces wishing to resolve the twin crises of Western sovereignty and Western capitalism, one has to ask to what extent these forces were, subconsciously or consciously, urging war before September 11? The current war is a war against terrorism we are told, which has suddenly become a global and immediate threat, though we were not generally told this before the catastrophe. And in fact there is much evidence that global terrorism has been recently in decline rather than to the contrary. Therefore there is every reason to suspect that this war is not simply a war against terrorism but is also a war against multiple targets, designed to ensure the continued legitimacy of the American state and the global perpetuation of the neocapitalist revolution of the 1980s.

Ever since January 2001 at the very least, crisis has surely been in the air. Bush withdrew from international agreements on ecology, weaponry, debt, and the pursuit of justice—most ironically of all he refused to acknowledge that any American could ever be a war criminal, thereby undercutting the legitimacy of international juridical procedures against someone like bin Laden. Meanwhile Communism in the East had been reemerging, anticapitalism was reasserting itself in Western Europe and under the banner of antiglobalization it was starting to coalesce with resistance movements in the South. Right along the Atlantic seaboard from Britain to Portugal a growing irritation with America in the face of economically disastrous flooding probably linked with global warming was evident, but was scarcely reported in the United States at all. Anti-Americanism in France and Italy was increasing at an alarming rate. In Great Britain the Conservative Party faced possible extinction, and public opinion, moving to the left of Tony Blair, now favored action to reduce drastically corporate greed.

More seriously still, the socialist president of Venezuela (and friend of Fidel Castro), Hugo Chavez, had been flexing considerable political muscle in the face of the general failure of neoliberal regimes in his subcontinent. In the face of American and European opposition, he had encouraged the OPEC countries to sustain a middling level of oil prices where market demand would have forced a drop. This, obviously, had implications for Middle Eastern politics and for the U.S. hegemony in that region. For some time now, reliance even on Saudi oil had become dubious.

Suddenly then, American and capitalist hegemony looked surprisingly fragile—although of course this should not be exaggerated. But it must have appeared fragile enough to powerful right-wing think tanks, who are in any case prone to apocalyptic scenarios: a frightening possible convergence of a protesting South America, Islamic nations rich in oil, revivified communism, and a Europe more wobbly and more prone to anti-U.S. sentiment than at any time since World War II.

Finally, the United States was and is itself a potentially unstable polity. Cultural and political shifts in South America would have ripple effects among Latino populations in the United States; low election turnout reveals a vastly indifferent and often alienated population; an eighteenth-century constitution produces constant stasis and deadlock that cannot deliver normal modern state infrastructures and welfare provisions that form a buffer against dangerous discontents of the underprivileged; the cultural gap between coastal and middle America could erupt into something serious; edgy rival oligarchies do not trust democracy to deliver security but believe they have to manipulate the outcome of elections (as occurred in November 2000). In the face of this potential hydra, it is clear that the U.S. establishment and the Bush administration were deeply divided and inconsistent. Pure isolationism had been one response, yet it was clear to many that this is a very risky course. Those advocating a more aggressive and interventionist strategy on the assumption that American supreme power must never be challenged (a doctrine initiated by Madeleine Albright: the Democratic Party is as guilty as anyone else in all this) were delivered, by good fortune or otherwise, a supreme present on September 11.

Not only could national security henceforward override democracy without question, but the immediate threat of terror for the moment pulled Europe, Russia, South America, moderate Arab States, and China in line behind the United States. They have been enlisted with varying degrees of enthusiasm and begrudgingness behind a military action that will assault all those who resist the sway of the global market, as well as behind police deployments to ensure that the market and flow of information are not themselves used against the market and against this flow. In addition, a new unity of Americans, rich and poor, behind a resurrected patriotism, has been put into place. The fractures lurking ever since November 2000 are for the moment sealed, although any manifest failure of "the war" might cause them to appear again with a vengeance.

Thus, while indeed in one respect "the war" is not simply to do with September 11 and is commanded by the West's pursuit of its own economic interests, in another respect its specific mode has been dictated by the need to react symbolically and cathartically in the face of public outrage, and in this respect the terrorists have truly dictated the pace and character of recent events. A balanced analysis must do justice to both the economic and the symbolic aspects, and try to comprehend just how they interact.

In neither aspect, however, is one really talking about the tracking down of evildoers, as we have been led to believe. Supposedly "the war" in Afghanistan was pursued against bin Laden, and yet it doesn't seem likely that if he were ever caught he would be treated in accord with the Geneva Convention. If terrorism were *really* the issue, then much the safer thing would be to stick to the discourse of crime and the practice of regular policing and due juridical process. Anything else, as the bitter experience of the French and British shows, only tends to increase the support of terrorist groups and legitimate their operations. The ethical evil of terrorism is that, more than certain modes of conventional warfare, it directly instrumentalizes human life. But this means that any response that tends to do the same thing is uniquely ineffective: in losing the ethical high ground, it also tends to lose the strategic high ground. This has already happened to America, which has now bombed and killed innocent villagers supposed to be "harboring" terrorists (the results could not be seen on American television); which, together with Britain, has bombed a prisoner of war camp at Qala-i-Jhangi fortress from the air; which has caused all the major aid agencies to flee Afghanistan for the duration of the conflict, and which has delayed the arrival of humanitarian aid even after the fall of Kabul—thereby cumulatively causing thousands of innocent deaths. Even were those who say that only "massive force" stops terrorism correct (and they are unlikely to be proved right in the long term because of the delayed "blowback" phenomenon), the implication would be that only a permanently terroristic state can stop terrorism—once again wiping out all moral distinctions between the respective parties.

The use of cluster bombs, of heavy bombers where there were no hard targets, and the attack on unquestionably non-Taliban places like the village of Gardez show that one is not even speaking about "collateral damage" here. Most crucial of all has been not capturing bin Laden, nor even overthrowing the Taliban, but rather exhibiting a show of terror intended to cow the entire region for the foreseeable future and bend it and parallel terrains to the Western will. From the war against Spain to capture the Philippines, through Hiroshima and Vietnam and the Gulf conflict (where bombing secretly continued long after Operation Desert Storm), the United States has deployed the terrorizing and murder of civilians (five million dead in the Vietnam conflict in the whole of Southeast Asia), the massacre of disempowered individual combatants, and the use of poisonous or torturing weapons (condemned ever since antiquity by civilized nations) as a primary instrument of military and political policy. Cumulatively this reveals the relatively genocidal tendency of specifically Republican imperialism (commencing domestically with the treatment of Native Americans), and it amounts to an atrocity almost on a level with the Holocaust and the Gulags—raising the suspicion that U.S. and indeed European domestic democracy is a kind of harmless theatrical indulgence for the globally privileged. And this circumstance reveals to us that the trouble is not "totalitarianism" pure and simple, but the emptiness of the secular as such, and its consequent disguised sacralization of violence. There is a desperate need for the United States to reach behind its current Machiavellian, Hobbesian, and Lockean norms for its deeper and more truly radical legacy of Christian (and at times Jewish) associative agrarian and civic Republicanism, which has truly to do with just distribution and the inculcation of social virtue. Among much of the American populace, the spirit of this legacy is still extraordinarily and creatively alive, as anyone who has lived in the United States can testify. Yet it is today rarely able to achieve any conscious political articulation.

Were this a war against terrorists it would not be a just one, primarily because it would be a lunatically "disproportionate" action. A case against Al-Qaeda should have been brought before the International Court in the Hague, which could have sponsored many effective means to reduce their influence. In any case, not the perpetrators (still at large after thousands of deaths and the sowing of the seeds of untold future misery and future terroristic movements) but a sovereign state—which was ready to hand over the supposed perpetrators, and with whom the British Foreign Office recommended a deal—have been attacked. As I have already said, the idea that Britain or the United States cares about the iniquities of the Taliban is ludicrous: they helped to create them; they are happy to tolerate the convenient Islamic atrocities of the Saudis; and having totally failed to carry out their own ground war, they were ready to let the Taliban be displaced by the equally obnoxious Northern Alliance.

One must assume that the powers that be are cynically aware of all this. So one must also assume that the war against terrorism is a cover for other operations and purposes, as well as being an unpremeditated symbolic response to an overwhelmingly symbolic event. Indeed, since terrorism is a now permanently possible form of behavior, the idea of a "war" against it is as absurd as the idea of a "war on drugs."

Unfortunately, the chance for the Western state and the Western market to ensure its continued hegemony in the face of dire symbolic and real threat is also the chance of specifically modern Islamic fanaticism. Bin Laden's following among those who in other circumstances would deplore him has probably been vastly increased by the recent actions of the West and Israel.

A war against a civilization cannot be won. And Islam could prove to be more united, less decadent, and more resilient than we imagine. Prophecy is perilous, but we may have reached the point where the only way out of a catastrophe that could potentially destroy the West is to abandon our global idolatrous worship of sacralized absolute sovereignty, and the formally neutral market, with their empty pursuit of power, in West and East alike.

Both empty secular power and arbitrary theocratic power, in their secret complicity, show us no way forward. Neither enlightenment nor "fundamentalism" can assist us in our new plight.

STANLEY HOFFMANN

Sheriff and Missionary

Today more than ever, nobody loves a hegemon.

IT WASN'T INNOCENCE that the United States lost September 11, 2001. It was its naiveté. Americans have tended to believe that in the eyes of others the United States has lived up to the boastful clichés propagated during the Cold War (especially under Ronald Reagan) and during the Clinton administration. We were seen, we thought, as the champions of freedom against fascism and communism, as the advocates of decolonization, economic development, and social progress, as the technical innovators whose mastery of technology, science, and advanced education was going to unify the world.

Some officials and academics explained that U.S. hegemony was the best thing for a troubled world and unlike past hegemonies would last—not only because there were no challengers strong enough to steal the crown but, above all, because we were benign rulers who threatened no one. But we have avoided looking at the

Stanley Hoffmann is the Paul and Catherine Buttenwieser University Professor at Harvard University. This essay first appeared as "Why Don't They Like Us" in the November 19, 2001, issue of The American Prospect. *It appears here by permission of that magazine.*

hegemon's clay feet, at what might neutralize our vaunted soft power and undermine our hard power. Like swarming insects exposed when a fallen tree is lifted, millions who dislike or distrust the hegemon have suddenly appeared after September 11, much to our horror and disbelief. America became a great power after World War II, when we faced a rival that seemed to stand for everything we had been fighting against—tyranny, terror, brainwashing—and we thought that our international reputation would benefit from our standing for liberty and stability (as it still does in much of Eastern Europe). We were not sufficiently marinated in history to know that, through the ages, nobody—or almost nobody—has ever loved a hegemon.

Past hegemons, from Rome to Great Britain, tended to be quite realistic about this. They wanted to be obeyed or, as in the case of France, admired. They rarely wanted to be loved. But as a combination of high-noon sheriff and proselytizing missionary, the United States expects gratitude and affection. It was bound to be disappointed; gratitude is not an emotion that one associates with the behavior of states.

THE NEW WORLD DISORDER

This is an old story. Two sets of factors make the current twist a new one. First, the so-called Westphalian world has collapsed. The world of sovereign states, the universe of Hans Morgenthau's and Henry Kissinger's Realism, is no longer. The unpopularity of the hegemonic power has been heightened to incandescence by two aspects of this collapse. One is the irruption of the public, the masses, in international affairs. Foreign policy is no longer, as Raymond Aron had written in *Peace and War*, the closed domain of the soldier and the diplomat. Domestic publics—along with their interest groups, religious organizations, and ideological chapels—either dictate or constrain the imperatives and preferences that the governments fight for. This puts the hegemon in a difficult position: it often must work with governments that represent but a small percentage of a country's people—but if it fishes for public support abroad, it risks alienating leaders whose cooperation it needs. The United States paid heavily for not having had enough contacts with the opposition to the shah of Iran in the 1970s. It discovers today that there is an abyss in Pakistan, Saudi Arabia, Egypt, and Indonesia between our official allies and the populace in these countries. Diplomacy in a world where the masses, so to speak, stayed indoors, was a much easier game.

The collapse of the barrier between domestic and foreign affairs in the state system is now accompanied by a disease that attacks the state system itself. Many of the "states" that are members of the United Nations are pseudo-states with shaky or shabby institutions, no basic consensus on values or on procedures among their heterogeneous components, and no sense of national identity. Thus the hegemon—in addition to suffering the hostility of the government in certain countries (like Cuba, Iraq, and North Korea) and of the public in others (like, in varying degrees, Pakistan, Egypt, and even France)—can now easily become both the target of factions fighting one another in disintegrating countries and the pawn in their quarrels (which range over such increasingly borderless issues as drug trafficking, arms trading, money laundering, and other criminal enterprises). In addition, today's hegemon suffers from the volatility and turbulence of a global system in which ethnic, religious, and ideological sympathies have become transnational and in which groups and individuals uncontrolled by states can act on their own. The world of the nineteenth century, when hegemons could impose their order, their institutions, has been supplanted by the world of the twenty-first century: where once there was order, there is now often a vacuum.

What makes the American Empire especially vulnerable is its historically unique combination of assets and liabilities. One has to go back to the Roman Empire to find a comparable set of resources. Britain, France, and Spain had to operate in multipolar systems; the United States is the only superpower.

But if America's means are vast, the limits of its power are also considerable. The United States, unlike Rome, cannot simply impose its will by force or through satellite states. Small "rogue" states can defy the hegemon (remember Vietnam?). And chaos can easily result from the large new role of nonstate actors. Meanwhile, the reluctance of Americans to take on the Herculean tasks of policing, "nation building," democratizing autocracies, and providing environmental protection and economic growth for billions of human beings stokes both resentment and hostility, especially among those who discover that one can count on American presence and leadership only when America's material interests are gravely threatened. (It is not surprising that the "defense of the national interest" approach of Realism was developed for a multipolar world. In an empire, as well as in a bipolar system, almost anything can be described as a vital interest, since even peripheral disorder can unravel the superpower's eminence.) Moreover, the complexities of America's process for making foreign policy decisions can produce disappointments abroad when policies that the international community counted on—such as the Kyoto Protocol and the International Criminal Court—are thwarted. Also, the fickleness of U.S. foreign policymaking in arenas like the Balkans has convinced many American enemies that this country is basically incapable of pursuing long-term policies consistently.

None of this means, of course, that the United States has no friends in the world. Europeans have not forgotten the liberating role played by Americans in the war against Hitler and in the Cold War. Israel remembers how President Harry Truman sided with the founders of the Zionist state; nor has it forgotten all the help the United States has given it since then. The democratizations of postwar Germany and Japan were huge successes. The Marshall Plan and the Point Four Program were revolutionary initiatives. The decisions to resist aggression in Korea and in Kuwait demonstrated a commendable farsightedness.

But Americans have a tendency to overlook the dark sides of their course (except on the protesting left, which is thus constantly accused of being un-American), perhaps because they perceive international affairs in terms of crusades between good and evil, endeavors that entail formidable pressures for unanimity. It is not surprising that the decade following the Gulf War was marked both by nostalgia for the clear days of the Cold War and by a lot of floundering and hesitating in a world without an overwhelming foe.

STRAINS OF ANTI-AMERICANISM

The main criticisms of American behavior have mostly been around for a long time. When we look at anti-Americanism today, we must first distinguish between those who attack the United States for what it does, or fails to do, and those who attack it for what it is. (Some, like the Islamic fundamentalists and terrorists, attack it for both reasons.) Perhaps the principal criticism is of the contrast between our ideology of universal liberalism and policies that have all too often consisted of supporting and sometimes installing singularly authoritarian and repressive regimes. (One reason why these policies often elicited more reproaches than Soviet control over satellites was that, as time went by, Stalinism became more and more cynical and thus the gap between words and deeds became far less wide than in the United States. One no longer expected much from Moscow.) The list of places where America failed at times to live up to its proclaimed ideals is long: Guatemala, Panama, El Salvador, Chile, Santo Domingo in 1965, the Greece of the colonels, Pakistan, the Philippines of Ferdinand Marcos, Indonesia after 1965, the shah's Iran, Saudi Arabia, Zaire, and, of course, South Vietnam. Enemies of these regimes were shocked by U.S. support for them—and even those whom we supported were disappointed, or worse, when America's cost-benefit analysis changed and we dropped our erstwhile allies. This Machiavellian scheming behind a Wilsonian façade has alienated many clients, as well as potential friends, and bred strains of anti-Americanism around the world.

A second grievance concerns America's frequent unilateralism and the difficult relationship between the United States and the United Nations. For many countries, the United Nations is, for all its flaws, the essential agency of cooperation and the protector of its members' sovereignty. The way U.S. diplomacy has "insulted" the UN system—sometimes by ignoring it and sometimes by rudely imposing its views and policies on it—has been costly in terms of foreign support.

Third, the United States' sorry record in international development has recently become a source of dissatisfaction abroad. Not only have America's financial contributions for narrowing the gap between the rich and the poor declined since the end of the Cold War, but American-dominated institutions such as the International Monetary Fund and the World Bank have often dictated financial policies that turned out to be disastrous for developing countries—most notably, before and during the Asian economic crisis of the mid-1990s.

Finally, there is the issue of American support of Israel. Much of the world—and not only the Arab world—considers America's Israel policy to be biased. Despite occasional American attempts at evenhandedness, the world sees that the Palestinians remain under occupation, Israeli settlements continue to expand, and individual acts of Arab terrorism—acts that Yasir Arafat can't completely control—are condemned more harshly than the killings of Palestinians by the Israeli army or by Israeli-sanctioned assassination squads. It is interesting to note that Israel, the smaller and dependent power, has been more successful in circumscribing the United States' freedom to maneuver diplomatically in the region than the United States has been at getting Israel to enforce the UN resolutions adopted after the 1967 war (which called for the withdrawal of Israeli forces from then-occupied territories, solving the refugee crisis, and establishing inviolate territorial zones for all states in the region). Many in the Arab world, and some outside, use this state of affairs to stoke paranoia of the "Jewish lobby" in the United States.

ANTIGLOBALISM AND ANTI-AMERICANISM

Those who attack specific American policies are often more ambivalent than hostile. They often envy the qualities and institutions that have helped the United States grow rich, powerful, and influential.

The real United States haters are those whose anti-Americanism is provoked by dislike of America's values, institutions, and society—and their enormous impact abroad. Many who despise America see us as representing the vanguard of globalization—even as they themselves use globalization to promote their hatred. The Islamic fundamentalists of al-Qaeda—like Iran's Ayatollah Khomeini 20 years ago—make excellent use of the communication technologies that are so essential to the spread of global trade and economic influence.

We must be careful here, for there are distinctions among the antiglobalist strains that fuel anti-Americanism. To some of our detractors, the most eloquent spokesman is bin Laden, for whom America and the globalization it promotes relentlessly through free trade and institutions under its control represent evil. To them, American-fueled globalism symbolizes the domination of the Christian-Jewish infidels or the triumph of pure secularism: they look at the United States and see a society of materialism, moral laxity, corruption in all its forms, fierce selfishness, and so on. (The charges are familiar to us because we know them as an exacerbated form of right-wing anti-Americanism in nineteenth- and twentieth-century Europe.) But there are also those who, while accepting the inevitability of globalization and seem eager to benefit from it, are incensed by the contrast between America's promises and the realities of American life. Looking at the United States and the countries we support, they see insufficient social protection, vast pockets of poverty amidst plenty, racial discrimination, the large role of money in politics, the domination of the elites—and they call us hypocrites. (And these charges, too, are familiar, because they are an exacerbated version of the left-wing anti-Americanism still powerful in Western Europe.)

On the one hand, those who see themselves as underdogs of the world condemn the United States for being an evil force because its dynamism makes it naturally and endlessly imperialistic—a behemoth that imposes its culture (often seen as debased), its democracy (often seen as flawed), and its conception of individual human rights (often seen as a threat to more communitarian and more socially concerned approaches) on other societies. The United States is perceived as a bully ready to use all means, including overwhelming force, against those who resist it: Hence, Hiroshima, the horrors of Vietnam, the rage against Iraq, the war on Afghanistan.

On the other hand, the underdogs draw hope from their conviction that the giant has a heel like Achilles'. They view America as a society that cannot tolerate high casualties and prolonged sacrifices and discomforts, one whose impatience with protracted and undecisive conflicts should encourage its victims to be patient and relentless in their challenges and assaults. They look at American foreign policy as one that is often incapable of overcoming obstacles and of sticking to a course that is fraught with high risks—as with the conflict with Iraq's Saddam Hussein at the end of the Gulf War; as in the flight from Lebanon after the terrorist attacks of 1982; as in Somalia in 1993; as in the attempts to strike back at bin Laden in the Clinton years.

Thus America stands condemned not because our enemies necessarily hate our freedoms but because they resent what they fear are our Darwinian aspects, and often because they deplore what they see as the softness at our core. Those who, on our side, note and celebrate America's power of attraction, its openness to immigrants and refugees, the uniqueness of a society based on common principles rather than on ethnicity or on an old culture, are not wrong. But many of the foreign students, for instance, who fall in love with the gifts of American education return home, where the attraction often fades. Those who stay sometimes feel that the price they have to pay in order to assimilate and be accepted is too high.

WHAT BRED BIN LADEN

This long catalog of grievances obviously needs to be picked apart. The complaints vary in intensity; different cultures, countries, and parties emphasize different flaws, and the criticism is often wildly excessive and unfair. But we are not dealing here with purely rational arguments; we are dealing with emotional responses to the omnipresence of a hegemon, to the sense that many people outside this country have that the United States dominates their lives.

Complaints are often contradictory: consider "America has neglected us, or dropped us" versus "America's attentions corrupt our culture." The result can be a gestalt of resentment that strikes Americans as absurd: we are damned, for instance, both for failing to intervene to protect Muslims in the Balkans and for using force to do so.

But the extraordinary array of roles that America plays in the world—along with its boastful attitude and, especially recently, its cavalier unilateralism—ensures that many wrongs caused by local regimes and societies will be blamed on the United States. We even end up being seen as responsible not only for anything bad that our "protectorates" do—it is no coincidence that many of the September 11 terrorists came from America's protégés, Saudi Arabia and Egypt—but for what our allies do, as when Arabs incensed by racism and joblessness in France take up bin Laden's cause, or when Muslims talk about American violence against the Palestinians. Bin Laden's extraordinary appeal and prestige in the Muslim world do not mean that his apocalyptic nihilism (to use Michael Ignatieff's term) is fully endorsed by all those who chant his name. Yet to many, he plays the role of a bloody Robin Hood, inflicting pain and humiliation on the superpower that they believe torments them.

Bin Laden fills the need for people who, rightly or not, feel collectively humiliated and individually in despair to attach themselves to a savior. They may in fact avert their eyes from the most unsavory of his deeds. This need on the part of the poor and dispossessed to connect their own feeble lot to a charismatic and single-minded leader was at the core of fascism and of communism. After the failure of pan-Arabism, the fiasco of nationalism, the dashed hopes of democratization, and the fall of Soviet communism, many young people in the Muslim world who might have once turned to these visions for succor turned instead to Islamic fundamentalism and terrorism.

One almost always finds the same psychological dynamics at work in such behavior: the search for simple explanations—and what is simpler and more inflammatory than the machinations of the Jews and the evils of America—and a highly selective approach to history. Islamic fundamentalists remember the promises made by the British to the Arabs in World War I and the imposition of British and French imperialism after 1918 rather than the support the United States gave to anticolonialists in French North Africa in the late 1940s and in the 1950s. They remember British opposition to and American reluctance toward intervention in Bosnia before Srebrenica, but they forget about NATO's actions to save Bosnian Muslims in 1995, to help Albanians in Kosovo in 1999, and to preserve and improve Albanians' rights in Macedonia in 2001. Such distortions are manufactured and maintained by the controlled media and schools of totalitarian regimes, and through the religious schools, conspiracy mills, and propaganda of fundamentalism.

WHAT CAN BE DONE?

Americans can do very little about the most extreme and violent forms of anti-American hatred—but they can try to limit its spread by addressing grievances that are justified. There are a number of ways to do this:

· First—and most difficult—drastically reorient U.S. policy in the Palestinian-Israeli conflict.

· Second, replace the ideologically market-based trickle-down economics that permeate American-led development institutions today with a kind of social safety net. (Even *New York Times* columnist Thomas Friedman, that ur-celebrator of the global market, believes that such a safety net is indispensable.)

· Third, prod our allies and protégés to democratize their regimes, and stop condoning violations of essential rights (an approach that can only, in the long run, breed more terrorists and anti-Americans).

• Fourth, return to internationalist policies, pay greater attention to the representatives of the developing world, and make fairness prevail over arrogance.

• Finally, focus more sharply on the needs and frustrations of the people suffering in undemocratic societies than on the authoritarian regimes that govern them.

America's self-image today is derived more from what Reinhold Niebuhr would have called pride than from reality, and this exacerbates the clash between how we see ourselves and foreign perceptions and misperceptions of the United States. If we want to affect those external perceptions (and that will be very difficult to do in extreme cases), we need to readjust our self-image. This means reinvigorating our curiosity about the outside world, even though our media have tended to downgrade foreign coverage since the Cold War. And it means listening carefully to views that we may find outrageous, both for the kernel of truth that may be present in them and for the stark realities (of fear, poverty, hunger, and social hopelessness) that may account for the excesses of these views.

Terrorism aimed at the innocent is, of course, intolerable. Safety precautions and the difficult task of eradicating the threat are not enough. If we want to limit terrorism's appeal, we must keep our eyes and ears open to conditions abroad, revise our perceptions of ourselves, and alter our world image through our actions. There is nothing un-American about this. We should not meet the Manichaeanism of our foes with a Manichaeanism of self-righteousness. Indeed, self-examination and self-criticism have been the not-so-secret weapons of America's historical success. Those who demand that we close ranks not only against murderers but also against shocking opinions and emotions, against dissenters at home and critics abroad, do a disservice to America.

G. JOHN IKENBERRY

Imperial Ambitions

9/11 removed America's inhibitions about exercising its power. But the resulting neoimperial strategy is fraught with peril.

THE LURES OF PREEMPTION

IN THE SHADOWS of the Bush administration's war on terrorism, sweeping new ideas are circulating about U.S. grand strategy and the restructuring of today's unipolar world. They call for American unilateral and preemptive, even preventive, use of force, facilitated if possible by coalitions of the willing—but ultimately unconstrained by the rules and norms of the international community. At the extreme, these notions form a neoimperial vision in which the United States arrogates to itself the global role of setting standards, determining threats, using force, and meting out justice. It is a vision in which sovereignty becomes more absolute for America even as it becomes more conditional for countries that

G. John Ikenberry is Peter F. Krogh Professor of Geopolitics and Global Justice at Georgetown University and a regular book reviewer for Foreign Affairs. *His most recent book is* After Victory: Institutions, Strategic Restraint, and the Rebuilding of Order After Major Wars. *This essay appeared in* Foreign Affairs *for September/October 2002 and is reprinted by permission.*

challenge Washington's standards of internal and external behavior. It is a vision made necessary—at least in the eyes of its advocates—by the new and apocalyptic character of contemporary terrorist threats and by America's unprecedented global dominance. These radical strategic ideas and impulses could transform today's world order in a way that the end of the Cold War, strangely enough, did not.

The exigencies of fighting terrorism in Afghanistan and the debate over intervening in Iraq obscure the profundity of this geopolitical challenge. Blueprints have not been produced, and Yalta-style summits have not been convened, but actions are afoot to dramatically alter the political order that the United States has built with its partners since the 1940s. The twin new realities of our age—catastrophic terrorism and American unipolar power—do necessitate a rethinking of the organizing principles of international order. America and the other major states do need a new consensus on terrorist threats, weapons of mass destruction (WMD), the use of force, and the global rules of the game. This imperative requires a better appreciation of the ideas coming out of the administration. But in turn, the administration should understand the virtues of the old order that it wishes to displace.

America's nascent neoimperial grand strategy threatens to rend the fabric of the international community and political partnerships precisely at a time when that community and those partnerships are urgently needed. It is an approach fraught with peril and likely to fail. It is not only politically unsustainable but diplomatically harmful. And if history is a guide, it will trigger antagonism and resistance that will leave America in a more hostile and divided world.

PROVEN LEGACIES

The mainstream of American foreign policy has been defined since the 1940s by two grand strategies that have built the modern international order. One is realist in orientation, organized around containment, deterrence, and the maintenance of the global balance of power. Facing a dangerous and expansive Soviet Union after 1945, the United States stepped forward to fill the vacuum left by a waning British Empire and a collapsing European order to provide a counterweight to Stalin and his Red Army.

The touchstone of this strategy was containment, which sought to deny the Soviet Union the ability to expand its sphere of influence. Order was maintained by managing the bipolar balance between the American and Soviet camps. Stability was achieved through nuclear deterrence. For the first time, nuclear weapons and the doctrine of mutual assured destruction made war between the great powers irrational. But containment and global power-balancing ended with the collapse of the Soviet Union in 1991. Nuclear deterrence is no longer the defining logic of the existing order, although it remains a recessed feature that continues to impart stability in relations among China, Russia, and the West.

This strategy has yielded a bounty of institutions and partnerships for America. The most important have been the NATO and U.S.-Japan alliances, American-led security partnerships that have survived the end of the Cold War by providing a bulwark for stability through commitment and reassurance. The United States maintains a forward presence in Europe and East Asia; its alliance partners gain security protection as well as a measure of regularity in their relationship with the world's leading military power. But Cold War balancing has yielded more than a utilitarian alliance structure; it has generated a political order that has value in itself.

This grand strategy presupposes a loose framework of consultations and agreements to resolve differences: the great powers extend to each other the respect of equals, and they accommodate each other until vital interests come into play. The domestic affairs of these states remain precisely that—domestic. The great powers compete with each other, and although war is not unthinkable, sober statecraft and the balance of power offer the best hope for stability and peace.

George W. Bush ran for president emphasizing some of these themes, describing his approach to foreign policy as "new realism": the focus of American efforts should shift away from

Clinton-era preoccupation with nation building, international social work, and the promiscuous use of force, and toward cultivating great-power relations and rebuilding the nation's military. Bush's efforts to integrate Russia into the Western security order have been the most important manifestation of this realist grand strategy at work. The moderation in Washington's confrontational rhetoric toward China also reflects this emphasis. If the major European and Asian states play by the rules, the great-power order will remain stable. (In a way, it is precisely because Europe is not a great power—or at least seems to eschew the logic of great-power politics—that it is now generating so much discord with the United States.)

The other grand strategy, forged during World War II as the United States planned the reconstruction of the world economy, is liberal in orientation. It seeks to build order around institutionalized political relations among integrated market democracies, supported by an opening of economies. This agenda was not simply an inspiration of American businessmen and economists, however. There have always been geopolitical goals as well. Whereas America's realist grand strategy was aimed at countering Soviet power, its liberal grand strategy was aimed at avoiding a return to the 1930s, an era of regional blocs, trade conflict, and strategic rivalry. Open trade, democracy, and multilateral institutional relations went together. Underlying this strategy was the view that a rule-based international order, especially one in which the United States uses its political weight to derive congenial rules, will most fully protect American interests, conserve its power, and extend its influence.

This grand strategy has been pursued through an array of post-war initiatives that look disarmingly like "low politics": the Bretton Woods institutions, the World Trade Organization (WTO), and the Organization for Economic Cooperation and Development are just a few examples. Together they form a complex layer cake of integrative initiatives that bind the democratic industrialized world together. During the 1990s, the United States continued to pursue this liberal grand strategy. Both the first Bush and the Clinton administrations attempted to articulate a vision of world order that was not dependent on an external threat or an explicit policy of balance of power. Bush the elder talked about the importance of the transatlantic community and articulated ideas about a more fully integrated Asia-Pacific region. In both cases, the strategy offered a positive vision of alliance and partnership built around common values, tradition, mutual self-interest, and the preservation of stability. The Clinton administration likewise attempted to describe the post–Cold War order in terms of the expansion of democracy and open markets. In this vision, democracy provided the foundation for global and regional community, and trade and capital flows were forces for political reform and integration.

The current Bush administration is not eager to brandish this Clinton-looking grand strategy, but it still invokes that strategy's ideas in various ways. Support for Chinese entry into the WTO is based on the liberal anticipation that free markets and integration into the Western economic order will create pressures for Chinese political reform and discourage a belligerent foreign policy. Administration support for last year's multilateral trade-negotiating round in Doha, Qatar, also was premised on the economic and political benefits of freer trade. After September 11, U.S. Trade Representative Robert Zoellick even linked trade expansion authority to the fight against terrorism: trade, growth, integration, and political stability go together. Richard Haass, policy planning director at the State Department, argued recently that "the principal aim of American foreign policy is to integrate other countries and organizations into arrangements that will sustain a world consistent with U.S. interests and values"—again, an echo of the liberal grand strategy. The administration's recent protectionist trade actions in steel and agriculture have triggered such a loud outcry around the world precisely because governments are worried that the United States might be retreating from this postwar liberal strategy.

AMERICA'S HISTORIC BARGAINS

These two grand strategies are rooted in divergent, even antagonistic, intellectual traditions. But over the last 50 years they have worked remarkably well together. The realist grand strategy created a political rationale for establishing major security commitments around the world. The liberal strategy created a positive agenda for American leadership. The United States could exercise its power and achieve its national interests, but it did so in a way that helped deepen the fabric of international community. American power did not destabilize world order; it helped create it. The development of rule-based agreements and political-security partnerships was good both for the United States and for much of the world. By the end of the 1990s, the result was an international political order of unprecedented size and success: a global coalition of democratic states tied together through markets, institutions, and security partnerships.

This international order was built on two historic bargains. One was the U.S. commitment to provide its European and Asian partners with security protection and access to American markets, technology, and supplies within an open world economy. In return, these countries agreed to be reliable partners providing diplomatic, economic, and logistical support for the United States as it led the wider Western postwar order. The other is the liberal bargain that addressed the uncertainties of American power. East Asian and European states agreed to accept American leadership and operate within an agreed-upon political-economic system. The United States, in response, opened itself up and bound itself to its partners. In effect, the United States built an institutionalized coalition of partners and reinforced the stability of these mutually beneficial relations by making itself more "user-friendly"—that is, by playing by the rules and creating ongoing political processes that facilitated consultation and joint decision-making. The United States made its power safe for the world, and in return the world agreed to live within the U.S. system. These bargains date from the 1940s, but they continue to shore up the post–Cold War order. The result has been the most stable and prosperous international system in world history. But new ideas within the Bush administration—crystallized by September 11 and U.S. dominance—are unsettling this order and the political bargains behind it.

A NEW GRAND STRATEGY

For the first time since the dawn of the Cold War, a new grand strategy is taking shape in Washington. It is advanced most directly as a response to terrorism, but it also constitutes a broader view about how the United States should wield power and organize world order. According to this new paradigm, America is to be less bound to its partners and to global rules and institutions while it steps forward to play a more unilateral and anticipatory role in attacking terrorist threats and confronting rogue states seeking WMD. The United States will use its unrivaled military power to manage the global order.

This new grand strategy has seven elements. It begins with a fundamental commitment to maintaining a unipolar world in which the United States has no peer competitor. No coalition of great powers without the United States will be allowed to achieve hegemony. Bush made this point the centerpiece of American security policy in his West Point commencement address in June: "America has, and intends to keep, military strengths beyond challenges—thereby making the destabilizing arms races of other eras pointless, and limiting rivalries to trade and other pursuits of peace." The United States will not seek security through the more modest realist strategy of operating within a global system of power balancing, nor will it pursue a liberal strategy in which institutions, democracy, and integrated markets reduce the importance of power politics altogether. America will be so much more powerful than other major states that strategic rivalries and security competition among the great powers will disappear, leaving everyone—not just the United States—better off.

This goal made an unsettling early appearance at the end of the first Bush administration in a leaked Pentagon memorandum written by then Under-Secretary of Defense Paul Wolfowitz. With the collapse of the Soviet Union, he wrote, the United States must act to prevent the rise of peer competitors in Europe and Asia. But the 1990s made this strategic aim moot. The United States grew faster than the other major states during the decade, it reduced military spending more slowly, and it dominated investment in the technological advancement of its forces. Today, however, the new goal is to make these advantages permanent—a fait accompli that will prompt other states to not even try to catch up. Some thinkers have described the strategy as "breakout," in which the United States moves so quickly to develop technological advantages (in robotics, lasers, satellites, precision munitions, etc.) that no state or coalition could ever challenge it as global leader, protector, and enforcer.

The second element is a dramatic new analysis of global threats and how they must be attacked. The grim new reality is that small groups of terrorists—perhaps aided by outlaw states—may soon acquire highly destructive nuclear, chemical, and biological weapons that can inflict catastrophic destruction. These terrorist groups cannot be appeased or deterred, the administration believes, so they must be eliminated. Secretary of Defense Donald Rumsfeld has articulated this frightening view with elegance: regarding the threats that confront the United States, he said, "There are things we know that we know. There are known unknowns. That is to say, there are things that we know we don't know. But there are also unknown unknowns. There are things we don't know we don't know. . . . Each year, we discover a few more of those unknown unknowns." In other words, there could exist groups of terrorists that no one knows about. They may have nuclear, chemical, or biological weapons that the United States did not know they could get, and they might be willing and able to attack without warning. In the age of terror, there is less room for error. Small networks of angry people can inflict unimaginable harm on the rest of the world. They are not nation-states, and they do not play by the accepted rules of the game.

The third element of the new strategy maintains that the Cold War concept of deterrence is outdated. Deterrence, sovereignty, and the balance of power work together. When deterrence is no longer viable, the larger realist edifice starts to crumble. The threat today is not other great powers that must be managed through second-strike nuclear capacity but the transnational terrorist networks that have no home address. They cannot be deterred because they are either willing to die for their cause or able to escape retaliation. The old defensive strategy of building missiles and other weapons that can survive a first strike and be used in a retaliatory strike to punish the attacker will no longer ensure security. The only option, then, is offense.

The use of force, this camp argues, will therefore need to be preemptive and perhaps even preventive—taking on potential threats before they can present a major problem. But this premise plays havoc with the old international rules of self-defense and United Nations norms about the proper use of force. Rumsfeld has articulated the justification for preemptive action by stating that the "absence of evidence is not evidence of absence of weapons of mass destruction." But such an approach renders international norms of self-defense—enshrined by Article 51 of the UN Charter—almost meaningless. The administration should remember that when Israeli jets bombed the Iraqi nuclear reactor at Osirak in 1981 in what Israel described as an act of self-defense, the world condemned it as an act of aggression. Even British Prime Minister Margaret Thatcher and the American ambassador to the UN, Jeane Kirkpatrick, criticized the action, and the United States joined in passing a UN resolution condemning it.

The Bush administration's security doctrine takes this country down the same slippery slope. Even without a clear threat, the United States now claims a right to use preemptive or preventive military force. At West Point, Bush put it succinctly when he stated that "the military must be ready to strike at a moment's notice in any dark corner of the world. All nations that decide for aggression and terror will pay a price." The administration defends this new doctrine as a necessary adjustment to a more uncertain and shifting threat environment. This policy of no regrets errs on the side of action—but it can also easily become national security by hunch or inference, leaving the world without clear-cut norms for justifying force.

As a result, the fourth element of this emerging grand strategy involves a recasting of the terms of sovereignty. Because these terrorist groups cannot be deterred, the United States must be prepared to intervene anywhere, anytime to preemptively destroy the threat. Terrorists do not respect borders, so neither can the United States. Moreover, countries that harbor terrorists, either by consent or because they are unable to enforce their laws within their territory, effectively forfeit their rights of sovereignty. Haass recently hinted at this notion in *The New Yorker*:

> What you are seeing in this administration is the emergence of a new principle or body of ideas . . . about what you might call the limits of sovereignty. Sovereignty entails obligations. One is not to massacre your own people. Another is not to support terrorism in any way. If a government fails to meet these obligations, then it forfeits some of the normal advantages of sovereignty, including the right to be left alone inside your own territory. Other governments, including the United States, gain the right to intervene. In the case of terrorism, this can even lead to a right of preventive . . . self-defense. You essentially can act in anticipation if you have grounds to think it's a question of when, and not if, you're going to be attacked.

Here the war on terrorism and the problem of the proliferation of WMD get entangled. The worry is that a few despotic states—Iraq in particular, but also Iran and North Korea—will develop capabilities to produce weapons of mass destruction and put these weapons in the hands of terrorists. The regimes themselves may be deterred from using such capabilities, but they might pass along these weapons to terrorist networks that are not deterred. Thus another emerging principle within the Bush administration: the possession of WMD by unaccountable, unfriendly, despotic governments is itself a threat that must be countered. In the old era, despotic regimes were to be lamented but ultimately tolerated. With the rise of terrorism and weapons of mass destruction, they are now unacceptable threats. Thus states that are not technically in violation of any existing international laws could nevertheless be targets of American force—if Washington determines that they have a prospective capacity to do harm.

The recasting of sovereignty is paradoxical. On the one hand, the new grand strategy reaffirms the importance of the territorial nation-state. After all, if all governments were accountable and capable of enforcing the rule of law within their sovereign territory, terrorists would find it very difficult to operate. The emerging Bush doctrine enshrines this idea: governments will be held responsible for what goes on inside their borders. On the other hand, sovereignty has been made newly conditional: governments that fail to act like respectable, law-abiding states will lose their sovereignty.

In one sense, such conditional sovereignty is not new. Great powers have willfully transgressed the norms of state sovereignty as far back as such norms have existed, particularly within their traditional spheres of influence, whenever the national interest dictated. The United States itself has done this within the western hemisphere since the nineteenth century. What is new and provocative in this notion today, however, is the Bush administration's inclination to apply it on a global basis, leaving to itself the authority to determine when sovereign rights have been forfeited, and doing so on an anticipatory basis.

The fifth element of this new grand strategy is a general depreciation of international rules, treaties, and security partnerships. This point relates to the new threats themselves: if the stakes are rising and the margins of error are shrinking in the war on terrorism, multilateral norms and agreements that sanction and limit the use of force are just annoying distractions. The critical task is to eliminate the threat. But the emerging unilateral strategy is also informed by a deeper suspicion about the value of international agreements themselves. Part of this view arises from a deeply felt and authentically American belief that the United States should not get entangled in the corrupting and constraining world of multilateral rules and institutions. For some Americans, the belief that American sovereignty is politically sacred leads to a preference for isolationism. But the more influential view—particularly after September 11—is not that the United States should withdraw from the world but that it should operate in the world on its own terms. The Bush administration's repudiation of a remarkable array of treaties and institutions—from the Kyoto Protocol on global warming to the International Criminal Court to the Biological Weapons Convention—reflects this new bias. Likewise, the United States signed a formal agreement with Russia on the reduction of deployed nuclear warheads only after Moscow's insistence; the Bush administration wanted only a "gentlemen's agreement." In other words, the United States has decided it is big enough, powerful enough, and remote enough to go it alone.

Sixth, the new grand strategy argues that the United States will need to play a direct and unconstrained role in responding to threats. This conviction is partially based on a judgment that no other country or coalition—even the European Union—has the force-projection capabilities to respond to terrorist and rogue states around the world. A decade of U.S. defense spending and modernization has left allies of the United States far behind. In combat operations, alliance partners are increasingly finding it difficult to mesh with U.S. forces. This view is also based on the judgment that joint operations and the use of force through coalitions tend to hinder effective operations. To some observers, this lesson became clear in the allied bombing campaign over Kosovo. The sentiment was also expressed during the U.S. and allied military actions in Afghanistan. Rumsfeld explained this point earlier this year, when he said, "The mission must determine the coalition; the coalition must not determine the mission. If it does, the mission will be dumbed down to the lowest common denominator, and we can't afford that."

No one in the Bush administration argues that NATO or the

U.S.-Japan alliance should be dismantled. Rather, these alliances are now seen as less useful to the United States as it confronts today's threats. Some officials argue that it is not that the United States chooses to depreciate alliance partnerships, but that the Europeans are unwilling to keep up. Whether that is true, the upgrading of the American military, along with its sheer size relative to the forces of the rest of the world, leaves the United States in a class by itself. In these circumstances, it is increasingly difficult to maintain the illusion of true alliance partnership. America's allies become merely strategic assets that are useful depending on the circumstance. The United States still finds attractive the logistical reach that its global alliance system provides, but the pacts with countries in Asia and Europe become more contingent and less premised on a vision of a common security community.

Finally, the new grand strategy attaches little value to international stability. There is an unsentimental view in the unilateralist camp that the traditions of the past must be shed. Whether it is withdrawal from the Anti-Ballistic Missile Treaty or the resistance to signing other formal arms-control treaties, policymakers are convinced that the United States needs to move beyond outmoded Cold War thinking. Administration officials have noted with some satisfaction that America's withdrawal from the ABM Treaty did not lead to a global arms race but actually paved the way for a historic arms-reduction agreement between the United States and Russia. This move is seen as a validation that moving beyond the old paradigm of great-power relations will not bring the international house down. The world can withstand radically new security approaches, and it will accommodate American unilateralism as well. But stability is not an end in itself. The administration's new hawkish policy toward North Korea, for example, might be destabilizing to the region, but such instability might be the necessary price for dislodging a dangerous and evil regime in Pyongyang.

In this brave new world, neoimperial thinkers contend that the older realist and liberal grand strategies are not very helpful. American security will not be ensured, as realist grand strategy assumes, by the preservation of deterrence and stable relations among the major powers. In a world of asymmetrical threats, the global balance of power is not the linchpin of war and peace. Likewise, liberal strategies of building order around open trade and democratic institutions might have some long-term impact on terrorism, but they do not address the immediacy of the threats. Apocalyptic violence is at our doorstep, so efforts at strengthening the rules and institutions of the international community are of little practical value. If we accept the worst-case imagining of "we don't know what we don't know," everything else is secondary: international rules, traditions of partnership, and standards of legitimacy. It is a war. And as Clausewitz famously remarked, "War is such a dangerous business that the mistakes which come from kindness are the very worst."

IMPERIAL DANGERS

Pitfalls accompany this neoimperial grand strategy, however. Unchecked U.S. power, shorn of legitimacy and disentangled from the postwar norms and institutions of the international order, will usher in a more hostile international system, making it far harder to achieve American interests. The secret of the United States' long brilliant run as the world's leading state was its ability and willingness to exercise power within alliance and multinational frameworks, which made its power and agenda more acceptable to allies and other key states around the world. This achievement has now been put at risk by the administration's new thinking.

The most immediate problem is that the neoimperialist approach is unsustainable. Going it alone might well succeed in removing Saddam Hussein from power, but it is far less certain that a strategy of counterproliferation, based on American willingness to use unilateral force to confront dangerous dictators, can work over the long term. An American policy that leaves the United States alone to decide which states are threats and how best to deny them weapons of mass destruction will lead to a diminishment of multilateral mechanisms—most important of which is the nonproliferation regime.

The Bush administration has elevated the threat of WMD to the top of its security agenda without investing its power or prestige in fostering, monitoring, and enforcing nonproliferation commitments. The tragedy of September 11 has given the Bush administration the authority and willingness to confront the Iraqs of the world. But that will not be enough when even more complicated cases come along—when it is not the use of force that is needed but concerted multilateral action to provide sanctions and inspections. Nor is it certain that a preemptive or preventive military intervention will go well; it might trigger a domestic political backlash to American-led and military-focused interventionism. America's well-meaning imperial strategy could undermine the principled multilateral agreements, institutional infrastructure, and cooperative spirit needed for the long-term success of nonproliferation goals.

The specific doctrine of preemptive action poses a related problem: once the United States feels it can take such a course, nothing will stop other countries from doing the same. Does the United States want this doctrine in the hands of Pakistan, or even China or Russia? After all, it would not require the intervening state to first provide evidence for its actions. The United States argues that to wait until all the evidence is in, or until authoritative international bodies support action, is to wait too long. Yet that approach is the only basis that the United States can use if it needs to appeal for restraint in the actions of others. Moreover, and quite paradoxically, overwhelming American conventional military might, combined with a policy of preemptive strikes, could lead hostile states to accelerate programs to acquire their only possible deterrent to the United States: WMD. This is another version of the security dilemma, but one made worse by a neoimperial grand strategy.

Another problem follows. The use of force to eliminate WMD capabilities or overturn dangerous regimes is never simple, whether it is pursued unilaterally or by a concert of major states. After the military intervention is over, the target country has to be put back together. Peacekeeping and state building are inevitably required, as are long-term strategies that bring the UN, the World Bank, and the major powers together to orchestrate aid and other forms of assistance. This is not heroic work, but it is utterly necessary. Peacekeeping troops may be required for many years, even after a new regime is built. Regional conflicts inflamed by outside military intervention must also be calmed. This is the "long tail" of burdens and commitments that comes with every major military action.

When these costs and obligations are added to America's imperial military role, it becomes even more doubtful that the neoimperial strategy can be sustained at home over the long haul—the classic problem of imperial overstretch. The United States could keep its military predominance for decades if it is supported by a growing and increasingly productive economy. But the indirect burdens of cleaning up the political mess in terrorist-prone failed states levy a hidden cost. Peacekeeping and state building will require coalitions of states and multilateral agencies that can be brought into the process only if the initial decisions about military intervention are hammered out in consultation with other major states. America's older realist and liberal grand strategies suddenly become relevant again.

A third problem with an imperial grand strategy is that it cannot generate the cooperation needed to solve practical problems at the heart of the U.S. foreign policy agenda. In the fight on terrorism, the United States needs cooperation from European and Asian countries in intelligence, law enforcement, and logistics. Outside the security sphere, realizing U.S. objectives depends even more on a continuous stream of amicable working relations with major states around the world. It needs partners for trade liberalization, global financial stabilization, environmental protection, deterring transnational organized crime, managing the rise of China, and a host of other thorny challenges. But it is impossible to expect would-be partners to acquiesce to America's self-appointed global security protectorate and then pursue business as usual in all other domains.

The key policy tool for states confronting a unipolar and unilateral America is to withhold cooperation in day-to-day relations with the United States. One obvious means is trade policy; the European response to the recent American decision to impose tariffs on imported steel is explicable in these terms. This particular struggle concerns specific trade issues, but it is also a struggle over how Washington exercises power. The United States may be a unipolar military power, but economic and political power is more evenly distributed across the globe. The major states may not have much leverage in directly restraining American military policy, but they can make the United States pay a price in other areas.

Finally, the neoimperial grand strategy poses a wider problem for maintenance of American unipolar power. It steps into the oldest trap of powerful imperial states: self-encirclement. When the most powerful state in the world throws its weight around, unconstrained by rules or norms of legitimacy, it risks a backlash. Other countries will bridle at an international order in which the United States plays only by its own rules. The proponents of the new grand strategy have assumed that the United States can single-handedly deploy military power abroad and not suffer untoward consequences; relations will be coarser with friends and allies, they believe, but such are the costs of leadership. But history shows that powerful states tend to trigger self-encirclement by their own overestimation of their power. Charles V, Louis XIV, Napoleon, and the leaders of post-Bismarck Germany sought to expand their imperial domains and impose a coercive order on others. Their imperial orders were all brought down when other countries decided they were not prepared to live in a world dominated by an overweening coercive state. America's imperial goals and modus operandi are much more limited and benign than were those of age-old emperors. But a hard-line imperial grand strategy runs the risk that history will repeat itself.

BRING IN THE OLD

Wars change world politics, and so too will America's war on terrorism. How great states fight wars, how they define the stakes, how they make the peace in its aftermath—all give lasting shape to the international system that emerges after the guns fall silent. In mobilizing their societies for battle, wartime leaders have tended to describe the military struggle as more than simply the defeat of an enemy. Woodrow Wilson sent U.S. troops to Europe not only to stop the kaiser's army but to destroy militarism and usher in a worldwide democratic revolution. Franklin Roosevelt saw the war with Germany and Japan as a struggle to secure the "four great freedoms." The Atlantic Charter was a statement of war aims that called not just for the defeat of fascism but for a new dedication to social welfare and human rights within an open and stable world system. To advance these visions, Wilson and Roosevelt proposed new international rules and mechanisms of cooperation. Their message was clear: If you bear the burdens of war, we, your leaders, will use this dreadful conflict to usher in a more peaceful and decent order among states. Fighting the war had as much to do with building global relations as it did with vanquishing an enemy.

Bush has not fully articulated a vision of postwar international order, aside from defining the struggle as one between freedom and evil. The world has seen Washington take determined steps to fight terrorism, but it does not yet have a sense of Bush's larger, positive agenda for a strengthened and more decent international order.

This failure explains why the sympathy and goodwill generated around the world for the United States after September 11 quickly disappeared. Newspapers that once proclaimed, "We are all Americans," now express distrust toward America. The prevailing view is that the United States seems prepared to use its power to go after terrorists and evil regimes, but not to use it to help build a more stable and peaceful world order. The United States appears to be degrading the rules and institutions of international community, not enhancing them. To the rest of the world, neoimperial thinking has more to do with exercising power than with exercising leadership.

In contrast, America's older strategic orientations—balance-of-power realism and liberal multilateralism—suggest a mature world power that seeks stability and pursues its interests in ways that do not fundamentally threaten the positions of other states. They are strategies of co-option and reassurance. The new imperial grand strategy presents the United States very differently: a revisionist state seeking to parlay its momentary power advantages into a world order in which it runs the show. Unlike the hegemonic states of the past, the United States does not seek territory or outright political domination in Europe or Asia; "America has no empire to extend or utopia to establish," Bush noted in his West Point address. But the sheer power advantages that the United States possesses and the doctrines of preemption and counterterrorism that it is articulating do unsettle governments and people around the world. The costs could be high. The last thing the United States wants is for foreign diplomats and government leaders to ask, How can we work around, undermine, contain, and retaliate against U.S. power?

Rather than invent a new grand strategy, the United States should reinvigorate its older strategies, those based on the view that America's security partnerships are not simply instrumental tools but critical components of an American-led world political order that should be preserved. U.S. power is both leveraged and made more legitimate and user-friendly by these partnerships. The neoimperial thinkers are haunted by the specter of catastrophic terrorism and seek a radical reordering of America's role in the world. America's commanding unipolar power and the advent of frightening new terrorist threats feed this imperial temptation. But it is a grand strategic vision that, taken to the extreme, will leave the world more dangerous and divided—and the United States less secure.

CHARLES S. MAIER

Imperial Limits

In a post-9/11 world, America's own penchant
for unilateralism may pose the greatest threat
to its empire.

ONLY A YEAR AND A WEEK separated the events of September
11, 2001, when Americans felt so vulnerable, from a presidential
declaration in which their leaders spoke so imperiously. The so-
called Bush Doctrine—more formally a White House–issued
document called *The National Security Strategy of the United
States*—reaffirms laudable support for democracy, religious tolerance, and economic development, but further claims the right to
act preemptively against terrorist states who arm themselves with
weapons of mass destruction. We have no cause to be surprised:
the Bush Doctrine has emerged from a public discussion by policymakers and journalists that has increasingly transgressed an earlier American taboo: what Edmund Burke would have called one
of the "decent draperies of life," or in this case, of political dis-

*Charles S. Maier is the Saltonstall Professor of History at Harvard University and
served as director of Harvard's Minda de Gunzburg Center for European Studies
from 1994 until 2001. This essay first appeared in* Harvard Magazine *(Novem-
ber/December 2002) and is reprinted by permission of the author.*

course. Increasingly, that is, Americans talk about themselves, and others talk about America, as an empire.

A decade ago, certainly two decades ago, the concept aroused righteous indignation. How could the United States be compared to Rome—with its conquering legions, its subjugation of peoples, its universalist claims to law and order—or even to Britain, the former ruler of millions of subjects in India, the Middle East, and Africa? If an empire, post–World War II America was the empire that dared not speak its name. But these days, on the part of friends and critics alike, the bashfulness has ended. "The Roman and the British empires have had their day. Why should we begrudge the new American Empire the right to protect its citizens from a jealous and hostile world?" writes a former British European Union official to the *Financial Times*. The historian Paul Kennedy cites the overwhelming preponderance of military power the United States possesses. In full agreement, the Bush administration has vowed to preserve that decisive margin against any rivals.

Except for a minority of tough-minded realists, Americans have tended to reject the idea that our own high-minded republic might be imperial (much less imperialist). Empire has traditionally been identified with conscious military expansion. Washington may have organized an alliance, but it did not seek to conquer territory nor, supposedly, to dominate other societies. President Kennedy, certainly an activist in foreign policy, declared explicitly that the United States did not aim at any Pax Americana. But British imperial historians also long denied that there was anything intentional about the creation of the Victorian domains in Asia and Africa. Modern liberal internationalists prefer to think of empire as the reluctant acceptance of responsibility for peoples and lands who must be rescued from the primitive violence that threatens to engulf them if left on their own.

In fact, some historians of international relations, myself included, have resorted to the concept of a quasi-American empire for a long time. Still, we believed it was an empire with a difference—a coordination of economic exchange and security guarantees welcomed by its less powerful member states, who preserved their autonomy and played a role in collective policymaking. We used such terms as "empire by invitation" or "consensual" empire. What, after all, distinguishes an empire? It is a major actor in the international system based on the subordination of diverse national elites who—whether under compulsion or from shared convictions—accept the values of those who govern the dominant center or metropole. The inequality of power, resources, and influence is what distinguishes an empire from an alliance (although treaties of alliance often formalize or disguise an imperial structure). Distinct national groupings may be harshly controlled within an empire or they may enjoy autonomy. At least some of their political, economic, and cultural leaders hobnob with their imperial rulers and reject any idea of escaping imperial influence. Others may organize resistance, but they, too, have often assimilated their colonizers' culture and even values. Empires function by virtue of the prestige they radiate as well as by might, and indeed collapse if they rely on force alone. Artistic styles, the language of the rulers, and consumer preferences flow outward along with power and investment capital—sometimes diffused consciously by cultural diplomacy and student exchanges, sometimes just by popular taste for the intriguing products of the metropole, whether Coca Cola or Big Macs. As supporters of the imperial power rightly maintain, empires provide public goods that masses of people outside their borders really want to enjoy, including an end to endemic warfare and murderous ethnic or religious conflicts.

Two kinds of empire existed before World War I: "old" landed empires, products of centuries-long expansion over contiguous territories (and still largely agrarian and semi-authoritarian); and overseas colonial realms. Among the first group—Russia, Austria-Hungary, the Ottoman domains, China—the states were empires and were vulnerable to new forces of national self-determination. Members of the second group—the British, French, Dutch, Spanish, and Portuguese, and more recently the Japanese, Germans, and Americans—had empires. When the internal crises of the first group combined with the interlocking rivalries of the second, the result was the First World War. Indeed the history of twentieth-century world politics was one long imperial transition—from the domination and then the destructive rivalries of the Europeans, to the Soviet and American spheres of influence that emerged from the Second World War, and finally to the ascendancy of the United States as "the only remaining superpower."

THE IMPORTANCE OF FRONTIERS

Empires claim universality but accentuate divisions between inclusion and exclusion, both on a world scale and within their own borders. Consider these external and internal effects in turn. The principal preoccupation of the guardians of empire is the frontier: what the Romans called the limes. The frontier separates insiders and outsiders, citizens and/or subjects within from "barbarians" without. This does not mean that barbarians cannot enter the empire: they can and they do and they are often actively recruited—as professional soldiers in Roman days, as industrial workers, as gardeners and house-cleaners, as hospital orderlies, and also as skilled professionals. But the empire seeks to control their flow from the frontiers of antiquity to the fences along the Mexican border. (The European Union is only a supranational association, not an empire, but it has the same preoccupation, now enforced at dozens of airports under the provisions of the Schengen Treaty framework.)

A major consequence of this preoccupation with the frontier has been a new political agenda. The salient issues today have shifted from the controversies over distribution that troubled the politics of the West, indeed of developed societies more generally, from the 1950s through the 1980s: income for farmers, the relative shares for labor and capital, the creation and costs of the welfare state. They have become questions of citizenship, residence, and belonging: who will be in and who will be outside our polities, and what intermediate rights—such as employment, welfare entitlements, and local suffrage—they might be granted.

Frontiers are important, not only at the geographic edge of

empire but as social gradients within. The distinction that preoccupies contemporary citizens, however, seems less the poverty line—which focuses attention on the deprivation of the least fortunate—than the affluence line, epitomized today by the air travelers' boundary between business or first-class and economy seating. Empires can provide increasing welfare for the less well-off in the home society, can advance the democratization of taste and access to education, but at the same time they sharpen differentials of prestige, exclusivity, and wealth. Here is the irony (or the artfulness) of empire: no matter what absolute increases in educational opportunity or income accrue either to the mass of the population at home or the subjects abroad, relative stratification seems to increase—or at least hold its own. Empires reward those who run them with goods, honor, and celebrity status. And for all the disclaimers about the white man's burden or its contemporary equivalent, few of us who get the chance to share these rewards disdain them. Helping to run an empire may not be exactly fun, but it appears to be deeply fulfilling.

Empires mitigate their inequality at home through a two-level management of public life. At one level is a serious effort to debate issues of distribution, environment, infrastructure, and development. This debate is carried on among communities of experts whose decisions must sometimes be ratified by a court or legislature. Those who take part in this "conversation," even if only as public commentators, are convinced that it represents an adequate and a real form of democracy. They denigrate those who are less convinced as populists (which they often are). But empires also operate on a second and more theatrical level. All politics involves some public performance, but empires emphasize dramaturgy. All societies may celebrate prowess, but from the Colosseum to the Super Bowl, in the West at least, empires particularly rely on the sports of the amphitheater that reward star players with fame and fortune. They nurture a culture of spectatorship to create rituals of shared experience.

IMPERIAL EDGES AND WORLD ORDER

Is an American empire good for the world? And is it good for us? What does an empire mean for international politics in general? Is it a source of order or disorder, cooperation or conflict? There are always powerful justifications for the dynamic of empire: by the second half of the twentieth century, when the United States emerged supreme, the reasons included "development" and "productivity." American supremacy quickly developed a clear military component, but it emerged by virtue of more than half a century of economic prowess: the assembly line that turned out Model Ts, the "arsenal of democracy" that armed British and Russian allies and mass produced aircraft and Liberty Ships, that subsidized the reconstruction of Europe after World War II, and commercially developed electronic computation.

This country, moreover, enjoyed advantages of geography and timing. Other countries had been devastated by war, not us. The Soviet Union offered enough competition to thrust Washington into a leadership role that was accepted by its allies, but not enough to overwhelm the American effort. We developed the technology to take a brief but critical lead in the new, decisive, atomic weaponry of the postwar world.

There are always propagandists to point out empire's achievement: recall Virgil's *Aeneid*:

Roman, remember by your strength to rule
Earth's peoples—for your arts are to be these:
To pacify, to impose the rule of law,
To spare the conquered, battle down the proud.

J. M. Coetzee's 1980 fable *Waiting for the Barbarians* suggests otherwise: "One thought alone preoccupied the submerged mind of Empire: how not to die, how to prolong its era. By day it pursues its enemies. It is cunning and ruthless, it sends its bloodhounds everywhere. By night it feeds on images of disaster: the sack of cities, the rape of populations, pyramids of bones, acres of desolation. A mad vision yet a virulent one. . . ."

Contemporary history suggests that both Virgil and Coetzee

are correct. Empires may have helped to suppress traditional wars in large areas of their domains, although many students of international politics have proposed that democratic states assure an end to war among themselves by virtue of their liberal constitutions, and still other analysts simply credit the balance of power maintained by any large-scale states. We cannot be certain which cause has been operative; nonetheless, throughout the nineteenth century and again after World War II, imperial systems helped stabilize a balance of power within Europe and North America. An international system based on national self-determination—even though complemented by commitments to collective security, such as the Paris peace conference of 1919 sought to institute—remained fragile and broke down within 20 years.

No stable imperial structures reemerged until the Cold War. Then the Soviet side relied on its own enthusiastic communist cadres and, when these were challenged in the streets, on the calculated use of force: in 1953 in Berlin; 1956 in Hungary; 1968 in Czechoslovakia. The competing U.S. model of a liberal capitalist order (or of market democracies) rested on a combination of championing economic regulatory principles (market capitalism, productivity, and growth) and of military prowess. Military action involved strategic deterrence at the European frontier and at the Thirty-eighth Parallel following an open conflict in Korea. But American administrations also intervened openly or covertly, among other places, in Iran (1953) and Guatemala (1954), and unsuccessfully in Cuba (1961) and Vietnam (1963–75).

It remains an open question whether a major imperial structure can ever work through consensual principles or economic means alone. Establishing and stabilizing a periphery seems always to require a military effort: in this sense, Coetzee's bleak indictment is correct. Empire must inevitably generate a resistance that rulers will perceive as shortsighted, bloody-minded, and even fanatic: recall the Jewish rebels at Masada. Our filmmakers may view imperial history through the eyes of Luke Skywalker, but policymakers, or at least their intelligence agencies, tend to share Darth Vader's perspective.

Empire-builders yearn for stability, but what imperial systems find hard to stabilize is, precisely, their frontiers. Historians of empire point out that colonizing countries were drawn into expansion by the disorder that seethed just outside the last domain they had stabilized. But researchers explore less often how staking out a new frontier can generate a further zone of "chaos" that requires imperial policymakers to intervene anew. The Romans wanted to pacify territory across the Rhine. Britain found itself moving ineluctably up the Nile after what it believed would be a limited occupation to sort out Egyptian finances in the 1880s. The U.S. presence in Vietnam embroiled Cambodia. Vice President Dick Cheney warns that once we have overthrown Saddam Hussein, we shall have to help ensure stability in the country for a long time. But the use of force that stabilizes conditions within any given boundary often upsets a precarious peace among the tribes or weakened states that abut the frontier. Can there be successful "nation-building" in just one country? Southeast Asia, the liberated African colonies, areas of Central America, and the Caucasus became in their turn areas of endemic and bloody violence with tremendous human costs. The boundaries within societies can also become sites of conflict and tragedy. Something there is that doesn't love a wall.

Americans today face choices about empire with consequences far outrunning the stakes of any immediate military action. Teachers, scholars, the university more generally can at best help reflect on possible alternatives. The organizations of international commerce and civil society—whether McDonald's, Microsoft, and Deutsche Bank or Oxfam and *Médecins sans Frontières*—may help enhance world welfare, but they will not assure world order. Empires are in the business of producing world order. But not all orders are alike: some enhance freedom and development; others repress it.

I believe that American empire has served some beneficial functions, above all in opposing far more authoritarian and repressive contenders for international dominance and in defending ideals of liberty and opportunity. Still, no matter how benevolent the intentions, the exercise of empire will generate some violence.

The problem is that for every greater inclusive effort, there must still be those left outside the expanded walls clamoring to enter, or those not willing to participate vicariously in the lifestyles of the rich and famous—and those, indeed, embittered by the values of secular consumerism (which contemporary empires rely on to generate public loyalties) and imbued with far more zealous and violent visions of fulfillment. These issues of inclusion and exclusion, belonging and estrangement, the peace of empire and the violence it generates despite its efforts, is what twenty-first-century politics, certainly since September 11, is increasingly about.

Nonetheless, one can choose alternatives likely to lead to less bitterness and less violence. For at least 50 years, Americans sought to exercise leadership by seeking to establish institutions that did not depend solely on our own force: the United Nations, the organs of the Marshall Plan, the North Atlantic alliance, the World Trade Organization, among others. Of course, Washington often had to animate their collective resolve. Still, we achieved ascendancy by accepting the need to restrain our own unilateral action (admittedly with significant lapses in our own hemisphere) and generally to persuade allies and neutrals that cooperation did not have to diminish their interests or status. Now, for the first time in the postwar history of the United States (at least for vast regions outside the Americas), our policymakers, elated by supposedly unmatchable military technology, have formally outlined a different vision. Eventually, I fear—if not this year or even this decade—historians will have fateful consequences to narrate if we persevere in this myopic option.

STEPHEN PETER ROSEN

Imperial Choices

Military strength alone will not suffice to maintain American preeminence.

IF THERE IS, or soon will be, an American empire, it will face questions different from those to which it is accustomed, and it will need to learn forms of statecraft different from those to which it has become habituated in the 19th and 20th centuries. This is because the range and nature of the issues facing an empire differ qualitatively from those facing a merely powerful state.

Empire is the rule exercised by one nation over others both to regulate their external behavior and to ensure minimally acceptable forms of internal behavior within the subordinate states. Merely powerful states do the former, but not the latter.

The central—one may say the necessary but not sufficient— imperial task is the creation and management of a hierarchical interstate order. From that key task of regulating the external behavior of other states proceeds the imperial problems of main-

---

Stephen Peter Rosen is the Kaneb Professor of National Security and Military Affairs at Harvard University, and the director of the Olin Institute for Strategic Studies. This essay first appeared in the Spring 2003 issue of The National Interest *and is reprinted by permission.*

taining a monopoly on the use of organized military power, and of using its monopolistic but still finite military power efficiently: a problem captured in the military concept of "economy of force" operations. But an empire must also assure the security and internal stability of its constituent parts, extract revenue to pay the costs of empire, and assimilate the elites of non-imperial societies to the metropolitan core, tasks that presuppose influence over the internal affairs of other societies.

By this definition, for example, the Wilhelmine empire was an empire over the Germanies, but not in central Europe. Imperial Britain included its crown colonies, but not Argentina or, for very long, Afghanistan or Persia. As to the United States, it was a de facto imperial power in much of the Western Hemisphere beginning in the late 19th century, and formally over the Philippines from 1898 to 1946.

Today, the picture for the United States is mixed. The United States exercises effective if less than formal hierarchical authority in the Western Hemisphere, in the Asian rimland, on the Arab side of the Persian Gulf, and in the NATO area. At the start of 2003, it was trying to extend its hierarchical interstate order to the Balkans and Afghanistan, and was preparing to intervene into the internal affairs of Iraq. China, Russia, and India cooperate opportunistically with the United States but have been willing to challenge American dominance when possible. They certainly reject the right of the United States to intervene in their internal affairs and thus remain the major countries outside the U.S. hierarchical order.

But what of the three internal governance functions of empire? The United States does tend to the internal security and stability of its constituent parts, but it does so selectively. It does this in manifold ways: humanitarian intervention, aid and assistance programs, intelligence sharing, the stationing of U.S. military forces abroad, and other means besides. The new post–September 11 concern with the security implications of failed states suggests an even greater focus on internal governance issues, and indeed the language of the new National Security Strategy document points sharply in that direction. As for extracting revenue to pay the costs of empire, only the 1991 Gulf War stands as a direct example of that. American influence over the main international economic organizations—the WTO, the IMF, and the World Bank—may be construed, at least indirectly, as a revenue extraction process, as may the international trading of the dollar, but this is to really stretch the imperial point. And as to the absorption of elites from the periphery to the core, the nature of globalization changes how we even think about such a question. If the United States does do this, it is not a function of an imperial governmental core that can tightly manage or control such things, but a by-product of social and economic phenomena intrinsic to the culture.

ESTABLISHING HIERARCHY

Because the problems of running an empire differ from the problems of interstate primacy, there is more to imperial statecraft than knowing "how to conduct a 'humble' foreign policy," a theme to which students of American hegemony constantly return. Humility is always a virtue, but the dominant male atop any social hierarchy, human or otherwise, never managed to rule simply by being nice. Human evolutionary history has produced a species that both creates hierarchies and harbors the desire among subordinates to challenge its dominant member. Those challenges never disappear. The dominant member can never do everything that subordinates desire, and so is blamed for what it does not do as much as for what it does. This is why empires never rest easy.

It is a naive and perhaps uniquely American notion that those states inferior to the United States in power ought not resent their own subordinate status; that, if it is nice enough, Washington can build a "benign" imperium in which all love it. This does not mean that the United States should dispense with tact. Ritual plays a role in ameliorating tensions in a social hierarchy by creating and confirming expectations of how members of the hierarchy are treated, but rituals do not fundamentally change reality or the attitudes of those subordinate in power. Acting in a humble manner is a ritual worth much respect, so the United States does well to consult the United Nations and NATO councils before it acts. But such rituals will only reduce, not eliminate, the resentment toward the United States that springs from the fact that the United States can do what it must in any case. And what it must do, if it is to wield imperial power, is create and enforce the rules of a hierarchical interstate order.

The organizing principle of interstate relations, Kenneth Waltz famously wrote, is anarchy: in the absence of an overarching power that creates and enforces rules for state behavior, states help themselves by "balancing" against other centers of power that could hurt them—either by building up their own forces or by joining with other states. The organizing principle of empire rests, in contrast, on the existence of an overarching power that creates and enforces the principle of hierarchy, but is not itself bound by such rules. In turn, subordinate states do not build up their own capabilities or join with others when threatened; they call instead on the imperial power for assistance. In so doing, they give up a key component of state sovereignty, which is direct control of their own security.

This condition, in which superior power is not merely predominant but functions as the guarantor of the security of others, is the result of two sets of factors. The first is the ability and willingness of the imperial power to acquire and maintain something close to a monopoly on the organized use of military power. The second is the abdication by states within the empire of their responsibility to build their own effective military capabilities. How does such overarching power come to exist?

The formation of a monopoly on military power is greatly facilitated by the decision of other potential powers not to compete. The Roman Empire effectively had two components, one in the west and one in the east centered on Byzantium. As is well known, the eastern empire persisted long after the sack of Rome in 476 CE. Less well known is the fact that the internal factors associated with the fall of the Roman Empire—the rise of Christianity, increasing social rigidity, and the bureaucratization of imperial governance—

were just as powerful in the east as they were in the west. The difference was that there were fewer organized military challenges in the east, and one potential challenger to Byzantium, the Parthian empire, chose to accept Rome's dominant role. Similarly, the British monopoly on seapower began to emerge in the early 18th century, when French continental concerns led to the virtual disappearance of the French battle fleet. The withdrawal of competitors was even more marked following the wars of the French revolution, at which time British naval mastery rested, according to Paul Kennedy, on the "simple wish of other nations not to spend the time or energy to challenge the British."[1]

The same phenomenon is at work today. The American empire did not emerge simply as the result of the growth of American power but as a result of the collapse of Russian power, the decline of European and Japanese military spending relative to the United States, and the unwillingness of those countries to take military action or make military preparations in response to a host of security problems. A surprising number of major states are not now engaging in the self-help that Waltz says is at the heart of interstate relations, but are relying instead on the United States for their security.

The creation and maintenance of an American monopoly, or near-monopoly, of organized military power could not and did not arise simply from the abdication of non-imperial powers, however. Historically, either enduring differences in the social organization of the imperial versus the non-imperial powers, or active and effective imperial strategies, have led to gross disparities in military power. The ability of republican Rome to develop military power from a population of free adult males from Rome and its Italian allies (totaling approximately 2.75 million men) was the basis of Roman expansion. From this base it built an army that controlled an imperial population of approximately fifty million people. Rome's ability to develop more military power than its rivals rested

---

[1]Paul M. Kennedy, *The Rise and Fall of British Naval Mastery* (London, 1976), pp. 82–83, 157.

primarily on the organizational practices of the Roman Legions, which created a unified and coordinated fighting force that could routinely defeat opposing armies five times larger. Drill and discipline produced formations that could withstand uncoordinated infantry and cavalry attacks mounted by less well-organized adversaries. The internal divisions and lack of social cohesion among the rivals of Rome, with the exception of the armies of Hannibal, created an enduring military advantage that cascaded over time, for as Rome's area of control expanded, the population base from which it could draw military recruits expanded, too.

Other empires also benefited from large asymmetries in the ability to generate military power from their populations. Those asymmetries often arose from the military capabilities of nomadic pastoral societies relative to sedentary agricultural populations. Thus the total population of the Manchu empire in the period before it expanded to include Xinjiang and Tibet has been estimated at approximately 150 million. The records of the Manchu empire in China suggest that the number of bannermen (the Manchu and northern Chinese military personnel who swore allegiance to the Manchu rulers) was not much larger than the Roman Legionnaires, and they controlled an even larger population. As was the case with the Roman Legions, the decline in effective Manchu military power took place as military training and discipline declined in peacetime. Artillery practice, for example, was cut back in 1795 so as not to disturb the silkworms of local silk producers. The result was that 2,100 British and Indian soldiers were sufficient to bring about the Manchu army's initial defeat in 1841.

Similarly, the Mughal empire in India was established in 1526 when Babur conquered the armies defending Delhi with a cavalry army of only about 5,000 soldiers. Babur's small but effective force faced a local Indian population with levels of social cohesion so catastrophically low that local leaders were happy to provide him with the information that allowed him to defeat his enemies. The prospect of being on the winning side swelled the number of soldiers who switched their allegiance to Babur, which diminished the forces available to his foes.

In the context of the history of empires, as opposed to the history of interstate relations, the position the United States now holds is not that unusual. Military competence, arising from superior training and long periods of active military engagement, builds forces that are proficient at converting human resources into fighting power. Indeed, the lopsided military outcome of the 1991 Gulf War was probably more the result of organizational competence than technological superiority. While there has been much talk of the way in which information technology has improved weaponry, and hence of a "Revolution in Military Affairs," much less attention has been paid to the revolution in American military training practices that flowed from problems associated with the Vietnam War. Post-Vietnam innovations at the National Training Center at Fort Irwin made possible highly realistic training for combined arms warfare. The U.S. Navy instituted its Top Gun program for realistic training in air-to-air combat, the Air Force its Red Flag exercises for the same purpose. Advances in data processing made possible computer-supported, fully networked training for armored warfare. By the time of the 1991 Gulf War, data from ongoing military operations were being used to develop and adjust combat training simulators. Movement from a conscript military to an all-volunteer force, too, made it both possible and necessary to institute these intensive training methods on a vast scale, and repeated military deployments after the end of the Cold War created powerful incentives to maintain these rigorous training programs.

Progress continues to be made. Advances in technology are making it possible for seamen to train for duty at sea on simulators while ashore, using real-time data from the ships at sea to which they will be deployed. No other country in the world, except Israel, profits from this combination of intensive training and repeated operational deployments. The result is a military instrument that improves with use, even as the military capabilities of other countries atrophy from disuse. That U.S. capabilities continue to draw away from other competitors strikes many as improbable because the concept we have inherited from the history of interstate relations tells us that interstate competition inhibits any country from developing and sustaining outsized military capabilities. This concept ill equips us to recognize the conditions associated with the creation of empire.

MAINTAINING HIERARCHY

Empires ultimately rest on military predominance, but military predominance is not a static phenomenon. Imperial governance must sustain that position, but how does it do so? In the case of military practices and capabilities that emerged historically from the basic character of civilian society, it is easy to see why more mobile warrior societies had advantages over sedentary agricultural societies. In the more modern cases of military practices that can be taught to any soldier, or technology that can be transferred across international boundaries, the answer is less obvious. It seems to be related to the empire builder's ability and willingness to use its initial advantages in ways that prevent others from acquiring them as well.

We tend to assume that military knowledge and capabilities will diffuse quickly. This was certainly the case in modern Europe. The presence of a literary tradition—exemplified by Machiavelli and his work, *The Art of War*—focused modern Europeans on ancient Roman military writings, and eventually made it possible for the Dutch, Swedes, and others to recreate Roman military practices in the 16th century. The Dutch were then able to defeat Spanish Hapsburg armies many times their size. The existence of printing presses and a literary class fluent in Latin ensured the spread of the Roman army's tactical secrets. Given the power of the new practices, the diffusion of this knowledge made it impossible for the Dutch, or anyone else, to maintain a monopoly within Europe on the military advantage they initially gained; this precluded the creation of an empire based on those techniques.

Not so in Asia at the end of the 18th century when the British established and maintained their empire. In India, the military power of small but efficient European armies enabled the French and the English to win victories against local Indian armies ten times their size. Military skill, not just technology, was the dominant factor, and the ability of local Indian military leaders to learn the new techniques from Latin texts was essentially nonexistent. Nonetheless, the possibility that new military knowledge would diffuse to the Indians and neutralize the military advantage of European armies very much concerned the English. This, in turn, led them to take two courses of action: co-optation and preemption.

New military skills could be taught directly by European military trainers, and the French were the first to train Indian soldiers in hopes of using them to resist the British. So Arthur Wellesley, the military commander responsible for British military operations in India, ordered that any French officer training local Indians (Marathas to be specific) could receive safe conduct and free passage back to Europe. In this fashion Wellesley hoped to sustain the British monopoly on effective military power in India.

But by observation and learning, or as a result of their own thinking, Indian armies began to adopt or invent the new techniques even without European trainers. Richard Wellesley, Governor-General of the East India Company, believed that the only solution for this rising danger was to quickly capitalize on the waning British military advantage to lock in their superiority. Rather than hang back and avoid involvements in local Indian military struggles, Wellesley adopted an aggressive policy of offering British military assistance to selected local Indian rulers so that they could win their battles, but only if those helped by the British would thereafter disband their armies. It was a good idea, but even so, it was a near thing. By 1803, the British were still able to defeat a Maratha army twice the size of their own army, but only after suffering losses equal to half the British force.

As these examples illustrate, successful imperial governance must focus on maintaining and increasing, if possible, the initial advantage in the ability to generate military power. Putting matters in these terms casts an acute historical light on U.S. policies to control the proliferation of weapons of mass destruction and ballistic missiles. Americans see such efforts as part of a program to ensure global "stability"—something that is good for everybody, because it heads off "unnecessary" and costly arms races. Viewed through the lens of imperial practice, however, U.S. non-proliferation policies compose a classic case of an imperial effort to keep a monopoly on the forms of military power that provide its dominance. Complementary to efforts at arms control, the United States has a strategy similar to that of the British in India, of extending security guarantees to others in order to remove their need for independent military capabilities. This concept was explicitly raised in the now famous 1992 Defense Policy Guidance, which recommended that the United States be capable of defending other countries so that they would not feel compelled to build forces to defend themselves. External observers were left to make the point that this would have the consequence of reinforcing the dominant American military position.

American forces stationed abroad also help fulfill that function, even after the collapse of the Soviet Union, by reassuring host countries that the United States will ensure that they need not arm themselves further. American missile defense technology, the research and development costs of which have been carried by the United States for almost fifty years, has been offered to friendly countries, again reducing the likelihood that they will develop and control their own missile defenses.

At the same time, conventional naval challenges to the U.S. Navy, or those of its subordinate states, are unlikely because of American naval supremacy. But as was the case during the era of British naval mastery, adversaries of the United States have shifted to guerre de course, or commerce raiding, openly in the Persian Gulf in the 1980s and indirectly, by means of ballistic missiles launched into the waters around Taiwan, in 1996. In both the 19th and 20th centuries, the imperial response was the same: convoys to stabilize and reassure friendly nations, and remove the need for them to arm themselves for naval operations. So it will be, most likely, in the 21st century, too.

Imperial governance also involves the creation and enforcement of rules. The first rule of the empire must be to prohibit behavior that threatens its basic power position. Non-proliferation treaties and diplomacy are today part of the imperial set of rules drawn up and enforced by the United States. NATO and the U.S.-Japan defense agreement are not really alliances among equals but security guarantees offered by the imperial power to subordinates. As such they are mechanisms for codifying interstate hierarchy. The position advanced by the U.S. government in 2002, that it will act preemptively to destroy the programs of hostile states to construct weapons of mass destruction, is a logical extension of that policy, and one enabled by the improved power position of the United States after the end of the Cold War.

ECONOMY OF FORCE

The problem of sustaining hierarchy comes down, in the main, to achieving economy of force. This is because imperial powers have predominant but not infinite military power. While they have a near monopoly on the organized means of violence, they face numerous potential challenges from less well-organized groups and peoples both within the empire and, more particularly, outside of it. In an interstate system, the land boundary of one state marks the beginning of another state that is capable of maintaining order within its frontiers. The boundaries of an empire, however, are often marked by peoples who are less well organized socially and who do not accept imperial dominance. In the old and impolite language of empires, these are the barbarians at the gates.

This exactly was the problem shared by the Romans, the various Chinese empires, and the British in India and Africa. Lasting peace was difficult to establish with the peoples beyond the frontiers because of their fluid internal social orders and their hostility to the empire. They thus constituted a chronic problem that could drive up the cost of empire. The historical repertoire of imperial techniques employed to manage this problem is still relevant today. That repertoire was composed of three parts: walls, which were parts of a system of defenses in depth; the application of overwhelming force followed by withdrawal; and indirect rule.

Imperial strategy could combine or alternate among these techniques, but the fundamental goal was the same: economy of force. Each of these techniques was supposed to reduce the number of soldiers needed to maintain order at the frontier.

In *The Grand Strategy of the Roman Empire* (1976), Edward Luttwak provided an excellent, if controversial, analysis of the de facto Roman strategy that effectively combined barriers, mobile forces and client states to help the Roman Legions handle the multiple potential threats at the periphery of empire. Roman walls, he pointed out, were not meant to provide a continuous, impermeable barrier. Rather, they formed part of a zone of defenses in depth that served as an intelligence collection device and delaying mechanism. The existence of walls and strong points on the frontier meant that an outer zone would have to be breached in order to effect an incursion. This meant that incursions could be detected by small numbers of friendly forces along the frontier. Fortifications protected those small forces long enough for the Legions to react to their intelligence. Roads running from the interior of the empire to the outer walls reduced the time it took the Legions to arrive.

Defenses in depth meant that breaches of the perimeter were not catastrophic, since the enemy would be weakened the further he penetrated into the defensive zone, within which there would be strong points from which counterattacks could be launched. Since any heavy fighting would be done by the Legions when they showed up, perimeter defenses could be, and often were, manned by locally recruited mercenaries who accepted their status as imperial clients. When the system worked, the result was not only reduced defensive burdens on the Roman Legions but the enhancement of their deterrent offensive power.

This was crucial to the economy of force aspect of Roman strategy. Every challenger to the empire could not be handled simultaneously at an acceptable cost. Therefore, periodic offensive operations had to be conducted so that potential challengers were aware of the terrible things that could happen to them if they rebelled. In conventional interstate relations, the presence of rival powers of near equal strength creates the possibility that initial conflicts will escalate, and escalation may or may not favor the state that starts the war. Prudence therefore leads to at least the consideration of limits on military operations. Empires do not face the problem of escalation mounted by peers. They do face the problem of long, drawn out, small but multiple wars against peoples who have not yet gotten the message that resistance to the empire is futile. This is the source of the logic of overwhelming force—of which history provides many successful examples.

The Athenians crushed the Melians because they could not afford to wage war against every island state that might defy them. The Melians had to be crushed, therefore, so that no other island state would even think about rebelling against Athens. The same with Rome: the war against the Jews and the reduction of Masada, so carefully chronicled by Josephus and published by the Romans, was meant to enforce peace by demonstrating that no matter how fanatical or distant you were, offensive military operations would eventually and inevitably annihilate you. So, too, with China. The Great Wall was not a single continuous barrier but a series of walls running parallel to one another with many gaps. It was meant not only to handle hostile local peoples but to provide the base for massive punitive raids. Both the barriers and the punitive raids were responses to chronic threats that could not be met at acceptable cost by the permanent presence of regular military forces, as was the case in the Roman empire.

In 2003, the United States is trying to cope with essentially the same problems, and with the same conceptual range of responses. The military position of the United States, however strong, can still be stretched to the breaking point by multiple hostile peoples who cannot mount direct military challenges to the United States but who can create disorder by unconventional means. Even before the attacks launched by Al-Qaeda, the U.S. military was being worn out by the extensive operations needed to maintain an acceptable international order in places such as Haiti and Bosnia. The increase in international terrorism reflects the ability of the enemies of the American empire to take advantage of the porosity of its frontiers.

The American response to date has involved the application of force followed by withdrawal and indirect rule. Less attention has been paid to the development of barriers or defensive zones. As in the past, barrier strategies and offensive raids should not be expected to be completely effective, only to achieve higher levels of security within the boundaries of acceptable levels of defense expenditures. They should be judged in terms of their use as economy of force measures, not as instruments of absolute security.

The parallels between earlier empires and the United States today are suggestive, but they hardly exhaust the factors we need to understand in order to define what post–post cold war international relations may be like. The external structural characteristic shared by all empires is a sustainable near-monopoly on the organized means of violence, but each historical period has its own unique characteristics. In our own period, it appears that the United States has such a monopoly, but one factor could quickly put an end to it: the proliferation of nuclear weapons. If such weapons become available to forces sufficiently hostile to the empire that they are willing to use them, the non-nuclear military predominance of the United States would be essentially neutralized. This suggests that the war against Iraq was about much more than liberating the Iraqi people, and that other potential sources of hostile nuclear weapons use—such as a Pakistan that reverses its currently favorable stance toward the United States—will have much to do with whether and how long the United States can maintain its primacy.

The other unique problematic of American empire today, of course, is that it is a putative empire run by a democracy that embraces the principle of equality and values formal limits on state power. These principles contradict the imperial tendency to hierarchy and the use of unrestrained, extra-legal violence. The United States, to be sure, is capable of hypocrisy and brutality on massive scales. But its most naked expressions of imperial power have really been mere episodes—intense, but limited in time and scope. Since imperial governance must sustain itself for decades to really work, it is worth asking whether the United States, given its principles, can sustain the kind of actions that an imperial mission requires for years on end?

The answer depends on circumstances. As long as the personal and societal safety of American citizens is at risk from external threats, historical precedent suggests that rather few limits will be placed on the use of American military power, nor on the constraints the United States will impose on the peoples of other countries. Any use of weapons of mass destruction against targets in the United States, or against American soldiers abroad, will evoke the implacable rage of the American people against a clear enemy.

As for imperial rule over other peoples, the United States has always preferred indirect rule; i.e., the installation of local governments compatible with American policies. Direct rule will be seen as a temporary measure to prepare conditions for a transfer of government to local inhabitants. But effective transfer could be a long time coming in places like Afghanistan and Iraq, or in other places where the United States establishes military garrisons intended to be temporary. The United States is fully capable of enlarging its army to maintain such garrisons over long periods of time: in living memory, the peacetime U.S. military had over three million men and women. The real constraint will be political: will the elites and general population of the United States regard it as just to rule other people, some of whom hate Americans enough to engage in suicidal attacks, and many of whom exploit Americans for their own malign purposes?

The United States could give up the imperial mission, or pretensions to it, now. This would essentially mean the withdrawal of all forces from the Middle East, Europe, and mainland Asia. It may be that all other peoples, without significant exception, will then turn to their own affairs and leave the United States alone. But those who are hostile to us might remain hostile, and be much less afraid of the United States as well. Current friends would feel less secure and would, in the most probable post-imperial world, revert to the logic of self-help in which all states do what they must to protect themselves. This would imply the relatively rapid acquisition of weapons of mass destruction by Japan, South Korea, Taiwan, Iran, Iraq, and perhaps Algeria, Saudi Arabia, Malaysia, Indonesia, and others. Constraints on the acquisition of biological weapons would be even weaker than they are today. Major regional arms races would also seem very likely throughout Asia and the Middle East. This would not be a pleasant world for Americans or anyone else. It is difficult to guess what the costs of such a world would be to the United States. They would probably not put the end of the United States in prospect, but they would not be small. If the logic of American empire is unappealing, it is not at all clear that the alternatives are that much more attractive.

Nor is it obvious, as so many assume, that empire is somehow historically obsolete. If an American empire does endure, we may, in retrospect, come to understand the era of independent nation-states as something of an historical anomaly. William McNeill first advanced this idea in 1985, when he challenged the idea

> that it is right and proper and normal for a single people to inhabit a particular piece of territory and obey a government of their own devising. . . . [I]t is my contention that civilized societies have nearly always subordinated some human groups to others of a different ethnic background, thereby creating a laminated polyethnic structure.

It was only the particular circumstances of 18th-century western Europe and modern industrial economies, McNeill argued, that temporarily created the conditions conducive to the culturally cohesive and economically viable political units known as nation-states. Pre- and post-industrial economies, he suggested, required specialization of military and economic functions and large-scale integration that culturally and linguistically homogeneous societies could not support, but which supra-national empires could.

If McNeill was right, then the notion of American empire, far from being anomalous and ill-fitted to the 21st century, might comport nicely with it. That alone, however, is insufficient reason to seek it.

I V

Imperial Prospects

WENDELL BERRY

A Citizen's Response

The strategy of the American empire promises
peace but leads to war; Americans must resist.

THE NEW National Security Strategy published by the White
House in September 2002, if carried out, would amount to a radical revision of the political character of our nation. Its central and
most significant statement is this:

> While the United States will constantly strive to enlist the
> support of the international community, we will not hesitate
> to act alone, if necessary, to exercise our right of self defense
> by acting preemptively against such terrorists. . . . (p. 6)

A democratic citizen must deal here first of all with the question, Who is this "we"? It is not the "we" of the Declaration of Independence, which referred to a small group of signatories bound
by the conviction that "governments [derive] their just powers

Wendell Berry is a Kentucky farmer and the author of more than thirty books includ-
ing, most recently, In the Presence of Fear: Three Essays for a Changed World.
This essay, originally printed in an advertisement in the New York Times *and on*
OrionOnline.org, is an abridged version of the cover article in the March/April 2003
Orion Magazine. *Reprinted by permission of The Orion Society.*

from the consent of the governed." And it is not the "we" of the Constitution, which refers to "*the people* [my emphasis] of the United States."

This "we" of the new strategy can refer only to the president. It is a royal "we." A head of state, preparing to act alone in starting a preemptive war, will need to justify his intention by secret information, and will need to plan in secret and execute his plan without forewarning. The idea of a government acting alone in preemptive war is inherently undemocratic, for it does not require or even permit the president to obtain the consent of the governed. As a policy, this new strategy depends on the acquiescence of a public kept fearful and ignorant, subject to manipulation by the executive power, and on the compliance of an intimidated and dependent legislature. To the extent that a government is secret, it cannot be democratic or its people free. By this new doctrine, the president alone may start a war against any nation at any time, and with no more forewarning than preceded the Japanese attack on Pearl Harbor.

Would-be participating citizens of a democratic nation, unwilling to have their consent coerced or taken for granted, therefore have no choice but to remove themselves from the illegitimate constraints of this "we" in as immediate and public a way as possible. The alleged justification for this new strategy is the recent emergence in the United States of international terrorism. But why the events of September 11, 2001, horrifying as they were, should have called for a radical new investiture of power in the executive branch is not clear.

The National Security Strategy defines terrorism as "premeditated, politically motivated violence perpetrated against innocents" (p. 5). This is truly a distinct kind of violence, but to imply by the word "terrorism" that this sort of terror is the work exclusively of "terrorists" is misleading. The "legitimate" warfare of technologically advanced nations likewise is premeditated, politically motivated violence perpetrated against innocents. The distinction between the intention to perpetrate violence against innocents, as in "terrorism," and the willingness to do so, as in "war," is not a source of comfort.

Supposedly, if a nation perpetrates violence officially—whether to bomb an enemy airfield or a hospital—it is not guilty of "terrorism." But there is no need to hesitate over the difference between "terrorism" and any violence or threat of violence that is terrifying. The National Security Strategy wishes to cause "terrorism" to be seen "in the same light as slavery, piracy, or genocide" (p. 6) but not in the same light as war. It accepts and affirms the legitimacy of war.

The war against terrorism is not, strictly speaking, a war against nations, even though it has already involved international war in Afghanistan and presidential threats against other nations. This is a war against "the embittered few" "thousands of trained terrorists"—who are "at large" (p. 5) among many millions of others who are, in the language of this document, "innocents," and thus are deserving of our protection.

Unless we are willing to kill innocents in order to kill the guilty, the need to be lethal will be impeded constantly by the need to be careful. Because we must suppose a new supply of villains to be always in the making, we can expect the war on terrorism to be more or less endless, endlessly costly and endlessly supportive of a thriving bureaucracy.

Unless, that is, we should become willing to ask why, and to do something about the causes. Why do people become terrorists? Such questions arise from the recognition that problems have causes. There is, however, no acknowledgement in The National Security Strategy that terrorism might have a cause that could possibly be discovered and possibly remedied. "The embittered few," it seems, are merely "evil."

II

Much of the obscurity of our effort so far against terrorism originates in this now official idea that the enemy is evil and that we are (therefore) good, which is the precise mirror image of the official idea of the terrorists.

The epigraph of Part III of The National Security Strategy contains this sentence from President Bush's speech at the National Cathedral on September 14, 2001: "But our responsibility to history is already clear: to answer these attacks and rid the world of evil." A government, committing its nation to rid the world of evil, is assuming necessarily that it and its nation are good.

But the proposition that anything so multiple and large as a nation can be "good" is an insult to common sense. It is also dangerous, because it precludes any attempt at self-criticism or self-correction; it precludes public dialogue. It leads us far indeed from the traditions of religion and democracy that are intended to measure and so to sustain our efforts to be good. Christ said, "He that is without sin among you, let him first cast a stone at her." And Thomas Jefferson justified general education by the obligation of citizens to be critical of their government: "for nothing can keep it right but their own vigilant and distrustful superintendence." An inescapable requirement of true patriotism, love for one's land, is a vigilant distrust of any determinative power, elected or unelected, that may preside over it.

And so it is not without reason or precedent that a citizen should point out that, in addition to evils originating abroad and supposedly correctable by catastrophic technologies in "legitimate" hands, we have an agenda of domestic evils, not only those that properly self-aware humans can find in their own hearts, but also several that are indigenous to our history as a nation: issues of economic and social justice, and issues related to the continuing and worsening maladjustment between our economy and our land.

There are kinds of violence that have nothing directly to do with unofficial or official warfare. I mean such things as toxic pollution, land destruction, soil erosion, the destruction of biological diversity and of the ecological supports of agriculture. To anybody with a normal concern for health and sanity, these "externalized costs" are terrible and are terrifying.

I don't wish to make light of the threats and dangers that now confront us. But frightening as these are, they do not relieve us of the responsibility to be as intelligent, principled, and practical as we can be. To rouse the public's anxiety about foreign terror while ignoring domestic terror, and to fail to ask if these terrors are in any way related, is wrong.

It is understandable that we should have reacted to the attacks of September 11, 2001, by curtailment of civil rights, by defiance of laws, and by resort to overwhelming force, for those things are the ready products of fear and hasty thought. But they cannot protect us against the destruction of our own land by ourselves. They cannot protect us against the selfishness, wastefulness, and greed that we have legitimized here as economic virtues, and have taught to the world. They cannot protect us against our government's long-standing disdain for any form of self-sufficiency or thrift, or against the consequent dependence, which for the present at least is inescapable, on foreign supplies, such as oil from the Middle East.

It is no wonder that the National Security Strategy, growing as it does out of unresolved contradictions in our domestic life, should attempt to compound a foreign policy out of contradictory principles.

There is, first of all, the contradiction of peace and war, or of war as the means of achieving and preserving peace. This document affirms peace; it also affirms peace as the justification of war and war as the means of peace, and thus perpetuates a hallowed absurdity. But implicit in its assertion of this (and, by implication, any other) nation's right to act alone in its own interest is an acceptance of war as a permanent condition. Either way, it is cynical to invoke the ideas of cooperation, community, peace, freedom, justice, dignity, and the rule of law (as this document repeatedly does), and then proceed to assert one's intention to act alone in making war. One cannot reduce terror by holding over the world the threat of what it most fears.

This is a contradiction not reconcilable except by a self-righteousness almost inconceivably naive. The authors of the strategy seem now and then to be glimmeringly conscious of the difficulty. Their implicit definition of "rogue state," for example, is any nation pursuing national greatness by advanced military capabilities that can threaten its neighbors—except *our* nation.

If you think our displeasure with "rogue states" might have any underpinning in international law, then you will be disappointed to learn on page 31 that

We will take the actions necessary to ensure that our efforts to meet our global security commitments and protect Americans are not impaired by the potential for investigations, inquiry, or prosecution by the International Criminal Court (ICC), whose jurisdiction does not extend to Americans and which we do not accept.

The rule of law in the world, then, is to be upheld by a nation that has declared itself to be above the law. A childish hypocrisy here assumes the dignity of a nation's foreign policy.

III

A further contradiction is that between war and commerce. This issue arises first of all in the war economy, which unsurprisingly regards war as a business and weapons as merchandise. However nationalistic may be the doctrine of the National Security Strategy, the fact is that the internationalization of the weapons trade is a result inherent in international trade itself. It is a part of globalization. Mr. Bush's addition of this Security Strategy to the previous bipartisan commitment to globalization exposes an American dementia that has not been so plainly displayed before.

The America Whose Business is Business has been internationalizing its economy in haste (for bad reasons, and with little foresight), looking everywhere for "trading partners," cheap labor, and tax shelters. Meanwhile, the America Whose Business is National Defense is withdrawing from the world in haste (for bad reasons, with little foresight), threatening left and right, repudiating agreements, and angering friends. The problem of participating in the Global Economy for the benefit of Washington's corporate sponsors while maintaining a nationalist belligerence and an isolationist morality calls for superhuman intelligence in the secretary of commerce. The problem of "acting alone" in an international war while maintaining simultaneously our ability to import the foreign goods (for instance, oil) on which we have become dependent even militarily will call, likewise, for overtopping genius in the secretary of defense.

After World War II, we hoped the world might be united for the sake of peacemaking. Now the world is being "globalized" for the sake of trade and the so-called free market—for the sake, that is, of plundering the world for cheap labor, cheap energy, and cheap materials. How nations, let alone regions and communities, are to shape and protect themselves within this "global economy" is far from clear. Nor is it clear how the global economy can hope to survive the wars of nations.

For a nation to be, in the truest sense, patriotic, its citizens must love their land with a knowing, intelligent, sustaining, and protective love. They must not, for any price, destroy its health, its beauty, or its productivity. And they must not allow their patriotism to be degraded to a mere loyalty to symbols or any present set of officials.

One might reasonably assume, therefore, that a policy of national security would advocate from the start various practical measures to conserve and to use frugally the nation's resources, the objects of this husbandry being a reduction in the nation's dependence on imports and a reduction in the competition between nations for necessary goods.

Agriculture, which is the economic activity most clearly and directly related to national security—if one grants that we all must eat—receives such scant and superficial treatment as to amount to a dismissal. The document proposes only:

1. "a global effort to address new technology, science, and health regulations that needlessly impede farm exports and improved agriculture" (p. 19). This refers, without saying so, to the growing consumer resistance to genetically modified food. A global effort to overcome this resistance would help not farmers and not consumers but global agribusiness corporations.

2. "transitional safeguards which we have used in the agricultural sector" (p. 19). This refers to government subsidies, which ultimately help the agribusiness corporations, not farmers.

3. Promotion of "new technologies, including biotechnology, [which] have enormous potential to improve crop yields in developing countries while using fewer pesticides and less water" (p. 23). This is offered (as usual and questionably) as the solution to

hunger, but its immediate benefit would be to the corporate suppliers.

This is not an agriculture policy, let alone a national security strategy. It has the blindness, arrogance, and foolishness that are characteristic of top-down thinking by politicians and academic experts, assuming that "improved agriculture" would inevitably be the result of catering to the agribusiness corporations, and that national food security can be achieved merely by going on as before. It does not address any agricultural problem as such, and it ignores the vulnerability of our present food system dependent as it is on genetically impoverished monocultures, cheap petroleum, cheap long-distance transportation, and cheap farm labor to many kinds of disruption by "the embittered few," who, in the event of such disruption, would quickly become the embittered many. On eroding, ecologically degraded, increasingly toxic landscapes, worked by failing or subsidy dependent farmers and by the cheap labor of migrants, we have erected the tottering tower of "agribusiness," which prospers and "feeds the world" (incompletely and temporarily) by undermining its own foundations.

IV

Since the end of World War II, when the terrors of industrial warfare had been fully revealed, many people and, by fits and starts, many governments have recognized that peace is not just a desirable condition, as was thought before, but a practical necessity. But we have not yet learned to think of peace apart from war. We wait, still, until we face terrifying dangers and the necessity to choose among bad alternatives, and then we think again of peace, and again we fight a war to secure it.

At the end of the war, if we have won it, we declare peace; we congratulate ourselves on our victory; we marvel at the newly proved efficiency of our latest weapons; we ignore the cost in lives, materials, and property, in suffering and disease, in damage to the natural world; we ignore the inevitable residue of resentment and hatred; and we go on as before, having, as we think, successfully defended our way of life.

That is pretty much the story of our victory in the Gulf War of 1991. In the years between that victory and September 11, 2001, we did not alter our thinking about peace and war—that is, we thought much about war and little about peace; we continued to punish the defeated people of Iraq and their children; we made no effort to reduce our dependence on the oil we import from other, potentially belligerent countries; we made no improvement in our charity toward the rest of the world; we made no motion toward greater economic self-reliance; and we continued our extensive and often irreversible damages to our own land. We appear to have assumed merely that our victory confirmed our manifest destiny to be the richest, most powerful, most wasteful nation in the world. After the catastrophe of September 11, it again became clear to us how good it would be to be at peace, to have no enemies, to have no more needless deaths to mourn. And then, our need for war following with the customary swift and deadly logic our need for peace, we took up the customary obsession with the evil of other people.

It is useless to try to adjudicate a long-standing animosity by asking who started it or who is the most wrong. The only sufficient answer is to give up the animosity and try forgiveness, to try to love our enemies and to talk to them and (if we pray) to pray for them. If we can't do any of that, then we must begin again by trying to imagine our enemies' children who, like our children, are in mortal danger because of enmity that they did not cause.

We can no longer afford to confuse peaceability with passivity. Authentic peace is no more passive than war. Like war, it calls for discipline and intelligence and strength of character, though it calls also for higher principles and aims. If we are serious about peace, then we must work for it as ardently, seriously, continuously, carefully, and bravely as we now prepare for war.

GABRIEL ASH

The Empire's Coming Crisis

George W. Bush's quest for global empire confronts American capitalism with its ultimate test.

THE AMERICAN RESPONSE to September 11th did not change the terms of international relations. It only enhanced and deepened a trend that was manifest in Bush's foreign policy from the beginning. Surprisingly, this trend should give pause to the corporate executives who lined up behind Bush's candidacy. Unsurprisingly, nobody else wins either. Bush is the ultimate lose-lose president.

Before the election of George Bush, the U.S. dominated a vast American empire. That empire had enormous military might, more powerful than anything ever dreamed of. U.S. military power was visible in a host of military bases around the world, from Germany and Saudi Arabia to Okinawa. However, since the end of the Cold War, U.S. military forces rarely functioned as forces employed to defend the United States per se. Rather, they

Gabriel Ash is a columnist for YellowTimes.org, where this essay first appeared in somewhat different form on March 6, 2002. Reprinted by permission of Yellow-times.org.

functioned as world police forces, intervening almost exclusively by invitation, with a mission to restore the peace or defeat local thugs.

In the space secured by this world police, America exercised its world domination, relatively peacefully, through a series of technocratic institutions that protected and extended the power of U.S. corporations over world production.

These institutions included the IMF, the World Bank, the WTO, the G7, and the UN. A host of NGOs, such as Amnesty International, mostly funded by American philanthropy, also participated in this world order, acting in lieu of a nonexistent world electorate to maintain the appearance of a social contract.

These NGOs supplied the necessary legitimacy for the U.S. "police interventions," a legitimacy expressed in terms of human rights and respect for the law.

In this manner, American foreign domination replicated the capitalist model of the domestic domination of production: police in the background, economic necessity in the foreground. Exploitation was, and is, relentless. Third World workers are squeezed to the limit in order to bolster the spending power of First World consumers. And those who cannot be squeezed are left to rot.

But for the dominators, the virtues of the system are significant. The abstract, diffuse, and apparently benign exercise of power makes resistance extremely difficult. It is difficult to organize against a power that manifests itself as destiny rather than as a concrete, nameable enemy. The U.S. professed commitment to human rights, democracy, and rule of law promised hope and gave the system respectability, even among its critics.

There were, to be sure, points of stress in this imperial idyll. U.S. police intervention sometimes failed to materialize, as in Rwanda, and sometimes simply failed, as in Somalia. All too often, U.S. foreign policy merely paid lip service to human rights. These flaws were real. But far from undermining the system, they generated calls for improving it.

A new movement of protest that emerged in Seattle challenged the economic logic of the American empire. But the deglobalization movement was not posed to create massive social unrest. As a rallying cry, the evil machinations of international institutions are too complex and abstract to generate a heated emotional response. The demonstrations dented the confidence of Western governments, but they were far from posing a threat to the survival of the system. On the contrary, the deglobalization movement is a feature of the U.S. imperial rule.

Bush changed all that. In a series of actions that started soon after he took office and culminated in his "axis of evil" speech, Bush switched U.S. foreign domination towards an older imperialist model. Like British and French pre-war imperialism, Bush's imperialism is unabashedly and openly nationalistic. "America first" became the motto of foreign policy, as Bush rejected international cooperation, arm-control treaties, the Kyoto protocol, and the very model of using the U.S. military as "world police."

For a brief moment, the September 11th attacks seemed to force U.S. policy back to the internationalist modus operandi. Urged by Secretary of State Colin Powell, and buoyed by an effusion of international solidarity, Bush could have responded to the obvious gangsterism of the attack with an international police action.

America's right to self-defense was not in doubt. But given that the terrorists never posed a real national security threat, an empty rhetorical gesture of magnanimity towards the world community would have solidified American imperial rule.

The U.S. could have come out of Afghanistan as the undisputed and unchallenged ruler of the world. Instead, Bush soon returned to the course he had already plotted before September 11, and the U.S. emerged from Afghanistan as the hated tyrant of the world.

One can point to several reasons for the tenacity of Bush's "doctrine."

First, the human reasons: the personal touch of George Bush, and the rise of the strategic hawks; Donald Rumsfeld, Paul Wolfowitz, and Richard Perle. What unites them is a willful incapacity to take into consideration the benefits and potential of the post–Cold War era.

Second, there are the interests of the oil and defense lobbies, dear to the Bush White House. It wasn't by chance that the Islamic fundamentalists who attacked New York came from the Middle East, a region in which old-fashioned oil politics blocked globalization. The oil and defense lobbies prefer old-style imperialism.

Third, the dynamics created by America's military superiority makes negotiated cooperation seem unnecessary, hence unpatriotic. Americans have as much difficulty as anyone grasping the strategic value of human rights, restraint, and "humanitarian interventions." It didn't help that Clinton never took the time to express a coherent foreign policy doctrine. That made it easier for Republican critics to portray his actions as incoherent and opportunistic.

Finally, holding it all together is the electoral policy of George W. Bush. As Karl Rove, Bush's senior political adviser, has explicitly stated, the swagger of the new muscular America would protect the GOP from having to confront voters over a bankrupt domestic agenda.

But there's the rub. Western capitalism moved away from both the pre-war model and the Cold War model of imperialism for a reason. The European empires died off because Third World nationalism made them too expensive to maintain. In Vietnam, the U.S. discovered that even superpowers cannot afford what it takes to secure a territory against a determined population. In response, capitalism transformed itself and learned to profit from the newly independent Third World.

Capitalism was also the prime beneficiary of the end of the Cold War. Consumer capitalism discovered the power of optimism. While containing the Soviet Union was a necessity, it could never be as sexy as the prospect of arming every Chinese peasant with an Internet-ready cell phone.

Thus the gospel of democracy and human rights proved to be a much more potent bourgeois ideology than anti-communism ever was. Furthermore, the end of the Cold War freed the U.S. government to concentrate on economic expansion. Instead of being blackmailed by unsavory dictators, the U.S. was itself able to engage in blackmail, all in the service of multinational capitalism.

George Bush's White House is oblivious to this recent history. By trying to turn back the clock, his policy is undermining the world hegemony of the United States.

First, the new focus on war interferes with the business of promoting business. Second, U.S. policy undermines the credibility of the institutions representing capitalism. And most importantly, by shedding the international institutional framework, Bush gives American domination a recognizable face and address.

During the Cold War, the Soviet threat balanced anti-Americanism. The ideological conflict masked the national issues. Today, there is no Soviet Union to scare the middle classes with.

As it emerges from behind its international cloak, the new American domination appears unmasked, as a purely foreign force. Bush's clumsy attempt to substitute "axis of evil" for the "evil empire" convinces nobody beyond the Rose Garden.

As a result, all over the world, unmasking power no longer requires making sense of complex Marxist arguments. Patriotism will do just as well. And patriots are easier to come by than Marxists. America-bashing is thus slated to become de rigueur for politicians far beyond the left.

We already see it happening. A ruling party parliament member in South Korea (of all countries) called Bush "evil incarnate" on the eve of his state visit. In France, U.S. hegemony became an election theme. The British tabloids are almost as critical of Bush as the Left-leaning *Guardian* is. This is just the beginning.

Now to the crux of the matter: no matter what ensues, the bad blood between the United States and the world can be expected to hurt American business interests. As America contracts behind its night-vision goggles, the spread of market capitalism is bound to lose steam. That will cause a split between American capitalism and Bush's imperialism.

The coming split could be glimpsed at the recent World Economic Forum (WEF) convention in New York City. Colin Powell and Secretary of the Treasury Paul O'Neill had to endure none-too-subtle criticism from both foreign diplomats and corporate magnates. Some of the criticism surprisingly echoed the posters protesters carried at the demonstrations outside. Even American energy companies, Bush's staunchest support base, cannot be amused by the growing coziness between the Iranian government and Europe.

A believer in historical determinism might conclude that the new old imperialism will be short lived; either George Bush will change his tune, or he will be replaced by the very people who put him in power.

But as tensions increase, the White House may conclude that, rather than change the tune, the best election strategy will be to raise the volume. Given the present popular support for saber-rattling in the U.S., that might be a winning strategy for George Bush. But it would drive America deeper into a vicious cycle of militarization and anti-Americanism. This is how empires self-destruct.

What can stop that from happening? Political dynamics could force Bush to calm down. Congress, for example, might take a hatchet to his "defense" budget. A showdown with North Korea might chill the U.S. appetite for confrontation. A military operation could go awry. If nothing else happens, however, capitalism will start voting with its feet.

Capital fleeing the U.S.? That might sound outlandish, but it's not. The huge American trade deficit means that capital doesn't need to move out. If enough stops flowing in, it will dramatically alter the American political landscape.

The U.S. economy looked iffy even before factoring foreign policy in. With debt mounting, credibility under fire, goodwill largely written off the book, and the Pentagon fast becoming a bottomless money pit, America Inc. looks less and less of a strong buy with every passing day.

Yet those who might welcome the weakening of American hegemony are probably in for a nasty surprise. In many corners of the world, the mixture of capitalism, rule of law, and half-hearted human rights that America promoted during the last fifteen years was considered progress. Not enough progress, sure. But nothing that a return to plain old Cold War barbarism can't improve upon.

The Bush presidency is likely to be remembered as one of those rare destructive forces in history that leave practically nobody better off.

JAMES KURTH

Who Will Do the Dirty Work?

Today, empire and immigration are inextricably linked; the implications of that connection are large.

THE FIRST DECADE of the twenty-first century, like the first decade of the twentieth, is an age of empire. A hundred years ago, however, there were many empires. They included both the overseas empires of the national states of Western Europe—particularly those of Britain, France, and the Netherlands—and the overland empires of the multinational states of Eastern Europe—those ruled by the Habsburg, Romanoff, and Ottoman dynasties. Today, there is only one empire—the global empire of the United States, a state which is neither national nor multinational in the traditional meaning, but which instead is more accurately described as multicultural and transnational. This new and strange American empire is the context and the arena in which all the great and global events of our time are taking place.

James Kurth is the Claude Smith Professor of Political Science at Swarthmore College and author of more than sixty essays on international politics and foreign policy. This essay first appeared in the Spring 2003 issue of The National Interest *and is reprinted by permission.*

The first decade of the twenty-first century, like the first decade of the twentieth, is also an age of immigration. A hundred years ago, however, large numbers of people were leaving the national states and imperial metropoles of Western Europe to emigrate to their colonies, or to the United States. At the same time, many people were leaving the rural hinterlands of the multinational states of Eastern Europe to migrate to their metropolitan centers, or again to the United States. Today, the direction of imperial migration is largely the reverse of the Western pattern while reminiscent of the former Eastern one. Large numbers of people have left the former colonies of the Western European empires to emigrate to their once-imperial metropoles. At the same time, many people have left the current dominions of the American empire to emigrate to the United States. A century ago, the United States was receiving many immigrants from Europe but not from its recently acquired empire in the Caribbean and the Philippines. Today, the United States is receiving many immigrants from its long-established empire in Latin America and East Asia, but not from Europe.

THE DOUBLE DYNAMIC

The former age of empire reinvented the national states of Western Europe into imperial states, but the imperial metropole remained a national state in the classical meaning. It still made sense to talk of the national interest of Britain, France, or the Netherlands, and it still made sense to talk of international politics. Our own age of empire is reinventing the United States into an imperial state. Because of the impact of imperial immigration, however, the United States is no longer a national state in the classical sense, or even in the traditional American sense as understood during much of the twentieth century. The conjunction of American empire—America expanding into the world—and American immigration—the world coming into America—has made the very idea of the American national interest problematic. There seems to be a causal connection between empire and immigration, so that the two have come together to utterly transform our world. Empire and immigration have reinvented and perhaps even displaced the traditional ideas of national interest and international politics with the new ideas of transnational interests and global politics.

Since September 11, 2001, these two features of the first decade of the twenty-first century have intersected with a third, which is the first war of the twenty-first century. This is the war between the United States and Islamic terrorists. It has often been observed that Al Qaeda and transnational networks of Islamic terrorists with global reach are another version, the dark side, of the globalization which the United States has so vigorously promoted and which has been a central feature of the American empire. And, of course, Muslim immigrants who are residing within Europe and the United States have been central components in these transnational terrorist networks. Muslim immigrants within Europe and the United States planned and prepared the attacks on the World Trade Center and the Pentagon, symbols of the American empire's economic and military power. The continuing threat of new terrorist attacks emanating from Muslim immigrants has pushed the issue of immigration to the top of the agenda of what was once called national security but what now may be more accurately seen as imperial security.

EUROPEAN AND AMERICAN VERSIONS OF EMPIRE

At first glance, it would seem that the European experience with empire and immigration has little relevance to Americans. For one thing, the Europeans explicitly and officially referred to their imperial systems with the term "empire," and they referred to subordinate territories with terms such as "colonies" and "dependencies." In contrast, Americans have rarely used these terms when referring to their own imperial relationships. The closest American counterparts to European-style colonies and dependencies were the territories that the United States acquired after its victory in the Spanish-American War, particularly the Philippines and Puerto Rico. However, each of these countries was soon designated a "commonwealth," and there was a common understanding that each would eventually become independent if and when it wished to do so. At any rate, these and several smaller formal dependencies of the United States (e.g., American Samoa, Guam, the U.S. Virgin Islands, and the Panama Canal Zone) never amounted to anything as important to America as the formal dependencies of the European empires were to the metropolitan nations in Europe itself.

A narrow focus upon explicit and official dependencies alone is misleading, however. Recall that European empires often included vast areas in which the imperial rule was informal or indirect. Local leaders could even be given the title of king, prince, sultan, or sheik, and retain some of the elements of sovereignty. This was the case with much of the British empire (e.g., the Indian princely states, the Federated Malay States, and the sheikdoms of the Persian Gulf) and even the French empire (e.g., Morocco, Tunisia, Laos, Cambodia, and Annam). These forms of imperial rule differed little from the hegemony that the United States exercised at the same time over the countries of the Caribbean and Central America in the 1910s–1920s.

Beginning in the 1920s, the European nations themselves started to replace the term *empire* with words that connoted more equality between the various territories in the imperial system. This development was partly due to the example and influence of the United States after the First World War. It was also accentuated by the rhetoric of freedom and democracy that figured so prominently during the Second World War. In the immediate aftermath of that war, Europeans could reasonably think that there was not that much difference between the three great imperial systems of Britain, France, and the United States—by then officially designated as the British Commonwealth, the French Union, and the Inter-American System.

Of course, each of the European overseas empires soon experienced a painful and sometimes violent period of decolonization. The British fought and more or less won wars in Malaya and Kenya. The French fought and lost wars in Indochina and Algeria.

The Dutch did much the same in Indonesia. Surely, it might be said, the United States never experienced anything like this violent decolonization, which might seem to be proof that it never really had colonies to begin with. From a European perspective, however, the various Marxist movements roiling the Caribbean and Central America (Guatemala 1944–1954, Dominican Republic 1965, Nicaragua 1978–1990, Grenada 1978–1983, and El Salvador 1980–1992) represented attempts by local populations to shed their colonial status. Furthermore, the Castro revolution in Cuba represented a successful (if eventually pyrrhic) effort at decolonization.

Oblivious to evidence that their own experience with empire in the twentieth century had much in common with the European one, Americans today insist that their global role—and rule—in the twenty-first century is something new and unique. Even if an American empire of sort exists, it is defined by the "soft power" of information networks and popular culture rather than by hard power of economic exploitation and military force. It is, in that sense, an empire suited to the information age rather than the industrial age. Still, Americans should not be surprised if Europeans and almost all other peoples around the world perceive in the new American empire similarities to the earlier empires in their own historical experience.

POST-IMPERIAL IMMIGRATION INTO EUROPE

One might think that decolonization marked the final chapter in the long narrative of European empire. But it did not. Beginning in the 1960s massive migration of formerly colonial peoples into the European metropoles added a postscript to that narrative. Thus Britain has received immigrants especially from India, Pakistan, and what had been the British West Indies; France especially from Algeria, Morocco, Tunisia, and what had been French West Africa; the Netherlands from Indonesia and Surinam; and Belgium from what had been the Belgian Congo. For the most part, large-scale immigration from the colonies into the metropole commenced about the same time that decolonization was occurring or not long after. It has continued until the present day.

What explains this massive and prolonged immigration from the successor states of the European empires into the European metropoles? Why has it occurred after the empires came to an end rather than at some earlier time? The answers to these questions seem to lie principally within the metropoles themselves.

Some historians of Europe have seen the period 1914–1945 to be another Thirty Years War. It certainly was a period of successive great catastrophes—the First World War, the Communist revolution, the Great Depression, the Nazi and fascist dictatorships, the Second World War, and the Holocaust. After 1945 it was natural that creative and constructive political leaders were determined to remove once and for all the causes of these catastrophes.

Fifty years later, we can see that these political leaders succeeded. To prevent the recurrence of war, totalitarianism, and genocide, they promoted supra-national and European institutions and also post-nationalist and post-racist ideologies. To remove the causes of the Great Depression, they promoted the managed economy and European economic integration. To remove the causes of class conflict and Communist revolutions, they promoted the welfare state and provided the working class with access to a middle-class lifestyle. Together these great and successful projects to remove the causes of the great catastrophes of the first half of the twentieth century represent the finest achievements of European civilization in that century's second half.

DOING THE DIRTY WORK

The last of these great achievements of European nations—that all their citizens were entitled to a middle-class lifestyle—had embedded within it an intrinsic flaw: there would no longer be anyone to do the decidedly non-middle-class work necessary in any modern economy—the dirty (and sometimes dangerous or degrading) jobs in farms, factories, the streets, hospitals, and even middle-class homes and gardens. The dirty little secret of the modern European nations is that none of their citizens want to do the dirty work—and with the declining European birthrate there may soon be precious few Europeans to do any work at all.

Thus as soon as the welfare state and middle-class expectations were fully established for the citizens of the European nations (by the early 1960s in many of them), there developed a need for workers who were not citizens, i.e., immigrants or "guest workers" (the term invented at the time). One obvious place where European nations could find these immigrant workers was in the countries to their south—e.g., Algeria for France and Turkey for West Germany. More generally, however, the obvious place to find immigrant workers was among the colonies or other dependent territories of the nation's empire. The colonial peoples had already been doing a good deal of the dirty work of the empire for several generations. It was natural, then, that as the working-class citizens of European nations ascended into some version of middle-class life (or at least middle-class pretensions) that their necessary and essential working-class functions were filled by working-class immigrants from the colonies. Colonial workers not only knew how to work; they also were more likely than non-colonial peoples to know the distinctive national language, codes, and rules of the citizens within the metropole.

MUSLIM IMMIGRANTS IN EUROPE AND AMERICA

The specter of Islamic terrorism now haunting the West has focused attention upon Muslim immigrants into Western countries. These immigrants form communities that have long been hostile to the culture—be it seen as either Christian or as secular—of the host countries. Muslim immigrants thus have an anomalous position in both Europe and America. The particular nature of the anomaly is different, however, in the two regions of the West.

For Europe, Muslim countries comprised major parts of the British, French, and Dutch empires. Accordingly, Muslim communities comprise 5–10 percent of the populations of Britain, France, and the Netherlands today, and they will form an even larger part in the near future. They also comprise more than 5 percent of the population of Germany and several other European countries. European political leaders will have to take Muslim political demands into account, and Muslim leaders will be able to exercise a veto power over some policy issues, most obviously in regard to foreign policy toward the Middle East.

For the United States and in contrast, Muslim countries have not been long-established parts of the American empire. Even such putative allies as Saudi Arabia and Jordan have often engaged in independent, unfriendly, and distinctly uncolonial behavior toward the United States. Accordingly, Muslim immigrant communities comprise only a small part (about 1 percent) of the population of the United States. Furthermore, given the uninviting environment in America for Muslim immigrants since the terrorist attacks of September 11, Muslim immigrant communities probably will not form a much larger part of the American population anytime soon.

Consequently, American political leaders will not have to take Muslim political demands into account. On the contrary, they very likely will reject these demands, in so far as they conflict with those put forward by American Jews, most obviously in regard to foreign policy toward the Middle East.

THE TWO NATIONS OF EUROPE

The most important division created by Muslim immigrants, however, will not be between Europe and America but within the European states themselves. In the next couple of decades, the prospects are for several European states, particularly the once-imperial ones, to become two nations. The first will be the European nation, descended from the European and imperial peoples; it will be secular, rich, old, and feeble. The second will be the anti-European nation, descended from the non-European and colonial peoples; it will be Islamic, poor, young, and virile. It will be a kind of overseas colony of a foreign nation (an obviously familiar occurrence in European history, but this time the foreign nation will be the *umma* of Islam, and the colonized country will be Europe itself), and it will form the beginnings of a kind of settler state. The two nations will regard each other with mutual contempt, but in the new anti-European nation there will be a growing rage, and in the old European nation there will be a growing fear. They will provide the perfect conditions for endemic Islamic terrorism, or at least for a terrified once-imperial people.

At the same time that some European states are becoming two nations, they are becoming subordinate states within the European Union, conforming to economic policies dictated by the European Commission in Brussels and to monetary policies dictated by the European Central Bank in Frankfurt. They have also become subordinate dominions within the American empire, conforming to military policies implemented through NATO in Brussels but largely made in Washington. In short, post-imperial immigration has resulted in European states which are becoming bi-national, while quasi-imperial subordination has resulted in European states which are becoming post-national or even sub-national.

The European metropoles began their imperial narratives as nation states. The creators and exemplars of the nation state were Britain and France, and the creators and exemplars of the overseas empires of the industrial age were the British Empire and the French Empire.

At the beginning of the twenty-first century, however, the long imperial narratives of Britain and France have reached the point that, in many ways, they are no longer nations at all. For about a century (i.e., from about the 1830s to the 1940s) the imperial narrative seemed to provide the latest chapters, indeed the fulfillment, of the much longer national narrative, and for both Britain and France this was a narrative that reached back more than a thousand years. The British Empire and the French Empire, each in their own way, seemed to be the consummation of the longest and grandest historical dramas since that of the Roman Empire. Now, however, a half-century after the end of these two empires, it seems that empire, in particular immigration from the empire into its metropole and heartland, may have actually brought about the end of the British and the French national narratives.

This melancholy tale of empire, immigration, and national disintegration may not merely be a history that is relevant only to Europe. Perhaps it provides a warning, or a prophecy, for America as well.

PRE-IMPERIAL IMMIGRATION INTO AMERICA

In some respects, the American immigration of our time resembles the massive immigration of the 1890s–1910s. In particular, some observers see Latin-American immigrants recapitulating the earlier path of Italian immigrants and Asian immigrants recapitulating the earlier path of East European Jews. In the early twentieth century, there was widespread concern that immigrants from Southern and Eastern Europe could not be assimilated into the American way of life. By the 1960s, however, these groups were largely integrated into American society. By analogy, one might expect Latin American and Asian immigrants to be assimilated within a few decades.

But America today differs from the America that existed a century ago. First, the United States was then a self-conscious and self-confident national state. The American political class and the federal and state governments promulgated what was known as "the American Creed" and vigorously promoted what was known as Americanization, i.e., assimilation of immigrants into "the melting pot."

Second, the growing industrial economy of the time enabled immigrants to gain a step on the ladder of upward social mobility (and also outward geographical mobility and dispersion). Third, the restrictive Immigration Act of 1924 sharply curtailed immigration for a period of four decades, until the very different and unrestrictive Immigration Act of 1965. This converted immigrant communities from the turbulent streams of the 1890s–1910s into the settled masses of the 1920s–1950s, upon which the Americanization program could steadily and relentlessly work its way.

Fourth, few immigrants came from areas that were in the existing American empire (i.e., from Latin America or the Philippines). Thus the immigrants who did arrive did not bring with them the resentments and grievances of colonized populations. On the contrary, many immigrants were fleeing the foreign empires of Eastern Europe.

Even with these four factors favorable to assimilation, however, some immigrants carried with them particular ideologies prevalent in the lands that they had left behind (e.g., anarchism among some Italians, Marxism among some Jews). For a few immigrants, these ideologies legitimated their sense of separation from and opposition to the dominant American culture of liberal democracy, the free market, and competitive individualism. This produced a few obstacles on the road to assimilation (e.g., the "Red Scare" of 1919–1920, the activities of the Communist Party in the 1930s–1940s, McCarthyism in the 1950s).

When considering the contemporary era of American immigration, these four factors favorable to assimilation have been largely absent. In particular, the reigning ideology of multiculturalism erects far greater obstacles to assimilation than anarchism and Marxism ever did.

IMPERIAL IMMIGRATION INTO AMERICA

The contemporary era of immigration into America began with the Immigration Act of 1965, which eliminated previous restrictions on immigration from non-European regions (and in effect also increased restrictions on immigration from Europe). In contrast to the earlier American experience, in the contemporary era most immigrants to the United States have come from within the American empire. By far the largest number have come from the oldest domains of the empire, i.e., those countries that fell under the hegemony of the United States as a result of its wars with Mexico (1846–1848) and with Spain (1898): Mexico, Puerto Rico, the Dominican Republic, Haiti, Central America, and the Philippines. In addition, many immigrants have come from imperial precincts that America established in the Western Pacific after the Second World War and the Korean War and also from the abortive domain of Indochina.

With respect to immigration coming principally from within one's own empire, the contemporary American experience has been similar to the contemporary European one. However, whereas in Europe the great surge in immigration was largely a post-imperial phenomenon, in the United States it has come in the high-imperial era, at a time when the American empire has been in its ascendancy.

As it happens, the United States has experienced its own version of the sociological, demographic, and ideological factors that we have described for Europe: the ascent of working-class American citizens into a middle-class lifestyle or at least into middle-class pretensions; the decline in the reproduction rate of the European-descended majority; and the establishment of a post-national, multicultural ideology. This has produced the same kind of structural demand for immigrant workers in the United States as in Europe. Once the structure of demand has been established in the imperial center, the imperial territories become the most practical source of supply, for reasons that are similar in both Europe and America.

TWO NATIONS?

Today, the largest immigrant communities in the United States are Latin American in their origin. Latino Americans now compose the largest minority in the United States, having recently surpassed African Americans in numbers. Latino immigrants obviously already perform functions essential to the American economic system, and Latino Americans are steadily acquiring political power, including a kind of veto power on many issues where they have a concern.

Will imperial immigration cause the United States to become two nations, as is now the prospect for some European countries? The first nation could be the Anglo nation, descended from European peoples; as in Europe, much of this nation would be secular, rich, old, and feeble. The second nation could be a Latino nation, descended from Latin American peoples; much of it would be religious, particularly Christian (evangelical and Pentecostal Protestant, as well as Roman Catholic), poor, young, and robust. These two nations would regard each other with mutual suspicion and, in a few aspects, with contempt. The gated communities of Anglos, already widespread in the southwestern United States, are likely to become an even more central part of the Anglo way of life, the distinctive architectural style and urban design of the Anglo nation.

Still, Latino-American culture is probably closer to Anglo-American culture than Muslim culture is to European culture, if only because the two American cultures share a common origin in the Christian religion. This may retard the development of the two distinct nations within the United States. More likely, perhaps already happening, is the development in the Southwest of something that is a blend of American and Mexican features, a sort of "Amerexico." This is a society whose upper or capital-owning class is Anglo-American, whose professional and middle classes are largely Anglo-American but partly Mexican-American, and whose working and lower classes—those that do the dirty work—are Mexican-American. It is characterized by a racial division of labor, a rough correlation between class and color. As such, it has important similarities to the colonial societies of the European empires, which were also characterized by a racial or ethnic division of labor. Indeed, as the ratio of Mexican Americans to Anglo Americans increases, Amerexico will more and more resemble something like Northern Ireland in the United Kingdom, or perhaps even all of Ireland as it was in the British Empire. If so, the United States would have become not only an empire abroad but also one at home.

EMPIRE AND EMIGRATION

Essential to every empire is an imperial class—the civil officials, military officers, and business managers who go forth from the empire's metropole to its dominions and colonies and who carry out its policies and practices. In other words, an empire requires imperial emigrants.

Who will comprise the imperial emigrants, the imperial class, of the American empire? Here it is useful to distinguish between the three different components—civil, military, and business—of an imperial class.

The military services of the United States have had more than a half-century of experience of peacetime service overseas, especially in Germany, Japan, and South Korea. More than any other American institutions, the military services are the true heirs to the legendary civil officials, and not just the dedicated military officers, of the British Empire. Moreover, America does not seem to lack business entrepreneurs, managers, and professionals who are willing to go overseas, especially to those countries which are long established (and more predictable) realms of the American empire, particularly Latin America, Western and now Eastern Europe, and East Asia. These American business people are the counterparts to the merchants, managers, and engineers of the British Empire.

The problem, perhaps the void, in the American imperial class lies in the civil officials. There is no obvious equivalent of the Indian Civil Service or the Colonial Civil Service of the British Empire, that distinguished cadre of graduates from Oxford and Cambridge who went out to serve for long and hard years as district officers in the remote regions of the empire. The graduates of the best American universities are "organization kids," intent on having a successful career within America itself. In any event, the U.S. State Department (and even the Central Intelligence Agency) can hardly be compared to the civil services of the British Empire, either in regard to effectiveness or to morale.

The real civil servants of the American empire are not American in their physical origin. They are, however, American in their intellectual apparatus. They are the foreign students who come to American universities and who learn American principles and practices. In particular, they are the economics majors and business school students who come to believe in the free market and the political science majors and law school students who come to believe in liberal democracy and the rule of law. When (and if) they return to their home countries, they will know both the culture and customs of their own society and the principles and practices of American society. These foreign students are both imperial immigrants—when they arrive in America for their studies—and imperial emigrants—when they return home for their careers.

From the perspective of the American empire, these imperial immigrants-emigrants—local in their outer appearance, American in their inner attitudes—are the perfect candidates for political and economic leadership in the empire's domains. And, indeed, a significant number of current officials in Latin America, Western and Eastern Europe, and East Asia are graduates of American universities, and an even larger cadre of graduates is now entering into official careers. The ability of the American empire to govern its domains will depend upon its success in producing this distinct kind of immigrant-emigrant to serve as its distinct kind of imperial civil official. In the empires of the past, the metropole served as the mind, and the colonies served as the body. The American empire is attempting to solve the imperial mind-body problem in a new way. In a sense, it seeks to perform a series of brain transplants, to put an imperial mind into a colonial body.

The earlier European empires—the empires of the industrial age—also made some effort to educate and enculturate the best and the brightest from the colonies in the principles and practices of the empire. But in the end they could not prevent—indeed they helped to cause—the rise of colonial nationalism and the demise of the empire. The American empire—the empire of the information age—is based even more upon ideas than the empires of the past. In essence, these are the same ideas that Thomas Jefferson wrote into the birth certificate of the United States, the Declaration of Independence—"life, liberty, and the pursuit of happiness." As long as the American empire appears to be providing some semblance of life, liberty, and the pursuit of happiness to the peoples of its vast realm, it has a good chance of thriving.

If, however, the American empire fails to prevent a series of wars, if new dictatorships arise, or if the global economy falters, then American ideas clearly would forfeit their authority, and America's particular and peculiar imperial civil service would lose its control over the empire's domains. The empire would then come to an end, like all the European empires before it. But one massive legacy from the imperial age would remain. That would be the vast population of imperial immigrants within the once-imperial and now-diminished metropole, the territory of the United States itself.

Index

Accountability, 8
Adams, John Quincy, 126–127, 128
Aeneid (Virgil), 207
Afghanistan: postwar interventions, 38,
  225; U.S. economic aid to, 153; U.S.
  military actions on, 50, 74, 169–171,
  194; U.S. reputation after war on, 240
Africa, economic aid, 40–41, 154
Agriculture, national security and, 235–236
Aideed, Mohamad Farah, 17
Albania, 13
Albanians, interventions on behalf of, 181
Albright, Madeleine, 56, 136, 168
Angell, Norman, 32–33
Anti-Americanism, 167, 172–182, 239–240;
  addressing, 181–182; antiglobalism and,
  177, 239–240
Anti-Ballistic Missile Treaty, 195
Anticapitalism, 167
Antiglobalism, 167, 177–179, 239–240
Anti-imperialism, ix–x, 35–36
Anti-Imperialist League, x
Antiochos IV, 84
Arab-Israeli conflict, 42–43
Aron, Raymond, 173
Ash, Gabriel, 238n; writing of, 238–244
Asia: Eurasian religions, 44–45; immigrants
  to U.S. from, 246, 254; U.S. relations
  with, 188, 195. *See also* countries by
  name.
Assimilation of immigrants, 254–255
Athens (ancient): U.S. compared to,
  144–145, 149, 150, 152. *See also* Greece
  (ancient).
Atlantic Charter, 200
Augustus, 91–92

Babur, 216
Bacevich, Andrew J., 93n; writing of,
  93–101
Baker, James, 13
Baywatch, 106–107, 108–109
Belgium, immigrants to, 249
Bender, Peter, 81n; writing of, 81–92

"Benito Cereno" (Melville), 125–126
Berry, Wendell, 229n; writing of, 229–237
Bettati, Mario, 11
Bin Laden, Osama, 169, 171, 178,
  179–181; appeal of, 180–181; Bush
  compared to, 115, 143
Biological Weapons Convention, 54, 194
"Birthmark, The" (Hawthorne), 126
Blair, Tony, 167
"Blue Sky" laws, 37
Bosnia: human rights issues, 15–16, 18, 23,
  181; postwar interventions, 38
Bright, 32
Britain: economic history, 32; English
  Liberalism, 32–33; immigrants to, 249,
  253–254; U.S. and, 117, 124, 139, 167,
  242. *See also* British Empire.
British Empire: in China, 216; economic
  aspects, 34–35, 112–114, 138–142, 151;
  fall of, 31–32, 35, 112–113, 117, 138,
  145; frontiers, 138–142, 209, 212,
  248–249, 253; as a homogenizing
  empire, 31; in India, 138, 139, 140,
  218–219; international legal systems,
  141; leadership, 38, 114; in the Middle
  East, 139–141, 181, 209; military losses,
  152; military strength, 49, 140–142,
  215–216; naval powers, 140–142, 215;
  postwar interventions, 41; property
  right protection by, 141–142; U.S.
  compared to, 112–118, 138–145,
  149–150, 203, 220, 258. *See also* LIEO.
Brooks, Stephen, 48
Buchanan, Pat, 48
Bull, Hedley, 29
Bush administration (George W. Bush):
  agricultural policies, 235–236; conflicts
  within, 168; economic policies, 76–77,
  187; international policies, 97–98, 117,
  130–131, 143, 166–167, 189–201,
  238–244; Iraqi campaign, 114–115;
  military policies, 66–77, 119–120,
  130–131, 151, 189–196, 202–203,
  212–213, 229–239, 240; short-term

A NOTE ON THE EDITOR

Andrew J. Bacevich is professor of international relations at Boston University and author of *American Empire: The Realities and Consequences of U.S. Diplomacy.* Born in Normal, Illinois, he studied at the U.S. Military Academy at West Point, served as an army officer for twenty-three years, and studied history at Princeton University, where he received a Ph.D. He has taught at West Point and at Johns Hopkins University, and now lives in Walpole, Massachusetts. He and his wife have four children.